The Stories They Tell
Volume 1

Edited By Colin J. Cutler

Presented by Young Voices Foundation

ISBN: 1489579338

ISBN-13: 978-1489579331

Table of Contents

Group 1 (Grades 1-2)

Group 2 (Grades 3-7)

Introduction

"A people is known by the stories it tells," wrote Flannery O'Connor, one of the greatest short story writers America has produced. The Young Voices Foundation exists to make known the stories that our young people tell.

Every quarter, we receive hundreds of submissions to our writing contests. We currently give cash prizes to the top three in each of three age categories. This volume started as our attempt to honor more of the excellent short stories we receive, stories which range from sci-fi (from the alien's perspective) to Biblical fiction to stories set in modern-day middle schools to serious stories about real-life joys and grief.

Make sure to read through to the end. Midway through this project, I was sent to Germany for a month of training with the Army. During some of our off-time, we toured the concentration camp memorial at Dachau. Christina Gibbs's daring exploration of guilt and redemption from the perspective of a German child in "Rising Heat," which ends this volume, resonated deeply with what I saw there.

A note to the parents of the younger writers: we understand that binding a 1st grade story in the same volume as a 12th grade story could be the parental equivalent of putting a lion to pasture with a lamb. We did, however, ensure that nothing in this volume is above PG-13 (and cut profanity). We hope that your young writers and readers can mature into these stories and that this volume can grow up with them. In the meantime, we encourage you to review the stories with them!

Many thanks to all the writers who participated in the contest and congratulations to all featured here. To all: keep writing! You tell the stories by which your generation will be known.

Colin J. Cutler
Editor
Author, *The Ward of Heaven and the Wyrm in the Sea*

Group 1
(Grades 1-2)

The Talent Show

Gabrielle Arroyo
2nd Grade

There was a talent show on Friday after school, but I do not have a talent for the talent show and I signed up. Should I show people how to do a forward roll or maybe a cartwheel? What should I do? When the bus came to take us home, everybody was talking about their talent, except me.

Mia asked, "Are you okay?"

"I don't have a talent for the talent show," I answered. "Mia," I asked, "do you have a talent?"

She said, "Yes, tricks with a jump rope."

"Can you teach me?" I asked.

She answered, "I do not have time, sorry."

I got worried. What should I do now? When I got home, Zac said, "I am doing magic tricks for the talent show." I didn't say anything. Mia did not tell anyone I did not have a talent for the talent show. She was my best friend. That's why. I went to sleep that night and I had a nightmare. It was about me not having a talent for the talent show. Everyone was laughing at me. I woke up after that.

I was doing a handstand for a long time. Then it hit me! I could do the longest handstand. It was only Tuesday. I could not wait, until my teacher said, "We do not have mats." I was thinking all day what I should do. I was thinking so hard; instead of biting my sandwich, I bit my eraser. Yuck!

The next day of school, it was bad. Brian said, "I can balance a bat on my pinky."

Then Lauren said, "I can not blink for an hour." I asked, "How can you do that?"

She said, "Years of practice."

Next Jake said, "I can hold my breath for 20 minutes."

"Wow!" I said, very loudly. "I can't even hold my breath for even a minute."

"I was not breathing for forty minutes after I came out of my mom's belly." Said Jake.

I got even more worried because a lot of people had talent, except me. I was mad at myself for not having a talent. At school that day, it was almost time to call the buses, when at the sink, Kaitlyn asked, "What is your talent?" My bus was called; I was walking away from the sink. I was in luck.

On the bus ride home I sat alone. What should I do, what should I do? I said to myself in my head. At home my mom said, "Go play with Mia." I said, "Okay."

I rode my bike to Mia's house. I rang the doorbell. Mia said, "Come in and play." She said, "Let's have a hula-hoop contest." I agreed. Mia shouted to her mom, "You can be the judge." She came down the stairs, and out the back door to the backyard where we were standing.

Mia's mom said, "Whoever is the best, gets the biggest piece of brownie." I was happy inside. Mia's mom said, "Ready, Set, Go!" Mia was good, but I could not see myself so I do not know what I looked like. Time was up. Mia's mom said, "Gaby was the best. Sorry, Mia." Mia was happy for some reason. She said, "That could be your talent for the talent show." I was happy too. Mia said, "You did good, Gaby."

Two days passed, it was the talent show. After school I did not go home on the bus. I stayed after school because I was getting ready for the talent show. I had a good time practicing in the gym.

When everyone was at the school, in the gym, watching the show, it was finally my turn. Everyone went, "OHH" and everyone went, "AHHH."

A couple days passed, the loud speaker said, "The winner of the talent show is...Gabrielle Arroyo."

"Gaby," said Mia, "that's you." I was so excited. The prize was a free trip to Disney. I thought I was dreaming, so I pinched myself. But, I was not asleep.

In the Jungle

Shylah Crawford
2nd Grade

One day, in the jungle, there were three little kittens in a crate. They were heading to France.

"Where are we?" said Mickey.

"I don't know," said Kitty.

"I know where we are. We are in a crate," said Licky.

"AHHHHH," said all.

It was quiet for a moment.

"Why aren't we moving and why was it so quiet for a moment?" asked Mickey.

"I think we're on the ground," said Licky.

"I think I can open the lid and we can get out," said Licky.

"Oof, ow, ouch!" said all.

"Get off my leg," said Mickey.

"Get off MY leg," said Licky.

"Raarrrrr," said Kity.

"What?" asked Mickey and Licky?

"Get off my face," said Kitty.

"Sorry," said Mickey and Licky, climbing off of Kitty.

"Let's explore," said Licky.

"OK," said Kitty.

"Hmmm...what is that thing on the ground creeping toward us?" asked Licky.

"It's a lion!" screamed Kitty.

"RUN!" yelled Mickey.

"That's what I was thinking," said Mickey.

They ran and ran until there was no sign of the lion. They stopped at the pond.

"I'm going to have a have a bath, good thing I brought my shampoo and my rubber ducky," said Licky.

"Hey, I'll be back I am going to get some food," said Mickey.

A few hours later:

"Wow, Mickey has been taking a long time. He might be in

the deep, deep woods slashing and snatching food," thought Kitty, "I'm going to see what's up with him."

"Where you going? Wait up." said Licky.

In the background they heard a lot of animals noises.
"Kaka kaka."
"Tweet, Tweet."
"Ooooo Aaaahhhh!"

"Silly monkeys," they said.

"Hey guys, over here," said Mickey.

"There you-" said Kitty stopping when she saw Mickey.

"What happened?" said Licky.

"Ah, can't you see I'm trapped in a huge spider's web." said Mickey.

"OK we'll help you get out," said Kitty and Licky.

"OK let's travel on," said Kitty.

"I'm still hungry," said Mickey.

"I'm hungry too, let's eat that coconut," said Licky, "Yum, yum, yum. Now let's go!"

"We're on the road again," said Mickey.

"And no one has come," said Licky.

"Hey, look, a car!" shouted Kitty.

"Hey you up there, stop," said Mickey.

"Huh?" said the driver.

"Hey that car could hit us, you know?" said Kitty.

"Here kitty, kitty, kitties," called the driver.

So they hitched a ride on to France with the driver. They lived happily ever after.

One Direction

Cierra Francis
2nd Grade

"Naaay," a young brown and white horse screeched while being trained for a Championship Horse Race. She wasn't doing well, so her trainer was very strict.

"Run, jump, go!" the man yelled.

A couple of days later, Breeze, a gentle, spotted horse, was in the field. She had just finished dinner, and her trainer had gone to eat out, when a shower of lightning began. Thunder and rain joined the storm after a few seconds. The wild animal skidded through the grass, leaving muddy tracks behind.

In the blink of an eye, the horse leapt over to the high wired fence, and with a big jump the animal ended up on the other side of the gate. Trotting softly through the midnight shadows, Breeze was frightened. She was only one year old, and she had never been alone in the wild.

Hunting for shelter, the horse noticed a shaking noise coming from a far off bush that paralyzed her for a moment. Then, out of no where, a huge wolf took two steps towards Breeze. For a moment or two, the wolf and the pony made serious eye contact. The next moment, the pony laid down, letting her bigger opponent hurt her. The wolf licked his lips, but did not move. The pony was confused. Why am I not dead by now? she thought, puzzled. She knew being here would lead to trouble, so slowly she got up, and raced off leaving the wolf behind, and once again she was alone.

Then suddenly, a hunter and a large dog walked up to Breeze. The horse closed her eyes thinking of her life before this, then took a step back from the scary man, but the man did not step back--or hurt her, either.

He showed the pony to a little cabin, and tied her up close by. "We'll go for a ride soon, girl," the man whispered softly to Breeze. And now she knew she was home, and that she was not the right horse for a race.

The Case of the Broken Pencil

By Lia Kim
2nd Grade

One day Sophie was sitting at her desk admiring her beautiful pencil. The pencil was sparkly and smelled like bubble gum. Daniel was looking at the pencil like it was irritating him. She went to the bathroom to get some wipes to clean her beautiful pencil. When she came back to her desk the pencil was broken into half. It was on her desk.

After a while, at recess, she got her friends Rebecca and Samantha to solve the case with her and find some clues to tell them who broke the pencil.

"Rebecca, can you get some powder from the kitchen?" Sophie said.

"Sure!" Rebecca said.

"Samantha, can you get a brush from the art room?"

"Of course!"

They put some powder on her desk where the pencil had been. They blew on it and they saw fingerprints. They looked at the fingerprints very carefully and they saw that it was Daniel's fingerprints.

"Oh my goodness!" Sophie said.

"Holy macaroni!" shouted Samantha

Rebecca just fainted. Sophie and Samantha splashed Rebecca with water until she woke up.

"Oh, okay! I'm ready to go!" she said.

They went outside and decided what to do. They tried to figure out a plan. Their plan was to trick Daniel into telling on himself about the broken pencil. Then after they tricked him, they thought they could sass him.

They found Daniel outside. He was playing basketball. The girls ran up to him.

"You have to go to the principal's office!" they said.

"Okay," said Daniel. They led him to the classroom.

"Sit down," commanded Rebecca.

"Okay," said Daniel. Then the girls started asking him

questions.

"Do you like sparkly pencils?" Sophie asked.

"No!" Daniel shouted.

"Would you break a sparkly pencil if you saw one?" asked Rebecca.

"Eh," said Daniel.

"Really?" said Samantha. As Samantha stroked her chin wisely, Sophie slowly took out the broken pencil and put it on the desk in front of Daniel. Daniel started laughing loudly and clapping his hands.

"I did it!" he shouted.

"Aha!" all three girls shouted. They jumped up and down and clapped.

"I knew it!" Sophie said. "Never do that again or touch my other stuff! Or else…"

"Or else what?" Daniel asked.

"We will tell on you!" Sophie, Samantha, and Rebecca yelled together.

"Okay, fine," Daniel said.

"You have to give us five dollars," Sophie said.

"Okay," grumbled Daniel. He handed her five dollars. The girls high fived each other.

"Case closed," said Sophie happily.

Stuck at Mars

Neel Maddali
1st Grade

One day, I was going to Jupiter. My spaceship crashed on the way. Oh no, my ship had exploded and I landed on Mars. I said; "It's hot!" 10 seconds after that, my spaceship landed. I dug for an ice pack and dug one out of my ice storage. That cooled me down. I saw a green flash with a white object. A squeaky voice said "A Human!" A sword with a jewel in it appeared in my hand. The green flash with a white object came closer.

And then…the top ten scariest aliens in the universe came. They asked "Do you want to play baseball?" in their squeaky voice. I said "yes". They seemed to know a lot about baseball and hit 10 home runs. Our team hit only five.
We lost.

At last, another astronaut found the "winning potion" and sprinkled it on the bat. It's a potion that has the blessings and smiles of our friends on earth.

I say "Ha! Ha!" to the aliens. They play my astronaut friends and me in the baseball game. We win….the next game and the one after! This means that the aliens lose.

"Hooray! The superhero saves the day" my friends cheer. "Awesome, we won!" This meant a huge prize for us and our friends on Earth.

The bad guys who control the scary aliens cry.

My friends and I fix the ship and are on our way to our next stop, Jupiter.

Leyroy, The Dragon Slayer

Jayden Maddox
2nd Grade

Once upon a time, there was a big scary dragon and a dragon slayer, named, "Leyroy". Leyroy was the son of the best dragon slayer in the world. Leyroy's dad trusted Leyroy to be a great dragon slayer like him. One day, Leyroy decided he was going to slay the strongest dragon in the world.

Leyroy searched and found a dark cave where the dragon was sleeping on the floor. The dragon woke up and Leyroy fought the dragon face to face.

Leyroy said, "You will no longer eat the poor people!" The dragon breathed fire in Leyroy's face. This did not stop Leyroy from slaying the dragon. Leyroy rushed to get his sword and cut the dragon across his neck.

The dragon died.

Leyroy was so proud of himself. He told his family about his journey. His parents were very proud of him too. Soon the whole town knew about Leyroy's journey. Leyroy became famous. There were no more dragons in the town. Everyone was safe from dragons!

The Bunny Escape

Madelyn Murray
1st Grade

I opened my eyes and looked out my window. The wind was blowing. I had soft silky fur and a tiny pink nose. I shivered and caught sight of an orange fox with a furry tail swishing in the cold breeze.

I got out of bed but suddenly the fox stopped eating and quickly saw me! In the distance I could hear giant footsteps coming to my door. Suddenly I heard a knock on the door. I opened the door and there it was--the fox! I was too late. The fox almost ate me! So I quickly hid under a pricker bush. Ouch! Ouch! OUCH! The fox ran past me and he was gone! Whew! That was a close one. I jumped back home but I heard footsteps behind me. But this time it was my mom. That was the worst adventure ever.

Chester and His Red Apple

Julia Niemeyer
1st Grade

Once a little cat was wandering around the garden. His name was Chester and he saw something bright red. Chester didn't know what it was, and he didn't know what to do with it. There was no one to ask.

Then he saw a little brown cat and said, "Do you know what it is?" showing him the bright red thing. "No, but I do know a very wise owl." he said. So he led Chester to the very wise owl.

Chester and his friend went to the very wise owl, but it turns out he wasn't very wise. Chester asked, "Do you know what it is?" "No" said the owl. "I do know a giraffe, he might know." So he took Chester and his friend to the giraffe.

So when he got there the owl flew away saying, "Hope he knows what it is!" Chester asked the giraffe, "Do you know what it is?" showing him the red thing. "No, but I know a horse," said the giraffe, smiling at Chester and his friend. So he led them to the horse.

The giraffe led them there. The horse was eating some hay, but he stopped. Chester asked the horse, "Do you know what this is?" "Yes" said the horse. Chomp! The apple was in the horse's tummy. It was too late to get it. "Thanks anyway" said Chester.

When Chester went home he saw something bright orange...and you know what happened next.

Group 2
(Grades 3-7)

Her

Megan Chen
5th Grade

I still remember the time I met Her. She helped me see the price of everything because nothing is free. I'm so glad I found Her. This is how this happened. All preserved in a 14-year-old diary entry I wrote in when I was 12 years old.

5/4/2003

Dear Diary,

Hello, my name is Andromeda. I am 12 years old and I have a mother, father, and a twin brother named Perseus, but I am 15 minutes older. Yes, Perseus and I came from the same Greek myth. It all started when Mom and Dad decided to go to England for April vacation.

We live in Greece, which is a long way from England. We decided to stay for a week, and we booked a 5-star hotel. I was extremely excited, and packed faster than I have ever packed for anything in my life.

So, I was packed a week before our trip. At school, I was bouncy and didn't concentrate very well. I was so glad that we didn't have a test, quiz, or serious assignment that week. When April vacation started on Saturday, I could barely do anything because of my excitement, for tomorrow was the starting of our trip!!!

The next day we all woke up at 5:00 in the morning and ate breakfast, checked our belongings, and drove to the airport. At 6:30 we finished getting through all the security and boarded the plane. After the long, boring four and a half hour airplane ride, it was 11:00. Then we took 30 more minutes to get through the British security and rent a car.

Finally we got to our magnificent hotel. It was called The Grand Hotel, in East Sussex. I totally agreed with the hotel's name, only that the name was bit boring, but the hotel was so awesome that nobody would even care! I seriously recommend this hotel to anybody who comes to Britain. It was like, a huge and long white long white castle that dominates the shoreline. The restaurants had wonderful food and everything was so fancy! The suite was even better. Mom and Dad outdid themselves and got us a Master Suite! The suite had four rooms. Mom and Dad got the extremely fancy Master bedroom. Perseus got the yellow-brown bedroom and I got ceiling to floor windows with a wonderful view of the famous English Channel.

For the rest of the day, we rested and unpacked our belongings. The next day, Monday, we explored the hotel, along with the rocky beach and crystal clear pool. The day after, the real adventure began when we went to the Bodiam Castle for a little tour.

On Tuesday morning, we all got up at 8:00 to go to the Bodiam Castle for a little self-tour. When I first saw it, I froze with my mouth in a comical "O". If you ever got the chance to see the Bodiam Castle, it's a majestic castle with a monumental moat and a huge, wooden portcullis. The beautiful and stately gray stone castle was a wonder of the world. When Perseus and I got in the castle, we kept running ahead and Mom would yell for us to stop and wait. Eventually Mom apparently got tired and told us to meet us at the portcullis at 4:00. Perseus and I went our separate ways in the colossal castle. At exactly 3:33 I saw something strange. I saw some silvery purple mist coming out of a dark corridor. That's strange, I thought. Then I took a deep breath and plunged into the fog.

I kept my hands right in front of me just in case I bumped into something that I didn't see. After a couple minutes of walking through fog, I came to a dead end. At the end was a picture with golden letters at the top that said, Beatrix Dalyngrigge. Underneath was a painting of a beautiful woman in royal English-style clothing. Suddenly, the woman in the picture moved! I blinked. Pictures don't move, I thought. Then to reassure myself I said out loud, "Pictures don't move!"

"Sure they do," said a mysterious, silvery voice.

"What?" I shouted.

"Shhhhhh, don't shout, everyone will hear us," the voice said again.

"Where are you?" I complained.

"Right here, just look, would you?"

Since I couldn't see anyone, I looked at the painting. I jumped. The painting was talking and moving! "Oi, don't be so still, move it!" ordered the picture. "Now, down to business."

"What is happening to me? Am I hallucinating?" I asked in a daze.

"I am the world's only painted genie!" said the painting proudly. "My name is Beatrix Dalyngrigge, and I will grant you three wishes!"

I was so dumbstruck the only thing I could think of to come out of my mouth was, "Where'd you learn how to say oi?"

"Off some American foreigner," said the genie promptly.

At that point I started cracking up. "So, returning to the topic. You are a genie."

"Check."

"You will grant me three wishes."

"Check."

"You are the world's only genie painting."

"Check."

"Great. Does purple mist come out of your corridor every day?

"Nope. I pop up once every century."

"So, can I wish horrible luck on my worst enemy?

"No, that's the only catch. You cannot wish for anything destructive or hurtful to yourself or others."

"Rats."

"Now, what are your three wishes?" The genie questioned. "You also must discuss what might happen to the world because of your wish."

"Genie, can I wish to be extremely charming only when it's okay? I decided after a while.

"Sure, it's fine to be charming and persuasive for the right thing. Tons of actors and actresses are extremely charming. Also, you cannot persuade a genie. By the way, I prefer being called Beatrix instead of Genie."

"Okay, Beatrix, I wish to be charming only when it's right." Then, a ball of silver light went into my mouth and disappeared.

"There," declared Beatrix. "Now, what's your second

wish?"

"Beatrix, can I wish for everyone to not hate me?"

"Hmmm....sure. Why not? Nobody wants people to hate themselves, and I'm guessing you probably don't want to be extremely popular."

I blushed. "You guessed that right, my friend. So, Beatrix, I wish that nobody would hate me." Then another ball of silvery light appeared, but this time huge, went around my body and also disappeared.

"Now, what's your third wish?" Beatrix inquired.

"Well, I really have nothing to wish for anymore so if you had a wish, what would it be?"

Beatrix froze. "What?" she exclaimed. "Really?" she started to tear up. "Nobody's asked me that before!"

"Well, quit blubbering, now, what would you wish for?"

Beatrix sniffled and mumbled, "I've always been so lonely. I would wish for company, like when the castle is empty, all the pictures would come to life and be able to go to any picture they wanted to."

I smiled and announced, "I wish for what Beatrix just said to be true."

Suddenly, a ball of silvery light went and lit up Beatrix's frame. Then Beatrix smiled thankfully and called out, "Thank you and good bye," and her picture went still.

I smiled sadly and replied, "Thanks, you too." Then I glanced at my watch and I swear I jumped a foot in the air. It was 3:55 and I needed to get to the portcullis in five minutes!

Hopefully my new persuasion would back me up. When I got to the portcullis, it was 4:05. Uh oh, I thought.

I said sweetly, "I'm sorry, I got so caught up in one of the paintings that I lost track of time." Which was true.

Mom and Dad relaxed and said, "It's fine dear, just try not to do that again."

I was shocked. It actually worked! I was about to scream with joy. The rest of the days flew by as a blur.

A nearby restaurant had a gift shop that sold diaries with pictures of the Bodiam Castle on them.

That diary is you. That is my story of Beatrix, the world's only painted genie.

Sincerely,
Andromeda

There. That's my 14-year-old diary entry. I am now 26, and I still have my effortless persuasion skills and nobody hates me yet. I'm living a happy life and I visit the Bodiam Castle every year. Here's a hint. The next time you go to the Bodiam Castle and you see some silvery purple mist, go and follow it. I'm sure Beatrix will welcome you with open arms.

Feeling Impish

Gibby Free
6th Grade

The demonic creature sat at his stainless steel desk tiredly, playing with his thick, armored digits. He turned to a smaller demonic creature, an imp, to his right.

"When were the loaves put into the oven, Gareo? I'm starving."

"Less than two minutes ago, sir. You were there."

"Ah," the General said. "Of course,"

"See?" Gareo, the small dark green impish creature said and pointed an accusatory finger at his employer. "This is what I'm talking about, sir. Your memory is going down a metaphorical toilet, I'm afraid."

The General shifted his gaze, and was rescued from the uncomfortable topic when the steel doors to his office clicked twice and slid open noiselessly.

What he assumed to be two imps entered the large office. They had the signature impish horns at the crowns of the head, roughly the size of two sharpened pencil erasers and the rhombus shaped armor plates along their arms. However, the only difference was that these creatures were not in traditional cloaks. They both wore a strapless gown of hot pink silk and a white doily-looking skirt with glittering gems all throughout. Atop their heads was a silver tiara with all kind of sparkling glitter and jewels making up the royal crown.

All in all, such intense colors and sparkling nearly melted the General's corneas.

"My eyes!" he screamed. "They are flaming, Gareo, help!"

Gareo scrambled into the color-sensitive figure of power's drawers, found a pair of dark sunglasses and handed them to him.

"Why are you wearing such horrifying attire, boys?" the General asked the very feminine-looking imps.

"We've come here to report our findings in a recent excursion to Earth." The smaller of them said.

"An excursion? Wonderful. What happened?"

The smaller looked to the larger and they exchanged a look of excitement. The pair had made dozens of trips to Earth before in search for the next big thing to add to their dimension; a get rich quick scheme that would set them above all of the other Scouts that had been assigned to Earth.

"This," the smaller one said simply and threw a bag towards Gareo, who caught it out of the air and brought it to the General.

"We already have plastic bags, boys," the General said, as the two had a good record of excitedly bringing in things which had already been discovered.

"Inside the bag, sir," Gareo explained.

The General pulled the bag open and examined the foreign objects inside. There were many little pointy, colorful things, colored white, orange and yellow. They were chalky to the touch.

"What is it?" he asked.

"A humanfolk delicacy," relayed the smaller of the imps. "They call it Canned Die."

"Canned Die?"

"Yes, very horrible-sounding, I know. Spelled C-A-N-D-Y. Canned die."

The General examined the small candy skeptically.

"I am expected to eat this?"

The larger imp, eager, nodded. "They taste magnificent, sir. The effect, though, that's the best part!"

The General reluctantly placed the treat on his rough, dark gray tongue and chewed it. Immediately the flavors exploded in his mouth and an almost sickeningly sweet feeling coated his tongue. His brain seemed to short circuit. A new energy filled his veins- an energy that he had never felt before. He felt the sudden urge to do something great, like lift a hovercraft off of a baby impling or at least run around in circles for a little bit.

"T-this is incredible!" he shouted, jumping up and down, totally wired from the sugar that coursed through him. "A wonderful advancement in our modern science! We can supply it to our military, Gareo! They would be unstoppable with this…this energy going through them!"

The two imps turned to each other and grinned hugely. The larger one whispered something unintelligible to his brother. Something like "I told you so,"

"And you!" the General cried, pointing to the imps. "You will be greatly rewarded for this find! Absolute genius, boys! Why the outfit, though?"

They looked down and, as if they for the first time, seemed embarrassed by their pink, frilly get up.

The larger imp opened his mouth to speak, but the smaller spoke first.

"I believe if you allow us to report our entire excursion you will understand,"

"Please, tell us all about it!" the General exclaimed. "Before I literally burst through my skin in excitement!"

The nine-year-old looking girl's boots crunched through the pleasant aggregation of warmly colored autumn leaves, her slightly more diminutive companion trailing close behind her. Although the field they were tromping through was open and little to no people surrounded them, the air felt thick with excitement as children rushed by them, Jack o' Lantern plastic baskets tightly in hand,

Despite this atmosphere, the taller girl seemed bothered.

"How can they just leave these decomposing dead appendages lying around like flower beds? Are they supposed to make this area appear more attractive? It's disgusting, frankly." She spoke with a peculiar accent, a bizarre twist of French and German, but still passably American.

The girls walked in a silence for a few meters, until the smaller of the girls expressed disdain.

"Why am I smaller than you?" she asked in a similar strange accent. "I'm larger than you on Infernom."

The taller girl, with ferocity very unlike that of a nine-year-old girl smacked her friend with the palm of her hand.

"You're betraying our presence," she growled. "Keep your mouth shut."

"Plus," the little girl continued, undeterred by the beating. "Why little girls, Kardo?"

"Silence, knave!"

"Doesn't it damage your pride a little? We're currently human girls. Let that sink in for a little bit."

"So? I bet you couldn't do better!"

"I could have turned us into, oh, I don't know…boys! I get it, though. Don't worry. You like being a little girl."

Again, the 'girl' known as Kardo sharp hit his companion's back of the head.

"Everyone is watching us," he hissed. "You are being so obvious. We only have a small amount of time to search. Pick up the pace."

Sure enough, the smaller girl looked up and noticed countless humanfolk glaring at the pair and whispering among themselves about their peculiar word choices and topics of discussion.

"Skirts!" Kardo suddenly shrieked. "Barbies!"

Such vocabulary confused his comrade thoroughly. Once they had shuffled away from the large open field the pair began shuffled toward a concrete path, which lead to a quiet suburban neighborhood.

"How does one 'Barbie' exactly, Kardo?"

"I never fully translated it," Kardo explained. "But I have reason to believe it is a form of entertainment."

"Like goat herding back home?"

Kardo's supernatural partner was referring to the planet of Infernom's most popular competitive sport, in which the players hurried to herd a group of horned goats.

"Just like it," solemnly confirmed Kardo.

Pausing at a street corner thoughtfully, Kardo's friend turned to him.

"What was the point of shouting that?"

"Ah, foolish Korad," chided Kardo. "Such lingo leads these silly humanfolk to believe that we are one of them."

Korad-who was incredibly thick-had yet to become enlightened.

"But we're not humanfolk. Why are we disguised? I like being an imp, Kardo. Mother always said we needed to be ourselves."

Kardo, noticing a group of genuine human girls staring at them from less than twenty feet away, shrilly cried, "Humorous tale, eh…Deborah! Cutty boys, yes?"

Korad nearly decided to continue their prior conversation and just neutralize the 'humanfolk calves' at a later time, but rolled with the punches for the sake of not being hit again.

"Very much so, comrade!" he said in his best feminine voice, although all he succeeded in was sounding like a talking piccolo.

Panicked by this abrupt rise in attention, Kardo grabbed his friend's slender disgustingly fleshy arm and hurried off into the thick of the neighborhood.

They pretended to stand and watch the children run about in their costumes.

"Cutty boys?" the appears-to-be-smaller-girl inquired in a low voice.

"Yes. Spelled C-U-T-E. Cutty."

Korad shuddered. "How violent this race has become,"

Kardo grimly nodded.

The shape-shifted imps approached a house cautiously and watched as the costumed children came and went. A little boy disguised as a demon-devil hybrid ran past them gleefully.

"What a disgusting caricature," spat Korad. "Real demonic horns do not look like withering carrots, thank you."

"Why are they all red, anyway?" continued Korad. "Back home, do you know how many red imps and demons I know? Two. I know a lot of imps and demons, too, so that really means something."

His rant was cut short when he noticed Kardo staring at the house, a fiery intensity burning in the apparent girl's eyes.

"How are you not convulsing with horror right now, Kardo? You typically convulse with horror on a regular basis. Why not now? Should I be worried?"

"Look at that." Kardo said firmly and pointed at the children.

Korad watched obediently as the children ran to the door, shouted some obscene phrase, seemed to rob the woman who owned the house and ran off laughing.

"Humanfolk calves disgracing their planet," he observed dryly. "Nothing new."

"It's a humanfolk ritual, actually," Kardo said quietly. "A trial of sorts. A calf approaches a den, states what I assume is a coded term, 'Trick or Treat', initiating the trial and subjects him or herself to either a trick or a treat. If the humanfolk elders deem their disguises worthy, they are given a treat."

"What treat?" excitedly whispered Korad.

"Canned Die," Kardo let out an involuntary squeak of vertigo.

Korad observed Kardo's sudden giggle fit with hesitance.

"I don't know, Kardo," he muttered. "This seems a lot like that time you thought those urinal cakes were actually meant to be eaten. You were vomiting for days, brother!"

"Oh, Korad," his brother began ecstatically. "Canned die is said to be sweeter than any triumph and twice as valuable.

At the word 'valuable', Korad perked up, but was still unnerved by the by the dozens of calves effortlessly passing their trials and shoveling the sweet-smelling treats into their faces.

"What if the disguises are not deemed worthy?"

Kardo turned to Korad with utmost steely seriousness and said, "Decapitation,"

Korad shook his head.

"How very misguided Earth is becoming,"

As one can imagine, the door of the house was approached with total caution.

Taking the lead for once, Korad carefully pressed the white button near the door as he had watched many other children do before.

When the melodic note rang through the air, the witchcraft of it all nearly had Korad wetting himself.

When the door finally opened, a matured humanfolk female stepped out, except unlike many other humanfolk females the two had seen in the past, this woman seemed to have applied makeup and used other disguising tools in order to look even more cadaverous and disgusting than humanfolk females typically did.

If this was done to intimidate the children before they completed their trial, then Kardo felt that the attempt was successful, because he was practically petrified.

The disturbing woman reached behind her and took out a large plastic bowl that appeared like a large bleached skull, and thoughts of possibly having his head taken off by this woman sank into Korad's thoughts and he also became petrified.

"Aw, aren't you girls just precious?" cooed the female in a voice much too soft and sweet for the sickly pale face it came from. "Would you lovely ladies like lollipops or chocolate?"

Kardo was completely unprepared for this sudden barrage of humanfolk language. What was a 'precious' and how was he expected to obtain it? Was a 'lollipop' a means of threatening someone? If so, she was lollipopping him really well, because he was about to turn hostile.

"Cutty boys?" Korad offered uncertainly.

The female seemed to become even more confused and scared of the two strange little girls with the strange accents and the haunted look in their eyes than they were scared of her.

Assuming they were troubled foreign exchange student frightened by her zombie makeup appliance, she dropped both into their extended hands.

Following Kardo's lead, Korad slowly backed away from the porch, nervous eyes never leaving the confused female with her human head storage device until they were out in the middle of the street.

"That was an electrifying experience," panted Kardo.

"I will never view life the same way again," numbly agreed Korad.

After regaining their composure and finding a comfortable grassy area to sit on, the pair began to attempt to remove the thin wrapping from the candy.

Korad opened his first.

He tentatively touched his bizarrely pink tongue to the dark brown rectangle, and his pupils grew three sizes.

When the taste of the sweet chocolate coated the tip of his tongue, he couldn't get enough. Before he knew what he was doing, he crammed the entire full-sized bar into his mouth, light brown dribble dripping down his chin.

Kardo was ultimately concerned by this sudden animosity that filled his usually pacifistic brother's eyes as he chewed the candy and swallowed it, licking the wrapper when the taste was no longer so strong on his tongue.

"Korad, are you becoming possessed?" he asked suddenly, shaking his shoulders. "I am worried for you. The nearly convulsing kind of worried."

Korad looked up and grinned at his brother.

"Kardo, this is the best thing I've ever eaten," he said, the thick amount of drool in the back of his throat muffling his voice. "We must bring this back."

"We need to get more, then!" exclaimed Kardo. "Hurry, though!"

Since the demonic race did not have candy, Korad was extremely unused to the feeling of sugar moving through his bloodstream, so the phrase 'hurry' was like lighting a match underneath him, because he moved faster than Kardo had ever seen him move.

"When is the portal to Infernom opening again?" Kardo yelled back to Korad, who was running towards him, not caring about the tremendous amount of humanfolk calves staring at them and pointing.

"About fifteen minutes!" he yelled to Kardo.

"Are you sure it's going to work?" Kardo tried to ask. "I thought your portals always showed open in different places!"

Korad didn't respond. He was too busy marveling in the large house before him, which had an elderly man passing out huge portions of candy.

Following the lead of the many children ahead of them, they stood in an orderly line, waiting for it to be their turn.

The imps were disguised as little girls, who were costumed as witches of some sort. They couldn't help but notice the even smaller girls dressed as some kind of pink explosion wearing tiaras were receiving fistfuls of candy from the adult humanfolk.

When they reached the front of the line, however, they only received two pieces. Small pieces of candy, at that.

Pink girl get big, Korad thought ravenously. Me get small. Unfair. Specieist.

In a regular situation, Korad would have felt a sudden urge to write a strongly worded letter to this humanfolk male and stamp his feet. However, the sugar flowing through him muddled his thoughts and common sense.

In a sugar-induced rage, he shouted, "Give!" and snatched the bowl full of candy away from the man and ran as fast as his female legs could go.

Kardo chased after him and watched as his younger brother manically threw the candies into the air as he darted through the crowded streets, with a bewildered man somewhere behind, being able to only watch as his ten dollars worth of candy corn was stolen by a little girl.

Korad began hallucinating, as was expected from a foolish, sugar-loaded imp. In his mind, dozens of large humanfolk were chasing him with all kinds of sharp objects and foreign tools. In reality, he was running through a street carrying a bowl full of cheap candy corn and screaming, "You are the only thing that matters," while throwing the candy at bystanders.

Being the larger female, Kardo caught up with Korad and grabbed him by his shoulders.

"Stop it!" he shouted as Korad loosened his entire body in attempt to wiggle out of his grip. "You're acting crazy! Snap out of it!"

Korad suddenly stopped and looked at Kardo with big, confused eyes. "Me go crazy?"

Kardo nodded. He grabbed his partner by his wrist and began to walk in the direction of the soon-to-open portal. Korad refused to move.

"Come on!" he urged. "We don't have much time!"

Korad still didn't move.

"Pink girl get big," Korad muttered, moving his free hand through the enormous amount of candy corn before him. There was a line of drool dripping from the side of his mouth and the candy was in between his teeth.

With a groan of impatience, Kardo picked up Korad by

his armpits and began to walk him back towards the field. He was pleasantly surprised when Korad didn't struggle, but a few minutes later realized it was because he was asleep.

He found the marked tree and waited for the vortex to appear so he could get home and take Korad to the hospital.

The vortex never came.

I set up the hex perfectly, he thought. Wait. I didn't set up the hex. Korad did.

He vaguely recalled prior times in which he had trusted Korad to create the hex and having had to go on a wild goose chase through the whole town looking for the misplaced portal.

He dropped Korad to the ground, unfortunately on top of a large ant pile.

"Korad!" he yelled, shaking him frantically. "Wake up! We need to get home!"

Korad stirred and his eyelids fluttered open. He stared at Kardo hazily. "What happen?" he mumbled, rubbing the back of his head where he had been hit a half hour or so before.

"Where did you set up the portal?"

Ignoring his brother like always, Korad continued his display of confusion. "Why am I covered in insects? Is this a joke? I am not in the mood to joke."

Kardo slapped Korad forcefully.

"Where did you set up the portal?" he repeated.

"The tree!" Korad snapped testily. "You were right there with me!"

"It's not here!" Kardo grabbed Korad's head and sharply twisted it in the direction of the marked tree, where there was no portal to be found.

Korad frowned in confusion. He then turned towards the neighborhood behind him.

"You don't think the portal is…" he trailed off and gestured towards the neighborhood.

As if destiny answered him, the sound of screams met their ears.the also troubled imps.

Elsewhere about five minutes before Kardo and Korad heard the hysterical screams, a group of troubled teenagers sat on the curb in the neighborhood less than two hundred yards away from the also troubled imps.

"What a lame Halloween," a male sophomore muttered. "All of these decorations are the same as last year."

The female sophomore next to him nodded. "Seems this place gets cheaper every year," She held up her nearly empty bucket of candy. "Old Man Roysen is practically giving out pennies this year."

"People say Halloween gets lamer as you grow up," a freshman male said sadly. "This neighborhood isn't really helping me get into the Halloween spirit."

A different, taller male sophomore gestured with his head towards the huge house behind him.

"The Kirkland family always does something cool at the end of the night, though," he said hopefully. "Remember in seventh grade when Mister Kirkland pretended to turn into a zombie and tried to attack you, Joel? That was awesome."

The first male sophomore, Joel, shook his head.

"That was seventh grade, though, bro. This is now."

"They haven't done anything cool since eighth grade," the girl agreed. "It's been going downhill since I was like nine, anyway,"

"Maybe they'll do something this year, though," the boy said hopefully.

As if destiny answered them, as well, a bright purple light suddenly flashed through the entire neighborhood.

The high school students turned around, and right behind them was a flashing, dark purple swirling vertical oval of light.

"Wow," breathed the freshman. "You seeing this, Ian?"

Ian, the hopeful sophomore grinned. "I knew they'd pull through this year,"

A few younger children from across the street saw the unexplained vortex and screamed at its sudden and noisy appearance, but the teenagers stood before it in awe.

They realized the vortex was shrinking.

"How on earth did they get it to do that?" the female sophomore wondered out loud.

As if the appearance of the beacon of light was not enough, they watched as two little girls dressed up as witches, one holding a huge bowl of candy corn emitted a bright white light and became some kind of strange demonic-looking creature. The two little girls had become utterly horrifying, with thick armored bodies, black emotionless eyes and short, sharp, twisted horns. The larger of the creatures was a pale gray, the other a disgusting mossy green.

The creatures jumped into the vortex right before it had completely disappeared, and in a flash even more purple and bright than the one before, the vortex was gone.

Realizing the vortex was probably just a silly prank that those silly Kirkland fellows pulled, the entire neighborhood burst into nervous laughter and applause.

"I told you so!" Ian laughed, applauding the bewildered looking family. "Those Kirkland kids are pretty cool!"

An hour or so later, Kardo and Korad sat in their modest den, sipping cups of hot deconstructed salt.

"What are we going to do with that stuff?" Korad asked, gesturing towards the enormous mound of candy corn sitting on the floor.

"We should get rid of it. Forever." Kardo said firmly. "That stuff messed up your head, Korad."

Korad did not like the idea of nearly killing himself from excessive sugar intake and not being rewarded for his scouting efforts.

"I was faking it," he lied cleanly. "I didn't want to have to walk around anymore. My feet hurt. Like, painful hurt. It felt like the bottoms of my feet were about to melt clean off. I did it for my feet's well being. Sorry."

"You seemed pretty loopy," Kardo said suspiciously. "I think you're lying."

"Nope. Not lying. Not at all. The canned die is normal. Doesn't do anything. Tastes good. Invigorating."

"Why did you freak out about that girl dressed as a princess?"

Unfamiliar with the term 'princess', Korad said indignantly,

"I princessed her on purpose."

Also somewhat unfamiliar with the term 'princess', Kardo assumed his brother was telling the truth.

"She got a lot more stuff than I did, though," Korad muttered, still stung by the elderly man's stingy candy corn distribution.

"Maybe her outfit hexed the humanfolk," Kardo suggested. "Maybe that's why."

Korad looked at his brother with an enormous grin.

"You're a genius."

Kardo shrugged modestly.

"We should recreate her hex," Korad began with enthusiasm. "I bet…I bet like soldiers could wear that stuff in the field!"

The imps immediately began to search for hot pink silk.

Three months after Kardo and Korad's pitch for the 'canned die', the Infernom military used the candy corn in the field of battle in order to reinvigorate themselves and fight with new-found strength.

Kardo and Korad became obscenely wealthy.

Initially, the treat was received well, but the General quickly caught wind of how, shortly after ingesting the canned die and feeling a sudden desire to run around in circles, soldiers experienced extreme drowsiness and fell asleep without warning.

He caught wind of it many times, actually, but never remembered to tell Kardo and Korad of the side effect, so Gareo had to tell them the bad news.

The princess dresses were met with skepticism, and all they accomplished was getting the somber soldiers who wore them to be mocked and ridiculed by the opposing militaries.

"I'm sorry," Gareo had said. "But your products are defective. We're going to need to stop distributing them,"

Korad had belligerently began on how binding the contract was and how they couldn't have predicted how 'sissy' the soldiers' nervous system was and how unjust the law system was.

Kardo accepted the terms quietly.

The two had moped around their apartment for days, until

Kardo had burst out of his room one afternoon, a thick book in hand.

"We must return to Earth!" he had eagerly told Korad. "Chuh-rist-mass is coming!"

"What is Chuh-rist-mass, exactly?" Korad muttered, downcast, clicking through channels on their television.

"A day in which humanfolk scramble to purchase each other gifts for some incomprehensible reason and sing songs to their neighbors- but that's not the point! Look at this!"

He held up what appeared to be a white piece of paper.

"I don't get it."

Kardo pointed at the paper again.

"It's called Suh-Now! S-N-O-W. It's supposed to be incredibly cold and fluffy and I read this book-" he holds up a thin, colorful book, with the words, "Frosty the Snowman" across the front. "where this Suh-Now can be used to create these strange supernatural men made out of snow, who sing something about bumping to traffic stops! Imagine an army of those incredible beings!"

Korad, still somewhat skeptical, got up out of his seat.

"Well," he said. "What are we waiting for?"

First Amnesiac

Brynne Herzfeld
6th Grade

Prologue

My heart pounded as I ran. Sweat was pouring down my face and back, making my shirt damp. I heard rapid barking behind me. I glanced toward the small mirrors at the edge of my sunglasses, allowing me to see behind me. The Chihuahuas were catching up. These Chihuahuas were genetically altered to carry an extremely poisonous bite. The first bite will paralyze you, they say. The second will kill you. The police forces had stopped using German Shepherds and Labradors over a hundred years ago. Chihuahuas were fast, small, lightweight, and these Chihuahuas could climb.

I came to the edge of the vast lake, Centuria. This was a

lake I had swum in all my life, the lake where I learned to swim. My mind whirled. I cursed myself for not thinking about this. I was supposed to be prepared! But instead, during the biggest crime of my thieving career, I had forgotten about the only expanse of water in Lacerton. I looked at the small, handheld control panel for my electronic backpack. Waterproof mode was on. I kicked off my shoes, pulled off my shirt, and dove.

The Chihuahuas whined in frustration. The one thing Chihuahuas couldn't do was swim. I laughed at my sheer luck. That was the closest I had ever come to being caught. I glanced to the edge of my sunglasses, only to find that they weren't there. I was swimming at high speed, and I knew the dangers of looking behind me. Too late. I turned my head around as far as it would go, to check if I really was safe. I was. I made for the far shore, slowing down now. I stumbled out of the lake, soaked to the bone, and my best tank top was ruined.

Rrrrrr. I nervously turned around. Three Chihuahuas stood snarling behind me. I cursed myself again. I had forgotten that, despite my swim team training, Chihuahuas could run faster than I can swim. I made no delay in turning around and sprinting. As I turned my head to check behind me, a shadow took out the Chihuahuas. But my skull collided with solid steel, and all was black.

Chapter 1

I groggily opened my eyes. I had to make sure they were working, because it was still pitch black. They were working. Suddenly a light flared, and I winced. A small flame that seemed to be encased in a flashlight lit up a man's -no, boy's- face. The boy looked to be about thirteen, with amber eyes and red hair.

The first word I managed to choke out was, "Ginger." The boy smirked. "Right back 'atcha." I started to scowl, but then I just barely remembered something. "You saved me from the Chihuahuas." The boy laughed. "Not on your life. If it had been my decision, I would've let you died. That was Arnold that saved you. I'm not telling you my name until I am ordered to. So, since you're not part of our little group, I can ask for your name. So what's your name?"

I automatically opened my mouth to respond, but as I groped through my memory, the only thing I could remember is Chihuahuas chasing me. "I don't know. I don't remember anything. Except for the Chihuahuas chasing me, and someone saving me. I don't know who I am!" The boy's face paled. "Oh crud. Arnold!" He shouted the last part, and immediately another face materialized, holding its own flashlight-flame.

My eyes widened. The new arrival was breathtakingly handsome. With pure black hair and bright blue eyes, I found it hard to concentrate on what he's saying. "My name's Arnold. Arnold Quisler. I hope those restraints aren't too much for you." He gestured downward. For the first time I noticed that I was on an ancient hospital bed strapped to the bed by padded restraints. I also notice that we were moving.

"Oh- oh no, of course they're not too much. I- I never noticed them. Where-" He held up his hand. "No time for questions. You took quite a hit. I noticed that your parents must have been very wealthy. They obviously had enough money to pay for genetically enhanced brain cells that grow back almost instantaneously," at this his face grew sour for a moment. "The brain cells grow back, so you don't lose the function of the brain, or tasks, but individual memories won't grow back. It's going to be awhile before we get there. You might as well relax." He undid the restraints and I flexed my arms, happy to be able to move them.

It looked like we were underneath the Earth. We were traveling in a long gaping tunnel, with steel cables running along the top and bottom of the tunnel. When my eyes wandered, I saw that there were steel bars running alongside a platform that my bed stood on. The bars were vertical, enclosing me totally. The platform was wide enough for twenty people to stand on comfortably and still have elbow room. Ginger Dude and Arnold were seated in chairs right next to my bed. The chairs were sleek and modern, with keypads on the armrests and a high-tech seatbelt. I looked up at the top of the cage, because that's what it was, and found there were pulleys running along the edges of the roof. Thick steel cables ran through them.

"This compartment is one of the many porta-rooms that the Peace De Resistance owns. The porta-rooms are well equipped for any period of travel, from a day to six months. There are many different types of compartments, but this particular kind is medical. There's food, water, entertainment, and, of course, medical equipment. We don't have fancy stuff, just the basics." Arnold had clearly done this before. I raised my hand. "Just one question." I pointed to Ginger Dude. "What's his name?" Ginger Dude scowled. "Ralph. Ralph Sawyer."

There was a small, touchscreen panel in my hand. I held it up to my face. It was password protected. I pressed my thumb against a heat sensitive fingerprint scanner, and ACCESS GRANTED flashed on the screen. "Welcome Alexandra Velotskye," a cool female voice said. Arnold stiffened, and Ralph stood up. "What's wrong?" I asked. Ralph was trembling. "Velotskye," he croaked. "Is the President's name. Alexandra Velotskye is her daughter."

Never Give Up

Dillon Jenkins
4th Grade

Chapter 1

It was a beautiful sunny day and I had just woken up from an enchanted sleep. Today was the day my mother and I were off to Puerto Rico. I was so excited because it was the first time I'd ever been to Puerto Rico, an island in the Caribbean. On the way to the airport I thought, "What a wonderful, easy life I have. I get to swim, play and just have fun for two weeks." The airport was crowded because it was a holiday but we had gotten there early, so everything was going smoothly. We boarded the plane and got ready to take off. I looked at my mom and said, "This is going to be the best vacation ever."

The flight was thirteen hours so I settled in. I played video games, watched a movie and started to doze off. I was dreaming of swimming with the dolphins, a warm breeze against my skin, soft sand, palm trees and coconuts when Wham!! My head hit the side of the plane. I woke up and saw luggage flying out of the overhead bins and people screaming. I heard my mother cry out, "Dillon"!! She tried to grab my hand but the plane was shaking violently and I couldn't hold onto her. Crash!! We hit the water and it felt like hitting a cement wall.

When I opened my eyes, I was under water, shocked, frightened and filled with horror. I fought my way to the top of the water. My legs were numb and my head was throbbing. How did I get out of the plane? Where was my mother? Was I even alive or was this just a bad nightmare? All I knew was that I was going to die if I didn't find land. I thought I saw something far off in the distance that looked like an island. I felt something on my back. It was a flotation device from the plane and I hung onto it for dear life.

I started to swim and swim and swim. I could no longer move my arms and was completely frozen. I was delirious but thought I saw my backpack and my mom's suitcase. Was I dreaming? I just wanted to be with my mom, home in my warm bed. I reached for both bags and pulled them towards me, or thought I did. This took every ounce of energy I had left. I felt dizzy, everything was a blur and then I passed out.

Chapter 2

My eyes were still closed when I felt something nibbling on my nose. I opened my eyes to the horrifying sight of a large crab looking me right in the eye. My eyes and mouth were so full of sand, I could hardly see or scream for help. I jumped and pulled the crab from his strong grip on my nose. Where was I? I closed my eyes in hopes that it would all go away and this was just a dream. When I opened my eyes nothing had changed. It was real. I was on an island alone…well, not entirely alone, the crab was staring at me.

I desperately tried to figure out what had happened. I turned and tripped on what I realized was my mom's suitcase. Next to it was my backpack. Where was my mother? I immediately started to cry out to her. I couldn't see her or anyone for that matter. I started to run towards what looked like a cave. I found a small cave that looked like it would be a good place to sleep but I was so hungry and thirsty, I thought I'd better find some food.

I stumbled upon a fresh water pond and dove in. I drank the water because it seemed clean. I saw fish near my feet and thought this would be a place I could catch my dinner. I love fish, but what was I thinking? I wasn't at a restaurant. I was alone on a deserted island. I looked to the left of the pond and saw banana trees, fruit trees and vegetables. I ran towards the food. I found a tree with a large, juicy, red apple.

As I went to pick it, I heard the scariest hissing noise. Right next to the tree was a snake, not just your average garden snake but what looked like a boa constrictor! If I remember correctly, the Discovery Channel had a show about these kinds of snakes. They like to wrap around animals and 10-year-old boys, squeeze them to death, and then swallow them whole. Run!!

I jumped into a berry bush, thinking my blood shot eyes might blend in with the red berries all around me. He slithered around the bush and seemed to look at me with the most evil, black eyes. "I'm dead", I thought. He must not have seen me because he slowly went away. My heart was pounding 100 miles per hour. Between the berries I could see banana trees and melon vines. I didn't know if I should move but thought, "If I don't eat, I might pass out." I carefully grabbed banana and continued my journey to explore the island. I wanted to remember this location. The food was delicious, but I wanted nothing more than a big plate of French fries and to be home with my mother, off this island.

I came across a big area of bamboo. I started to think about making spears and fishing poles. Who was I kidding? I never have been camping or done a day of Boy Scouts in my life. I've watched movies about surviving on an island. Maybe I could figure it out. As I was thinking, I looked down to my foot.

"Oh no", I said, "if there's one thing that scares me more than snakes, it's spiders, large, black, furry, huge spiders." This spider was the size of a jumbo pancake you get at IHOP on their kids eat free, Tuesday pancake special. I was paralyzed. How would I get out of this one? The spider was crawling up my leg and I could actually see his beady, red eyes and fangs that were going to puncture me and suck my blood.

Suddenly I heard e-e-e-e-e-oh-oh-oh-oh and a coconut was thrown at the spider just perfect enough to knock him off of my leg and allow me to run. There was no time to say thank you. I ran past two more caves. I thought I saw a big pair of eyes looking out of one of the caves so I continued to run.

I saw what appeared to be man's best friend – a dog. I realized it actually wasn't a dog but a wolf, so I ran even faster. I was very tired. I now know why my mother told me I should have gone out for the track team. I couldn't run any longer. I saw beautiful, tall coconut trees. I collapsed under one and tried to catch my breath, when a coconut hit me on the head. It hurt very badly but the good news is my hard head split the coconut open. There in front of me was a fresh, juicy coconut ready to eat. I love coconuts, so I started to eat when I heard someone say, "Hello".

"What?" I said. "Who's there?"

"Knock, knock", the voice replied, "Who's there"?

I was so tired at this point, I said, "Tell me who you are!"

"Knock, knock, who's there…ding dong, dum dum," somebody replied. I usually have a good sense of humor, but not today. I looked up and saw a large yellow and red parrot. I started to ask him questions as if he was going to tell me a way to get home. I realized I was acting crazy and had to get away from ding-dong dum dum.

I saw more mountains and ocean as I explored more of the island. Up ahead of me, I saw what appeared to be a boat. This could be my way home off the island! I reached the boat only to find what looked more like a pile of firewood. The bottom had so many holes, it looked like swiss cheese.

I sat down on a stump feeling hopeless. I put my head down and thought, "There's no way out of here." I started to pray when the ground began to move. Could it be an earthquake or was it God trying to give me a sign? Just then a head popped out of the stump I was sitting on. My stump was actually a giant sea turtle. All sorts of thoughts ran through my head… I could ride on his back through the ocean to get home. "Not at that pace", I thought.

"I won't be home until my 16th birthday." I got up and told the turtle I hoped to see him again, but for now I had to find a cave and get some sleep. It was getting dark so I started my journey back to the first cave, my mom's suitcase and my backpack.

Chapter 3

I found the cave and pulled my backpack and mom's suitcase inside. My mother used to joke about the gigantic size of her suitcase. I now knew why she called it "The condominium", you could actually sleep in it. It took up most of the small cave. I took everything out and climbed inside. I used some clothes as a pillow and fell fast asleep.

I woke up stuck in a curled position and was so stiff I could hardly move. This was far from my comfortable bed at home. My stomach growled and reminded me how hungry I was. I remembered all the things I'd seen and didn't want to see on the island the day before, so I started to make a plan. I looked through my backpack and my mother's things. My mother had a lot of girl things like shampoo, cream, razors, curling iron, hairbrush, soap, hat and make-up. I also thought I could fill her hat with fruit. I needed to find more than fruit, so I planned to find the bamboo I had seen before and make a fishing pole. I was ready to venture out to begin my journey of survival.

I crawled out of the cave and headed to the pond. I saw the crab that was starring at me when I washed up on shore. I kneeled down to say hello. He was such a cute little thing and I was desperate to talk to someone or something. I needed a friend! I put my nose close to him on the ground and told him my whole story. He didn't move. It was as if he was listening. I said, "I think you understand." He moved closer like he wanted to show me he cared and then he lunged forward and clamped onto my nose! I spun around trying to get him off, but he held on tightly. I finally pried his claws off and threw him across the beach. He scampered right back as if he wanted to play "throw the crab". I told him he wasn't my friend and headed to the pond.

The pond was fairly close to the cave. The water felt so nice. While I was washing my hair, I saw fish swimming around me. I needed to find that bamboo. On the way there, I found berries, bananas and a coconut. I filled my mom's hat with fruit and put it in my backpack. When I got to the bamboo I tried to break off the shoots. I couldn't believe how tough it was to break.

I was struggling when something jumped on my back and started screaming "ouh, ouh, awe, awe." My heart was racing. I was terrified. Was it a tiger, bear or flesh-eating native? I fell down and looked up to see a monkey with the biggest brown eyes. I could hardly breathe, but the monkey was calm and actually appeared to be friendly. He jumped on the bamboo and broke off a piece. He must have been watching me struggle. I grabbed a banana out of my backpack and offered it to him. I decided to call him"Jumper," because of how we met.

My stomach was growling more than ever, so I ate a banana and headed back to the pond. How was I going to catch a fish with just a bamboo shoot? I needed wire and a hook. I ran back to the cave to see what I could find. I felt like someone was following me. It was Jumper, right behind me. I think I found a friend.

I found some dental floss and tied it onto my bamboo shoot. I took some berries for bait and a rock as a sinker and fastened them on the dental floss. Jumper sat quietly and watched, then handed me a coconut I had found earlier. I wasn't sure why he did that, but realized I should bring back water from the pond and maybe I could crack open the coconut and fill it with water. Jumper was so smart! We headed to the pond to catch some fish.

After about an hour, I caught my first fish. I cracked open my coconut by hitting it against a rock. I drank the juice and filled it with water for the cave. Now I had to figure out how to cook the fish. I needed to start a fire. I collected sticks and dry brush and made a pile. I found two sticks and tried rubbing them together to create a flame, but wasn't having much luck. My uncle was a serious camper. I remember he told me once that if you put fuel on something and hit it with a rock you, could cause sparks and start a flame. Where could I find fuel? I looked in my mother's suitcase and found hairspray! I covered a medium size rock with it and rubbed another rock against the soaked rock. I created friction and sparks, then took a twig and caught it on fire. I poked the fish with a sharp stick and held it over the fire to cook. It was the best fish ever, but sure was a lot of work for one meal. I gave Jumper a banana and ate some berries. I was exhausted. Tomorrow I would try to find a bigger cave, find more food, make a weapon and try to think of a way off this island.

I woke up early and went to the pond to fill my coconut with water and collect more fruit. I found some more melons and berries. I now needed a weapon and another tool to hunt with. I needed to make a bow and arrow. I found a sturdy stick for the bow, feathers and several good sticks for the arrows. I had to make sharp tips for the arrows, so I looked for sharp rocks or broken glass. I always carry dental floss in my backpack so I thought that would be a useful tool again. I filled my backpack and went looking for another cave.

About 20 minutes from the pond, I found a large cave. I wanted to move my things there and find a way to close off the opening. I remembered there was an old, broken down, boat on the other side of the island. I found the boat and a few big pieces of wood for a door for the cave. I piled them on top of each other and tied one vine around them and another vine like a rope to pull them back to the cave. Jumper wore my backpack and I pulled with all my might. As I was heading back, I heard a horrifying, growling sound. "Oh no, not the wolf again!" I tried to walk faster but was so weighed down I didn't want to look back.

Suddenly I felt my leg being pierced by sharp teeth, the wolf had attacked me. Jumper screamed to distract him but he wouldn't let go. I felt dizzy and weak. I heard "No, No, dum dum." It was that parrot again! He swooped down and landed on the wolf's head. He pecked at his head and eyes with powerful strength. The wolf released my leg and ran away. The parrot saved my life. I named him "Swooper", because of how we met. I couldn't decide between that and Dum Dum, so I made Dum Dum his nickname. I had another friend. The three of us were like a little family now.

We made it back to the cave, but my leg was bleeding badly. I found an aloe vera plant, cleaned my wound and rubbed aloe all over it. I tore a tee shirt I had and wrapped it around my leg. I had to make my bow and arrows to protect myself from that wolf. I took the biggest stick I had found and tied dental floss to both ends. I made three arrows with the other sticks and tied feathers on each one to help them fly. I sharpened rocks with other rocks to make the tips of the arrows. I thought I should make a spear for protection in case I ran out of arrows. I took a piece of bamboo and secured my mother's razors on the end with strands from the coconut and more dental floss. My weapons were ready.

It was getting late so I pulled my wood into the cave and walked back to the pond to get some dinner. I brought my spear and fishing pole in case that wolf returned. I thought I would sleep in the small cave and bring my things over to the big cave in the morning. Good thing the condominium had wheels! I couldn't catch a fish and realized I had the whole ocean to use for food and the salt water would be healing for my leg. When the three of us arrived at the ocean, we saw crabs and clams everywhere. I collected several of them and filled my backpack. I pried open the clams and cracked open the crab shells with a rock. As I was doing this, the crab that clamped onto my nose earlier appeared. I felt terrible thinking he was watching me prepare to eat his family. I decided to make him my friend and name him Crabby (not because of how we met. If that were the case, I would have named him Clamper). I made a fire and cooked my dinner. "What a long, painful day," I thought.

The next day, I decided it was time to set up my new house. I packed up everything and headed to the bigger cave with my new family. When I got there the first thing I did was make beds for everyone. I used a big palm branch as a broom. I cleaned the cave and brought a large branch in and leaned it against the cave wall for Scooper to perch on. I filled the bottom of the condominium with sand and placed a jacket over it to make a soft surface to sleep on. I filled a tee shirt of mine with grass and tied the ends for a pillow. I made a bed for Jumper by digging a hole and filling it with soft grass and leaves. I used wood from the boat to set a shelf up between rocks on the wall of the cave. I used clamshells for spoons, my Frisbee from my backpack for a plate and carved out coconuts for bowls and glasses. I made forks out of sharp branches. I collected vines and wove them into baskets and floor coverings. Jumper helped me with everything. He was like a human being.

For the outside of the cave, I dug a pit and laid branches over it to make a fire pit for cooking. I took hundreds of rocks and made a wall around the cave for protection. I piled them almost five feet tall with a small hole dug underground to crawl through. I put two large pieces of wood in front of the cave entrance for doors. I strung vines from one side to the other as a clothing line to hang my clothes after I washed them in the fresh water pond. I collected wood, water, fruit, and vegetables and fished everyday.

I was surviving better than I ever thought I could, but I had to think of a way home off this island and back to my family. I missed them so much! It was time to plan my rescue. I told Jumper, Swooper and Crabby it was time to go home and not to worry. If we found a way home, they were coming with me!

Chapter 4

The days seemed to turn into months since I had arrived on the island. Ever since that first day I was washed onto the shore, I had collected a pebble each day to keep track of the time here. Today was the day I wanted to count the pebbles. There were 270! I had been here over nine months! I told Jumper and the others I was ready to plan my rescue weeks ago, but for some reason or another, just surviving seemed to take all my time. I was so homesick it hurt. Not a day would go by without thoughts of my family and friends. I had to believe my mom survived the crash and was going to find me or it would be too hard to go on.

I had been making a rescue plan in my head for some time. The first thing I needed to do was make a giant S.O.S sign. I collected large rocks and found the most open, visible part of the beach to spell S.O.S. Jumper helped carry rocks while Swooper directed the whole operation with annoying orders of where to place the rocks. "Over there, here, no not there dum dum," were just some of his many helpful words. The rocks were arranged 20 feet high and 30 feet wide. We placed them on the white sand so a plane flying by could spot them. I then took three sturdy bamboo shoots and tied my red Junior Lifeguard sweatshirt on the top to make a red flag. I dug a hole in the area close to the S.O.S rocks and firmly secured the flag. I then took my mom's makeup mirror and tied it on a tree facing the ocean. I thought when the sun shone on the mirror it would be a signal for a plane or boat.

My next plan was to find the old broken down boat on the other side of the island and see if I could rebuild something that could float. If my signs and signals didn't work, I needed another plan. I sat down and talked to Jumper, Crabby and Swooper and told them my plan. If I could build a raft or sail boat and was rescued, I assured them I would come back for them. I spent days putting the broken pieces of wood, bamboo and large tree branches together with vines. I used several pieces of my mom's clothing and tied them together to make a sail attached to bamboo. It had been almost a month since I started to build my boat. Nobody had seen my S.O.S sign, so I knew it was time to set sail. I packed as much food as I could in my backpack, a compass I made, my spear and lots of water. I know this was crazy, but ten months on this island was too much to bear. I left as soon as the sun had risen and said a tearful, "I'll be back," to my island family. The waves were big and it took me a long time to get past the shore break. It was windy and I felt like I was moving fast. I started to get scared. All the things that could happen ran through my mind…starvation, drowning, being eaten by man-eating sharks… I had to remain calm, though. Hours had gone by and it was starting to get dark and cold. The wind was getting strong, I started to pray and then fell asleep.

I woke up in the daylight to a loud thump! I was lying on half of what was left of the boat. My sail was gone, but I was clinging onto my backpack and paddle. I had been washed up on a beach. When I came to my senses, I realized it was the beach on the other side of my island. I had gone in a circle and ended right back where I started on this deserted, lonely, far away from home, place. For the first time, I felt completely hopeless. I thought I would never be rescued. I made my way back to the cave and went to sleep for a long time.

The next day I woke up and convinced myself I couldn't

quit! My mother always told me, "Never give up!" She'd remind me often by saying "NG up!" I had to believe I was going to be rescued and I had to go to drastic measures to make it happen. I called a family meeting and told them my plan. "I know you are going to think I've lost my mind", I said. "I'm going to burn the island down with bombs made by my mom's cans of hair care products." Jumper turned his head to the side in shock. Swooper said "dum dum" and Crabby ran away towards the water. I guess that didn't go over so well. I explained my reasons for the fire. I told them if a whole island were on fire, somebody would have to see the flames. On the other hand, if they didn't, I just burned down our home. It was worth the chance and I was desperate to be rescued.

I began to collect all the cans of flammable hair care products. Half of my mom's suitcase was dedicated to her hair, so I had a lot. I thought if I caught the aluminum cans on fire they would explode like fireworks. I thought I would do this on the other side of the island so my cave would be the last to go. I prepared everything for the big day.

It had been over ten months and I was ready to take a chance to be saved. I planned on throwing five hair care product bombs into the burning brush. I'd then run back to my cave and the S.O.S sign. I hugged everyone and confidently told them this was going to work, even though inside I was full of fear.

The bombs worked better than I thought. The bamboo and palm trees caught on fire quickly as I ran back to the other side. By the time I got back I could see flames and smoke. I held onto Jumper and Swooper and prayed for a miracle.

Suddenly an incredibly loud sound, almost like thunder or the rumble of a huge earthquake, came out of nowhere above my head. The sand was blowing so hard against my face it felt like sand paper. I couldn't see anything. My eyes and skin were burning from the tornado of sand. I heard a voice say, "Dillon! Dillon, I'm here! Hold on!" For a moment I thought I'd gone to heaven, but I didn't think painful sand in my face was the way the entrance to heaven would feel.

The voice became louder and louder. "Dillon, it's me!

Hold on!" Just then something hit me on the head and almost knocked me out. It was a ladder from a helicopter. I could see a vague outline of a woman flying the helicopter. I heard the voice again. "Dillon, it's mom! Pull yourself up!" I said, "Mom??? Are you flying the helicopter???" "Yes, Dillon. I'll explain later," she said, "Just get in." I grabbed onto the ladder. Jumper was clinging to my head, Swooper was hanging onto my arm and Crabby was clamped onto my nose. It took every ounce of my strength to pull everyone up the ladder towards the helicopter. The wind was blowing hard and we were swaying back and forth, but we managed to make it inside.

I held onto my mom so tightly, she could hardly steer the helicopter. This was the happiest day of my life! I had so many questions like… What happened to her the dreaded day the plane crashed and when did she learn how to fly a helicopter? But more importantly, how did she find me? She looked at me with tears in her eyes and said, "Dillon, I always told you to never, ever, give up! I never gave up trying to find you." In that moment, I felt so loved. We didn't have to say anything else, I was home.

Working for Fluffy

Meghan Leong
8th Grade

On a brisk winter afternoon, nine-year-old Alisa walked happily home from school, thinking about all the fun she and her best friend Connie would have over Christmas break. As she skipped gaily down the snow-covered sidewalk, she thought: If only I had a puppy to play with, it would be so much more fun. Deep in thought, Alisa lost track of where she was heading and finally realized she was in an unfamiliar part of town.

Where am I? She wondered and twirled a strand of her shoulder-length black hair nervously. It was twilight and snowflakes daintily danced down from the darkening sky. Alisa shivered and looked around. She spotted a brown brick building across the street. The rusty metal sign read: The Tri-City Animal Shelter... what is that? *I need to use a phone, so I hope it's a friendly place. There's only one way to find out.*

She headed to the building and swung open the heavy wooden door. She stepped into a whole new world. From top to bottom and side to side, there were metal cages of dogs, cats, puppies, and kittens. Although the animals were cute, the place had a somber feel to it, and Alisa could see that the caged animals were miserable. One gray calico kitten mewed as she pawed at the cage lock. Alisa sensed they all wanted a nice warm, cozy home with a loving family. She tried to ignore the gloominess as she stared at the lonely animals that were looking at her with their forlorn eyes, curious to know what was going on. There was one extremely adorable West Highland terrier puppy that especially caught her eye. He looked inquisitively up at her as she neared his cage. His dirty cotton ball tail wagged immensely as Alisa reached through the cage to pet him. However, instead of giving a contented bark, he emitted a whimper and nuzzled her hand sadly.

"Hello! How may I help you?" A voice called out from behind her. Startled, Alisa whirled around to see a kind looking woman with short brown hair and a pleasant face. "Yes! May I please use a telephone?" Alisa asked.

"Sure," the woman indicated to a pay phone on the wall.

"Thank you," Alisa said, relieved. She inserted a quarter in the phone and dialed her home number and after a few minutes, her parents were on their way. While she waited, the nice lady explained the purpose of the animal shelter and how it was founded. She elaborated that saving the animals from cold and hunger was only part of the goal.

Finding a suitable owner and home for each animal was often the hardest part of her job. Alisa listened and thought about what the lady said as she walked back to the little Westie's cage. She opened the cage and picked the puppy up and cradled him. The puppy emitted a soft bark and nuzzled into her arms and licked her cheek. Alisa giggled and stroked his soft, fluffy fur. She looked out the window and saw her mother's car outside. Quickly, she stood up and coaxed the puppy back into his cage.

"See you soon," Alisa whispered to the puppy as she thanked the nice lady and headed home.

* * *

"For the last time, Alisa, no!" her mother cried. They had just gotten back from the Tri-City Animal Shelter, and Alisa had asked her parents about the Westie puppy.

"Why?" Alisa asked, "I am really responsible and efficient. I help with chores and I have straight A's."

"That's not the point," her father said wearily, "you're not old enough to take care of a puppy. Puppies are a lot of work, and you are just not ready for this type of hard work. You are only nine, and taking care of a puppy is almost like taking care of a baby."

"Can you guys tone it down a bit? Rock music is so much more interesting than arguing about a puppy! I can even hear you with my earphones on!" Alisa's older brother Sam complained while he stomped into the living room with headphones jammed in his ears.

"Yes, this talk is over," her mother agreed.

"That's so unfair! You don't even care about these animals that don't have a home!" Alisa cried and burst into tears. She ran to her room, slammed her door and stayed there the rest of the evening.

The next day, Alisa told Connie about the dilemma. Instead of getting angry at her parents though, Connie smiled and said, "I have an idea! Your parents probably think you are too immature and not ready for the big responsibility of taking care of a puppy, so you need to show them that you're responsible."

Bewildered and swiping tears away, Alisa asked, "How do I show them?"

"Easy," Connie replied, "Work for them and earn money. Do more chores. Wash windows, dust the whole house, clean the bathrooms, keep your room clean, be nice to your parents, and volunteer to clean people's houses. And blow your nose!"

The next few months Alisa set to work on this wonderful idea like a busy bee. She helped her parents wash the windows, cleaned and tidied every room until they were spotless, did the dishes, and helped with every single chore her parents didn't have time for.

Her parents were pleasantly surprised and thought Alisa was being so helpful that they increased her allowance. In private, they smiled and appreciated how their little girl was growing up and being more responsible. Every day, she kept doing more chores without being asked. Finally, Alisa saved enough money to buy one chew toy, two bags of dog food, and a dog bed.

However, Alisa knew she needed more money to save that little puppy. She and Connie hung posters around town that read: 'Housecleaning Service, Need Your Home Squeaky Clean? Call Alisa at 348-9012'. Sadly, nobody wanted to hire Alisa after they found out she was only nine. Very subdued, Alisa was just about to give up when the phone rang. After talking on the phone for a few minutes, Alisa jumped up with joy and shouted, "I'm hired!"

The next day Alisa rode her bike to her first customer's home. Nervously, she stepped on the whitewashed porch with her bag of cleaning rags and supplies and rang the doorbell. The door opened and Alisa gasped. It was the kind lady who she met at the Tri-City Animal Shelter.

"I know you. But…but…" Alisa stammered.

The lady smiled, "Hello. I don't think I've told you my name yet. I'm Mrs. Swan. Are you supposed to clean my house?"

"Hi Mrs. Swan," Alisa said brightly, "I'm ready to start." Suddenly, Alisa knew she could trust Mrs. Swan just by looking at her bright, twinkling brown eyes. She told her all about why she was doing all this work.

Mrs. Swan nodded and said, "Looks like you really want to help that puppy. You know what? Please take this and save that cute Westie." She rummaged through her purse and fished out a fifty dollar bill and pressed it in Alisa's palm. Alisa gasped again. That was enough money to buy everything else she needed.

"I-I haven't cleaned anything yet!" Alisa exclaimed surprised.

"Oh, don't worry about any of that. I have a feeling that you're going to be a wonderful owner for that puppy."

Alisa thanked Mrs. Swan and biked home in high spirits. Now she just needed to convince her parents. She closed her eyes and said a silent prayer. When she got home, she found Sam in the living room listening to his iPod. He looked up and called out, "Hey, crazy puppy freak." Alisa glared at him and went to her room to do homework and think.

Hours later, Sam called out and knocked at her room.

"Go away, Sam! I'm busy!" Alisa shouted out.

"Fine, don't come shopping with me," Sam replied.

Alisa jumped up. She loved shopping and needed a break from homework. Alisa poked her head out, "Hey! Wait, I'm coming!"

"Hurry up, slowpoke!" Sam teased. Alisa rolled her eyes, but she followed Sam out the door. After driving for a few minutes, Sam pulled up in front of the Tri-City Animal Shelter. Alisa was confused, "Why are we here?"

Sam turned around and said, "After you told me why you were doing all this cleaning, I persuaded Mom and Dad to let you get the puppy."

Alisa looked at him with genuine surprise, and then said with some skepticism, "But you're always making fun of me!"

"Just because I annoy you, doesn't mean I don't think about you. You deserve the puppy because you worked really hard, okay? You're a pretty awesome nine-year-old."

Alisa smiled wryly, "Since when did you start caring so much about me?"

"Hey! Wait a second..."

She laughed with joy, "I'm just joking! Thank you! Here, let me show you that adorable fluff ball." Alisa went straight for the Westie's cage and took him out. As Mrs. Swan helped, everyone was all smiles, including the Westie.

Sam then drove the very jubilant owner and puppy home. On the way Sam remarked, "What are you going to name him?"

Alisa thought for a long moment, "I'm going to name

him… Fluffy."

Sam scoffed, "I could have guessed that. He's so fluffy that I can't even see his eyes." Alisa smiled at her brother and thought about the long journey that led to saving this little puppy. She felt great that she could make a difference in one animal's life. She then thought about the other sad animals. Maybe Mrs. Swan needed some extra help at the shelter…

Kie and His Kite

Jacob Levin
3rd Grade

One nice afternoon Kie, the green fox, decided to buy a kite. As he walked to the store he saw a python threatening a bunny for his candy. The brave fox stood between the bunny and the terrifying python and exclaimed loudly, "Pick on somebody your own length!" The snake slivered away cowardly. Kie continued with his adventure to buy a kite. He walked in the store and immediately headed straight for the kite section. He knows where it is because he has been planning and savings his money for a kite for many months now. He is so excited when he picks out the most colorful kite of them all, and he proudly carries it to the cash register to pay for it with all his savings.

As Kie is skipping home the sneaky python spotted the fox with his brand new, colorful kite under his left arm. He gets an evil plan to sneak into Kie's house at night while he is sleeping, and steal his new, prized possession.

Later that night, the sneaky snake slipped into Kie's house unnoticed and got Kie's colorful kite and slivered home. The snake didn't know the bunny was watching, so after the python was gone the bunny races in to wake up the fox and alert him that the python stole his colorful kite. The fox and the bunny raced to the python's hole and surprised the sneaky snake. Kie demanded, "I want my kite back, please!" The python yelled, "Never!" Kie explained, "If it is a kite you want, I can share mine with you and I can teach you how to fly one." The snake said, "I always wanted a kite and would really love to know how to fly it."

As the days passed by the fox, the snake and the bunny became great friends. They played with their kites and had many fun afternoons together.

The Day the Thanksgiving Turkey Came to Life

Olivia Lewis
4th Grade

It was Thanksgiving morning, and my family and I were cleaning the house for dinner. Early in the morning my dad and I went to a new turkey farm outside of town. When we got there, we noticed an unusual light in the sky and a group of weird looking people. They were dressed like they were on their way to a costume party—long robes and pointy hats.

"Grace, I don't like these turkeys. That one is way too skinny, and that one is just plain fat," my dad criticized while we were picking out turkeys. "And I'm not too sure about that group of people either," my dad added.

"Just ignore them and focus on the turkeys. How about this one?" I asked pointing to a lovely turkey.

"Now that's a beauty," said my dad smiling. It was just perfect for eating!

We got home and started cooking our Thanksgiving dinner. Dad mashed the potatoes, mom boiled the corn, and my sisters and I started setting the table for dinner. Everything was running smoothly until my dad asked, "Where's the turkey?"

"Did you put it on the table girls?" asked my mom.

"Look!" yelled my sister Christie. We all saw that the turkey was alive!

It started running around the house, but we chased after it. The turkey's feathers were falling as it ran around frantically. My mom ignored the supernatural event and only noticed the mess. "Now I have to clean up again!" she cried. The bird ran out the back door and jumped onto a chair and then over the fence into the street. All we heard was a car coming and a loud GOBBLE!!!

Yes, the turkey was dead. "Well, who's up for hamburgers?!"

"Daddy!" I said while crying.

"What?"

"A turkey just got hit by a car and you want to make hamburgers?"

"Sure. Why not?"

It was a very insane day and a Thanksgiving Day I will never forget! We did have hamburgers, and then we all went to our rooms to think about what we had seen. I kept expecting someone to tell me the whole thing had been a joke, but no one ever did. Once I had time to think it over, I realized I had many, many questions. Why was that unusual light in the sky? Who were those strange people, and why didn't we ever see them again? How did the turkey come alive? Was it magic? I could only hope that next Thanksgiving my questions might be answered!

Fire, Fear, and I

Emily Ma
6th Grade

Smoke.

That's the first thing that registered in my drowsy mind. Then the smoke alarms. The constant beep, beep, beep rouses me enough to sit up and open my eyes. I rubbed my eyes, blinking slowly. Not that it helped much, my eyes immediately started watering, and I couldn't see much through the thick smoke that was slowly seeping into my room, from the crack under the door. Was this a nightmare? I slid out of bed, still trying to comprehend what's happening.

When the idea that my house is on actually on fire finally sunk into my sluggish head, panic coursed through me. Where were the firemen? Where were mom and dad? Where they safe? Or still asleep, unaware that our house was burning to the ground? I tried to remember what they had told us in school about fire safety, tried to remember the escape routes I had planned, but my mind came up blank.

I squinted and pulled my shirt up, to cover my mouth and nose. I grabbed the door knob and yanked the door open. The acrid scent of smoke overwhelmed my senses. The heat was intense. I instantly dropped onto my hands and knees, ignoring my stinging eyes and burning lungs. The hallway was filled with smoke and I could hear the crackling of fire somewhere downstairs.

I weighed my choices in my mind. I could either take my chances in the hallway and down the stairs, but possibly risk getting burned to death or suffocation or I could try going out my window, but since my room was on the second floor there was the chance I could injure myself. I shuddered at the image of my body going splat on the pavement. My prospects were great. Just great. I stood frozen with indecision. My eyes darted back and forth between the two options. I can still hear the smoke alarm beeping, but now it sounds like chanting, chose, chose, chose. I have to act like my life depends on the choice, because it does. No pressure. Yeah right.

My head pounds, I feel like someone is trying to drive a screw driver in it. I'm only eleven, too young to die, too young to be making life or death choices like this. I started cough. I've spent too much time thinking about it. I need to make a decision, and fast.

I screamed when I realized the bottom of my pants had caught on fire. The scream had been a mistake, I gagged and choked. Think! What had they told us in fire safety? Stop.....stop... Drop....STOP DROP AND ROLL! I shut my eyes and dropped onto the floor rolling as fast as I could. The world around me was a blur. I finally stopped moving and checked my leg. The fire was gone, but my lower left calf was already starting to blister. I gave an involuntary gasp when I got up and quickly shut my bedroom door. I had made my decision.

My calf burned as I stumbled my way over to the window. I fumbled with the latch, my fingers sweaty and clumsy. I finally managed to open the stupid window. I had started to get dizzy, my lower leg throbbing. I gratefully stuck my head out, breathing in the cool night's air. My head cleared a bit. I looked up. The moon was obscured by the thick, dark clouds. It looked like it might rain. Then I looked down. The ground looked so far away. My sense of vertigo increased and my breathing quickened. *I can do this* I told myself. I took a deep breath, and painfully attempted to slide out feet first. I grabbed the window frame tightly, my knuckles turning white. Maybe I should have chosen the hallway. Maybe I should have-

My train of thought was abruptly stopped as one of my sweaty hands slipped. I desperately tried to hang on with only one hand, my arm muscles burning. I watched, despairingly, as, one by one, my finger slipped.

I felt myself free-falling. A feeling of weightlessness engulfed me as I watched the ground get steadily closer. I opened my mouth to scream, but no sound came out. I closed my eyes and hoped for the best.

WHAM! My feet hit the concrete hard, pain shooting up my unburned leg. A second later my legs gave out from under me and my body slumped onto the asphalt, my head hitting something, was it the pot that my mom grew daises in? My vision swam, red spots clouding my sight. Everything was fading in and out of focus, but I wasn't burning to death, and wasn't that all that mattered? I would have yelled, but my throat was too raw. I needed to get help, call 911 or something, but pain would shoot through me when I tried moving. It became harder and harder to form coherent thoughts.

The last thing I heard before blacking out, was the sirens a fire truck and someone calling my name. Was it my mom? My dad? I felt a smile tugging on the corners of my mouth, as the first drops of rain fell from the sky. I was alive! Maybe scarred for life, but I was living and breathing and that's good enough for me.

The Colors of the Sunrise

Deepa Nandan
6th Grade

It is barely past five a.m. when the first rays of dawn penetrate the clouds. They paint the sky with golden hues as the sun gradually ascends and embraces the land with its warmth. The rooster marches to the post. He tosses back his bronze head, proudly puffs his scarlet chest, and crows confidently to signal the coming of dawn. The melody takes over the air, sending farmers flying out of beds and into the fields, while their wives struggle to wake their drowsy children and half-asleep cows.

A tear rolls down my cheek, and I wipe it away. It is the first time since I was born on this farm that I have gotten up in time to witness the sunrise – and it's absolutely breathtaking. I feel a soft tickle at my upper ankle. Scratch, my black and white kitten, has curled himself around my foot, as if pleading me not to go away. "Sorry, buddy," I tell him, gently lifting him up and pressing our cheeks together. Scratch is muddy most of the time, and his fur is tangled and matted. To me, however, he is the most beautiful creature in the world. But of course, I can't take him with me.

When the harvest sale ended last month, our family did not sell any crops. We became increasingly poor by day. Soon enough, our food supply was short, and there were too many mouths to feed. I, as the oldest of my four siblings, was relocating to London, England, to live with my Uncle Harry. I had never been anywhere outside of my farm in Kentucky before and the thought of leaving my beautiful home pains me, especially because I will have to spend the rest of my life without Scratch. My knees give away and I collapse onto my bed, which creaks loudly. I would love to sit on this bed forever, to never have to leave my wonderful farm. Of course, however, that's not an option.

Downstairs, my youngest sibling and only sister, Maggie, is perched on a wooden stool, carefully plaiting the golden hair of her doll. It is not a real doll, of course. My family could never afford such luxuries. My sister had simply fashioned one using an eggplant, hay, and some of Mama's old fabric. The moment she spots me appearing into the kitchen, she bursts into tears and flies toward me, her arms outstretched. I lift her into the air, and we hug.

"Gwenny, don't leave me," she cries. "Let me come with you!" I stroke her messy auburn hair, hold her freckled face in my palms, and look into her teary jade eyes.

"Listen, Maggie," I tell her tenderly. "If you were ready to travel, I wouldn't have rested until Papa let you come with me. But it's my duty as the oldest sibling to do what I can to make it easier for our family. You're eleven years old. You should understand what we're going through."

Maggie sniffles. "But Gwenny, I love you."

I feel tears starting to spring up in my own eyes. "I love you too, Maggie. You know I do. And I'd never want to leave you, but I have no choice. You'll take care of Scratch, won't you?" She nods vigorously. Apart from me, Maggie is the closest to my kitten.

Compassionate and shy by nature, my younger sister's home is among the critters. All the farm animals simply adore her. I suddenly detest myself. What am I doing? Why am I shoving Scratch, my siblings, and my parents away from me like this? Don't I love them the way they love me? "Maggie, I'll miss you" I say, choked by tears. I pull her into another embrace, and enjoy every moment of it, because I know this will be the last hug I share with Maggie in an extremely long time, if not forever.

"You'll write to me every day, promise?" Maggie's voice comes out in barely a whisper. All I manage to do is nod, as she sits back down on the stool and resumes her work on the doll's hair. I decide to stay outdoors for a while. I figure it will cheer me up, as it always does. The weather instantly urges me to take a leisurely walk around the farm. I slip into my walking shoes, and take in every single moment of my last trip around home. The briskness of the fresh autumn wind blows away my tears. How can I cry on such a beautiful day? My mind changes course and I try to think positively. My eighteenth birthday is a mere few weeks away.

However, this would be the first birthday I've ever spent away from my parents and my siblings. The tears return to my eyes, but I rub them away furiously. I'm not thirteen anymore. I'm a young adult, and I need to be strong. However, as I approach the wheat field, my favorite place on the farm, I feel as if the wind has blown away all my seventeen-year-old maturity. I sprint toward it as if I was five and had just seen an enormous candy. Rapidly losing control of my actions, I begin to sob, letting tears cascade down my face and splash upon the field. Soon, I cannot run any longer, and I collapse onto the ground, letting the wheat crops engulf me in a sea of gold.

By the time I reach home, my parents and siblings are waiting for me. My face is smeared with dirt and my hair is all over the place. I am still wearing my favorite denim overalls and plaid shirt. Mama convinces me to tie up my hair and wash my face, but no amount of begging and pleading can get me to change into the foreign scarlet dress Uncle Harry had sent me. Even in London, I still want to keep a piece of myself and my home. Mama lets me wear it on the plane, as long as I change at London. I agree to this, because I don't want to look like an outcast in my new home. When my bag is ready, and I have triple-checked to make sure I haven't left anything behind, Mama places a kiss on my forehead. "Good luck, Gwenny. We'll all miss you."

I nod. "I'll miss you too, Mama." She wipes a tear off of her cheek.

Papa, on the other hand, is his usual cheery self. "Why cry, pumpkin pie?" he chuckles, slapping my back. "Harry's not so bad. Why, I grew up my entire childhood with him. He's alright, and we got along just fine. Well-" his voice suddenly drops to a low, ominous tone. "Well, you've got to watch out too, because he can be a little…unpleasant at times, when you make the wrong move…"

Mama must have seen the horrified look on my face, because she instantly bursts, "Shut your mouth, Harvey, you're scaring her!"

Papa looks at me, his face suddenly bright again. "Why, I'm so sorry, Gwenny. I'll miss you so much when you're there! It's just that I'm maybe a bit scared of my baby girl going out into the world all by herself." I can tell he is a little depressed, although he tries to cover it with a laugh, coated with fake heartiness. I feel awful that I'm doing this, but it is for the benefit of my family and my household. I've said proper farewells to my parents, siblings, and Scratch, though I am still unsure of whether I should make this decision or not. Before I know it, however, I am on the airplane. I am going to London, and there is now nothing I can do to change it. There is also nothing I can do now to cure the feeling of vomiting that is caused by a mixture of homesickness and being airborne. My heavy eyes fall shut, and I wander into a dreamless slumber.

Bang! Bounce! Thud! A series of bumps on the plane instantly sends me awake and upright in my seat, as if I've been struck by lightning. At first, I'm bewildered and terrified. I think we've crash-landed or banged into another plane in the air. However, as I notice the glowing city lights, and a woman's voice appears on the speaker above, I know we've landed safely. I haul my bag into the London airport. Papa gave me some money in case of emergencies, but I highly doubt they use dollars here, and I want to avoid confusion. I stumble around from jetlag, shoving my way between the crowds.

When I notice the many signs pointing in many different directions, I stop dead in my tracks. I am lost. Wandering hopelessly around, I occasionally glance at the minuscule picture of Uncle Harry for reference, but he is nowhere in sight. Then, I see a line of people leading up to a woman checking passports. I recognize some people in the line, for they were on the same plane as I was. I figure this is where I am supposed to go, so after changing into my fiery red dress, I wait in line to get my passport checked.

"Madam, first and last name, please!" The lady at the desk drums her fingers impatiently. I realize that I am at the front of the passport line; the line that seemed never-ending when I first joined it. I must have dozed off because of time zone changes. "Huh?" I ask stupidly, having forgotten her request. "First and last name," she repeats, frowning disapprovingly. "Oh, you want my name?" I stammer, almost unconsciously. "Um…Gwenny…Gwendolyn. Gwendolyn Thompson." I hand her my passport.

As she adjusts her glasses and begins confirming it, I crane my neck to try to spot my uncle. He told my papa he'd be waiting at the main entrance. However, the only person I see there is a boy. He looks young- about my age. It dawns on me that perhaps he's seen Uncle Harry somewhere. Soon after the lady hands me my passport, I begin to walk tentatively toward the boy. I've always been somewhat shy toward strangers, and now that Papa and Mama aren't here, I'm feeling much more uncomfortable. But right now, I need as much help as I can get. "Hey! You over there! Yeah, I'm talking to you." The words flow out of me before I can stop them.

The boy looks at me with his piercing sapphire-blue eyes as if I'd just slapped him. "E-excuse me?" he stammers as his dark eyebrows ascend to the tip of his forehead, blending in with his rich chocolate-brown bangs. Embarrassment floods over me as I conclude that this must not be the proper approach to obtain one's attention. "I'm- I'm sorry. I'm new 'round this here uh… London," I stutter awkwardly. "Just wondering, but uh… have you seen this guy around by chance?" I yanked the photo out of Uncle Harry. He scans the photo, and suddenly his face lights up. "Aha!" he yells out triumphantly.

My heart suddenly floats with relief. "This man is Mr. Harold Thompson! You must be Miss Gwendolyn!" He grabs my hand and shakes it vigorously. "My name is Phillip, and I have been sent by your uncle to show you home. Oh, and I can carry that bag for you. It must be dreadfully heavy." He jerks the bag out of my arms and begins walking. I follow him curiously, wondering whether I can trust him or not. After all, this is an unfamiliar place, and strangers could be everywhere. But as I notice his warm smile, and his struggling to carry my bulky bag, I shove aside the thought that he is trying to kidnap me, and follow him to the taxi.

On the way to Uncle's apartment, I am dazed and worn out due to traveling, and I don't have much energy to speak. Phillip, however, is chatting and chatting. I am only listening to half of what he is saying. "You will adore it here, Miss Gwendolyn… I was waiting for hours there, thank goodness you arrived… I should have known it was you, the first words you said. Mr. Harold told me you were from somewhere uncivilized." The last word immediately gets my attention.

"Uncivilized?" I echo blankly. "My place is not uncivilized, just because it doesn't have all the fancy-shmancies y'all here have. You've got to be careful what you say, mister, or you'll be sorry" Phillip looks hurt at my retort, and turns to face the car window, but I don't care. He hurt me, too.

"I am sorry, but mind your manners, Gwendolyn," he mumbles softly. I can see a slight hint of disapproval in his eyes. I realize then that I am not going to like it here unless I really try, and if I am miserable here, it will only let my family down. "I'm sorry," I tell him a little hesitantly. "It's just that I'm trying to get used to this place instead of Kentucky. And, by the way, why'd my uncle send you to pick me up? Not that I don't like you or anything, but are you two like, best friends or something?" he shakes his head slowly. "I'm his butler," he mumbles. Because I don't have anything to say to that, the rest of the drive is spent in awkward silence.

Phillip knocks at the front door thrice. "It is I, with Miss Gwendolyn," he calls. A woman answers. She is dressed in a long gown and wearing an apron. "Ah, Miss Gwendolyn! Welcome home. The master's been expecting you." The woman gives a polite curtsy. "Thank you, Dorothy," said Phillip stiffly as she held the door for him. As Phillip leads me down the hall, I can see a few more women dressed the same as Dorothy. They must be maids, I think to myself. Back in Kentucky, there were barely any maids. Housewives did all the work themselves, with some help from their daughters. "Phillip!" booms a deep voice from down the hall. "Is Miss Gwendolyn here?"

I wonder why everyone here is calling me "Miss Gwendolyn". I've been "Gwenny" for as long as I can remember, and now the sound of my real name is almost alien. Phillip opens a door for me and holds it. Waiting on a leather armchair, is a thin and rather stern-looking man, wearing a formal black suit and tie with his other hand on a cane. The man's silver beard only hangs slightly below his chin. Shielding his head are shoulder-length locks that perfectly match his beard and thick eyebrows. "Ah, my niece," he says. So this is Uncle Harry! I can barely recognize him; he looked so much younger in the photo. "How are you doing, darling? How are you parents, Harvard and Angelina? How are your siblings?" I can tell he is trying hard to sound welcoming.

I haven't the slightest idea what to say next, so all I do is smile politely and say, "They're um… doing fine". I feel awkward then, not knowing how to carry on the conversation. Luckily, Phillip steps in and offers to show me around. "Go ahead, but bring her back immediately. I must know more about Gwendolyn if I am to take care of her."

"And this, my dear, is where you are to sleep." Phillip extends his arm to allow me into the room. The moment I step in, a bittersweet lemon fragrance flows through my nostrils, sending a wave of tranquility through my body. I exhale, feeling satisfied and relaxed. I wander around the rest of my room as if I am walking in a dream. My fingers delicately trace the patterns on my yellow tulip wallpaper. I carefully pull aside one of my velvety red window curtains, revealing a bustling city below. Reluctantly, I release the curtain, and the room becomes less bright.

Phillip is sitting patiently on my bed, letting me admire the luxury of my new room. I nearly faint as the sight of my bed catches my eye. The same feeling fills my heart as it did when I saw the wheat field on my last day at the farm. I run to the bed like a child and sink into the plush pillows and golden silk comforter. My brain is too relaxed for anything as I look above at the ornate violet canopy, and I laugh and cry at the same time. "Why, this is the most beautiful- I'm really going to live here?!"

Phillip frowns slightly. "I suppose you are… pleased with your bedroom, but that is no reason to act like an animal. You are, no doubt, uncivilized." His words slap me. I open my mouth angrily for a retort, but abruptly stop myself. Instead, I apologize and smooth out the bed sheets, embarrassed. "You should've seen my place. It's nothing like this," I mumble in a dry, toneless voice. He gives a curt nod and leads me out of the room.

"So what of your sister, Margaret?" asks Uncle Harry curiously. I've been stuck in this chair for hours, having an endless chat with him. I really need to learn how to have a conversation. I have never been sitting in one place for this long. At the farm, we were always active. "Maggie?" I ask. "She's fine, I think… I hope." He nods stiffly. "It was a simply delightful chat, Miss Gwendolyn. Pardon me, but I must leave now."

* * *

Dear Gwenny,

It's been a very lonely night without you. Mama and Papa made dinner, and we all ate at different times. No one's really talked much after you left. Your room's being emptied out. Scratch really, really misses you, and so do I. he is sleeping with me tonight. The brothers are doing fine. We all wish you were here with us. How is Uncles house so far? Are they really that uptight? Are there really no rodeo races? I hope you're doing fine. Please write back soon.

Love, Maggie

By the time I finish reading this letter, I am sobbing hysterically. Looking up, I see my reflection in the mirror hanging on my walls. My light blond hair is plastered to my face, and my cheeks and nose are a fiery red hue. My sapphire-blue eyes are puddles of tears. Thanks to my weeping, I look very unsightly. I know it won't help, but usually when I cry, I have someone there to comfort me. Now, I have no one. Phillip definitely won't do, and I'm just not comfortable enough with Uncle Harry to share my pain with him. This may sound childish, but right now, I really need a hug. I just want to be a kid again and cry until my uncle makes mama come to me. Obviously, at seventeen, that is not an option. Instead I collapse onto my bed and sob into the coziness of my comforters. I realize then that if I don't make friends soon, I'll be crying all day and all night.

"Now, I'm sure you unsophisticated folks don't know… hold the teacup handle between your thumb and index finger…" I am bored to the bone listening to Mrs. Samson from next door drone on and on about how to hold some tiny cup with a handle. This is only my second week living here, and I have already proven myself awfully uncivilized. Five days ago, after accidentally shoving off the fine fabric tablecloth during supper, (I needed the bowl of gravy on the other side of the table, and I thought it would be "rude" to ask) Uncle Harry thought I needed extra help fitting in with the sophistication of everyone else here. That's when he called in his neighbor Gertrude Samson to teach me how to "act like a lady"

Every morning she comes in with her graying hair and miniscule spectacles for a lesson, she gives me a look of pure disgust. Her obnoxious and annoying personality mixed with her tedious lessons just increases my already overflowing desire to return to the farm. Yesterday, we just completed a dull lesson on which of the three forks to use first during meals. This was a lesson we'd started the first day she came in. I personally think we could have covered this lesson in a mere two seconds. All she could have said to me was, "In the first meal, always use the fork to the farthest left" and we would be over with the lesson.

I tried to tell Uncle Harry that, but he scolded me, saying I should be "Thankful she is taking time off every morning to teach me how to act properly". To me, however, lessons on forks and teacups are absolutely pointless. Back at the farm, we each had only one fork, spoon, and knife. And none of the cups had handles. After about four hours, Mrs. Samson lets me take a break. I decide to write a brief letter to Maggie about my new life. I clench my teeth to prevent myself from crying as my quill brushes the paper, and I pour out my misery.

Dear Maggie,

I'm being trained how to act "properly" by Mrs. Samson, a cruel lady next door. She treats me like a nothing, and no matter how much I try to get along with her, she makes me as miserable as possible.

I stop to think if I should really be telling my little sister all this. I surely don't want to frighten her. Then again, I can't keep all my unhappiness inside myself forever.

Yesterday, I finally finished learning about the fancy-Nancy silverware, and now I have to go through a lesson about some specific manner of holding a stupid little cup. Tonight, we are having a dinner party (groan). It is nothing like the dinner parties we had at the farm. Here, there is no Papa playing the banjo, and certainly no rodeo races. It seems like the only form of fun here is playing poker. At least that's something I know how to do. I hope everyone's doing fine there. Are you all getting enough food? Did you guys plant the new seeds yet? I love you all.

Your loving sister, Gwenny

I finish off my letter by scrawling my signature. The moment I finish the "Y", someone knocks at the door. My heart sinks as Phillip's brown hair and piercing azure eyes come into view.

"Sorry to bother you, Miss Gwendolyn," he says with a slight hint of discomfort in his voice. "I just want to apologize about what I told you last week. I am merely your butler, and I had no right to say that to you. I am incredibly grateful that you hadn't told Mr. Thompson. Will you be kind enough as to forgive me?"

Phillip does look truly sorry.

Suddenly, I burst into tears. "Just go away, Phillip! I don't w-want to be here with you! I d-don't even want to be here at all! I want my family and f-friends. I want my home!" I sound awfully childish, but Phillip just stands there, waiting patiently for me to calm down. My wailing gradually dies down to weeping, and then I am sniffling.

When I've quieted down enough, Phillip clears his throat. "So, you are not content living here?" he asks weakly.

I shake my head. "Not at all" I bite my lower lip, afraid I might start crying again. Phillip tells me something but his voice is incoherent, and I am only half-listening. "What?" I ask.

He clears his throat again and repeats, "Tell me about your old home, if it doesn't bother you." So I swallow my tears and begin to describe my farm. His eyes widen in amazement as I reveal a land with a beautiful sunrise, and the rooster that awakens us every morning. I tell him about my closest friends and family. I choke on tears as I describe Scratch, my dear kitten that I was forced to leave. Then, I illustrate his mind with fields of corn, peas, and various flowers. I finish off with a vivid description of the wheat field. Tears block my throat, and I can say no more.

Phillip points to the beautiful pictures of flowers that are hanging on the wall. "Do you see those?" he asks. I look above, and nod. "Well, I painted them. If I wasn't a butler, I'd be an artist hanging my pieces in a museum." Then, he ambles out, leaving me to picture this young brown-haired boy holding a paint palette and wearing a French beret.

Dingdong! The doorbell's music sends Phillip sprinting toward the door. There stand our dinner guests, standing in a single file. First, Mrs. Samson comes in with her usual negative expression and disapproving frown. Then Mr. Bridges, a friend of my Uncle's, enters. "Good Evening," he says stiffly as he enters. A kind-looking couple, Benson and Belinda Rowan, arrives third. Mrs. Rowan is cradling a plump white cat in her arms. It makes me think of Scratch. "Why, you must be Miss Gwendolyn!" she greets me warmly. "How are you finding here so far. Your Uncle's told me your fondness for cats, so I brought along Princess." I gently stroke the cat's silky fur. "Lovely cat, Mrs. Rowan," I say, using my best manners. Dinner goes along okay. Mr. Bridges turns out to be quite dull, but I enjoy my conversation with the Rowans. Phillip brings along dessert at the end, and even if the pastries are nowhere close to apple pie, I enjoy it anyway. When I lay in bed that night, I am in a blissful mood. Finally, I am taking the Rowans' kind smiles more to heart than Mrs. Samson's cold stares. Finally, I am not sobbing, but smiling.

* * *

Happy birthday, Miss Gwendolyn," sings Uncle Harry as I finish reading my birthday letter from my family. "As an um… as a gift, I shall give you some money. The market is right down the corner. Spend wisely." He stuffs the money into my hand, and I rush out the door.

I realize that I haven't seen fresh air in weeks. Just being outside seems to make my eighteenth birthday. I find the market soon enough, but it is the choice of what I want to spend the money on that slows me down. I saunter past the shops, scanning each item carefully, but nothing really appeals to my interest.

I am just about to give up hope when something catches my eye. Through the clear glass of the widow, I witness a beautiful doll. It is nothing like the eggplant one that Maggie created. This doll has a delicate porcelain face, with perfect blue eyes, pink lips, and rosy cheeks. Her head is topped perfectly with ebony-black hair. The doll is for a little less than what is in my pocket, so I purchase her, and she reminds me of Maggie. I carry the doll with care and caution on the way home.

As I heave the door open, I see Phillip there, looking a little red in the face. "There's something I want to show you," he says shyly. I follow him to a room that must have been Phillip's, because it is filled with paintings wet and dry. He leads me to a quite gigantic painting, covered with tarp. "Happy birthday," he says while pulling off the tarp. I take one glimpse of the painting and almost faint. He has illustrated my farm, with the red barn, and all the fields lined up, ending with the golden wheat field. It is sunrise, and he has painted the sky in orange and yellow. A blissful feeling fills my heart as I recall my beautiful farm, with its fields and skies. Tears fill my eyes as I realize Phillip is my first real friend I've made here. "Oh. It's beautiful. Thank you!" I tell him.

The next few weeks at my Uncle's are much easier. I fly through Mrs. Samson's lessons, and I am a proper lady in no time. Whenever I feel down, I've got Phillip and the Rowans to talk to. I continue writing to Maggie, telling her how I am so happy here, and how much I miss her. I spend some of my free time playing with Mrs. Rowans' cat, Princess. I can't pretend that she is Scratch, but I love her just as much. As I am spinning the yarn around for Princess to follow, Uncle Harry approaches me. "Miss Gwendolyn, for you," he says, handing me a letter. The moment Uncle Harry exits the room, I begin gradually unfolding the letter. This time, it is not Maggie's handwriting, but Mama's. I read it carefully.

Dear Gwenny,
We are so sorry, but we've got awful news. The barn roof collapsed again yesterday. Everyone got out okay, but while your papa was repairing it, he hurt his back. He's okay, but he can't do any work for a pretty long time. We don't have enough people to help us, and we need you back home as soon as possible. I am so sorry to be doing this to you. If you can, try to bring someone else along to help with farm work.

Love, Mama Angie

I am shocked stiff, and I drop Mama's letter. Tears fill my eyes. I wonder furiously why this letter had to arrive now, when I'd just made friends and gotten adjusted to my sophisticated new life. I feel a fresh anger towards Mama, and how she made me go through all this pain if she was just going to make me come back home. However, that anger soon dies down. It is not her fault that the barn collapsed, or that Papa injured his back. I cannot take my disappointment out on my mother. I collapse onto the couch. If I had received this news a few weeks ago, I couldn't have been more overjoyed. Now, however, I bite my lower lip, trying not to cry.

"… So now, Mama wants me to return home". By the time I finish summarizing the letter to Uncle Harry, my lips are quivering. I can't say any more without crying. Uncle Harry nods grimly. "Very well, Gwendolyn. I cannot adequately express my disappointment to see you go, but if Angelina needs you back, you must leave." He reads over the letter once again. "Your mother is also saying she wants more people to help. I shall send Dorothy to assist you with housework. Go and pack up. You'll be off at precisely seven- thirty tomorrow morning."

Still in shock, I wander to my room and gather my belongings. Ever so deliberately, I place them in my bag. As I am folding my plaid shirt and overalls from the farm, Phillip comes in and waters the lavenders on my nightstand. "Phillip!" I cry. Startled, he whirls around. "I'm leaving!" I sob. "Papa broke his back, and now I've got to go home and help with farm work. I'll probably never see you again!" Phillip stands there, looking shocked. "You're leaving, Miss Gwendolyn? You're leaving… forever?"

I nod through tears. "I may never come back here again!" Phillip suddenly looks thoughtful after a while, he slowly begins speaking. "Do you think you can teach me farm work, because I've got an idea." I look up. I know exactly what he is thinking, and smile, because his idea is absolutely brilliant.

* * *

The airport is unusually empty today. I am holding Princess in my arms, and Phillip and Dorothy are standing beside me. Mr. and Mrs. Rowan have let me take Princess to the farm with me for a short time while they vacation in Paris. They are at the airport to say their farewells, and then catch the flight to their vacation. Uncle Harry is giving a list of instructions to Dorothy and Phillip.

When the Rowans leave, he turns to me. "It was delightful having you, and it is a pity to let you go. I have learned lots of lessons from you. I appreciate your sense of humor and carefree attitude. I am proud that you have learned how to be a lady. Goodbye… Gwenny". When he calls me "Gwenny," I cry, not bothering to stop myself. Then, Dorothy, Phillip, Princess, and I leave to board the plane back to… home.

Epilogue

I sit in the wheat field playing with Princess, Scratch, and their kittens. Phillip finally learned how to use a tractor. Maggie is playing with her two dolls (the eggplant one and the porcelain one). Mama and Dorothy are cooking dinner, and my brothers are with Phillip in the field. Papa is recovering rapidly, and soon, he will be able to work. Once Papa recovers, Phillip will be going to a painter's college in France. I'll miss him, but I'm glad he can finally follow his dreams. I watch as the sun slowly says his farewells to earth, sinking down into the hills, and tomorrow, the colors of the sunrise will reappear.

The Friends We Used to Be

Josie Pedretti
4th Grade

PART 1

I sat staring at the clock, willing it to turn 12 pm. Every second felt like an hour, tick, tick, tick. I blocked out everything else but…

"Lara," my teacher's eyes burned down on me. I felt like I was a tiny ant waiting for a giant to step on me. I knew she could tell I hadn't been listening. "Do you know what 8 times 7 is?"

I froze. I had no idea. "Um… is it…," I started trying to buy time. If there were anything I hated more than school, it would be feeling humiliated. I glanced up at the clock -- one more minute. I looked at Claire for help. She held up fingers but I think I misread them.

"Is it forty-five?" I asked still not certain it was the right answer.

"No," the teacher said sternly. "It's fifty-six. Were you practicing?"

My face turned red. I heard a few kids chuckle, but the teacher silenced them with a nasty look. I wondered whether or not I should lie about the teacher's question. I decided to lie. "Yes, I practiced." I mumbled, my eyes glued to the floor.

I glanced at the clock once more; it's a minute after 12! I glanced at Claire, then at the clock, then at Clair, then at the clock again. I didn't dare raise my hand to tell the teacher, not after that. But Claire raised her hand.

"Yes, Claire." The teacher sighed. "What is it?"

"It's time to go to lunch." Claire said happily.

"Very well, you may go."

And all at once, 30 heads, the whole class, rushed to the door.

PART 2

I met Claire in the lunch room. "Are you hungry?" she asked.

"Starving" I replied.

"Me too."

We sat down next to each other. The table was crowded, so we sat shoulder to shoulder. We talked, mostly about random things. I loved talking with Claire; she always had something to talk about. Something. Something like books, dogs, anything.

"So, what did you do today?" Claire's voice broke into my thoughts.

"I went to school?" I ask confused about what she meant.

"No, silly," she paused, "I meant what happened since I saw you last," she scolded.

"Oh. Uh… Nothing much." I tell her. It's true, last night I had eaten dinner, done my homework, and read.

"Really? Nothing?" She asked shocked. "Nothing at all? No finishing a book, or eating lots of ice cream, or a new TV show?" she continued. Everything she listed happened so often it wasn't really "special" anymore.

"I did finish a book…" I admitted. I was about to add "but

that's not so special," but I didn't have the time.

"We are going out to recess now!" one of the teachers announced in a extra loud voice.

"Meet you outside." I tell Claire and dashed for the line.

PART 3

I waited at the big tree for Claire. We waited for each other there because it symbolized our friendship. We met there in kindergarten, and have been friends ever since.

I spotted Claire walking toward the big tree. She didn't look very happy. Her short hair hung down in her face and her pretty hazel eyes were clouded with worry.

"Err… Lara… I promised someone I'd meet them at recess," she started, not meeting my gaze. "Um, so I have to go meet her…"

"OK, who?" I ask, just curious.

"Well, I promised Rachel-"

"Rachel? Why Rachel?" I cut her off. I knew Rachel wanted to be Claire's friend and all… but Rachel?

"Well, yeah. Why not Rachel?" Clair asked, puzzled.

"Um, Rachel's nice and all… but she's kind of rude," I replied cautiously.

"You're rude." She spat, "You're mean for calling someone rude! I'm allowed to play with whoever I want to play with!"

"Well! If I had to play with someone, I wouldn't want to play with you!" I raged. A look of shock crossed her face, and she looked like she was fighting back tears. Then I wasn't angry anymore. A wave of guilt stabbed me like a knife. How could I have said that to a friend like her?

I opened my mouth to say sorry, but nothing came out. It was like I was frozen in shock from my own words or my voice had run away from this horrible moment in time. But before I could say anything else, she turned around, and was gone in a heartbeat.

PART 4

A rush of anger flooded back into my body. Why did she always have to run away from her problems? My eyes followed her to where she was going. Rachel. She was going to Rachel. This was all Rachel's fault! If she hadn't asked Claire, this would have never happened! My gaze burned down on her.

No! I thought, I'm not going to depend on her anymore! I won't! I won't!

Both girls were staring at me. I had an uncomfortable suspicion that they were talking about me. I didn't want to look at them though, so I walked in the other direction. I tried to think about other things, but it didn't work.

I sat down next to a tree and waited for the lady to blow the whistle. My thoughts were clouded with anger and confusion. Why is she with Claire again? Why are they friends? Why are we in a fight? Because of Rachel. That's why we're in a fight.

Part 5

The bell rang and my class went inside for art. I walked as slowly as I could. I hated sitting in my assigned seat next to Clair, even worse, she sat next to Rachel. This was going to be one long, boring, frustrating art class.

And to make things even worse, my art teacher -- it's not like she goes around torturing the class, it's more like she tortures me. Everyone else loves her except me. That's why she tortures me. It's not easy to be the teacher's least-liked person.

As I approached the art class, I suddenly wanted to run away, not from the art room, the art teacher, Claire, nor Rachel. I wanted to quit. Quit life. And if I could, I would. But I guess I could... I pushed the thought away and entered the room.

"You're late." The teacher taunted sternly as soon as I entered the room. Behind me, a boy rushed into the room.

"I'm so sorry I'm late!" the boy apologized. I still stood frozen in the front of the room. The teacher nodded and smiled at the boy. But as soon as she turned to me, that smile whipped off her face, like it was never there.

"Sit down. Before the day is over." She pointed to my seat and I solemnly sat down. I tried to talk to some people out of pure boredom. But they either shushed me or the teacher did. It's frustrating to be the least-liked person in the class.

I finally gave up and sat down quietly.

The rest of art class went on, and it felt like it took hours! No, days! (but I knew it only took 20 minutes).

Though I tried to push the thought away, a dark thought lingered in my mind. It was, "What if she hates me? What if she wants to banish me from her life?"

PART 6

The rest of school passed by, but I felt like my soul had been banished from existence.

When I went home I didn't say a word. I simply pushed away my father who was asking about school. I didn't want to talk; I needed to think. Not about anything Claire said, not about how she acted. No, about what I said. The whole thing felt like I was spitting out random words or someone else took over my body for a short period of time. That thought made me shudder, so I stopped thinking about that.

I went to my bed and crawled into it. I closed my eyes but sleep did not come. I did not leave though.

"Life is like a nightmare that there is no waking up from," I thought.

PART 7

It felt like only a heartbeat before my dad's voice rang in my head like a flood. "Lara, it's time to go to school. Lara!" He pushed and pulled me as he spoke.

"It's school already? Only seconds ago it was three o'clock," I said drowsily.

"Will you look at the time?" he argued. "Get up, and get ready. Now, Lara."

I slipped out of the covers and onto the floor. The floor boards creaked under my feet. Cool air from them sent a chill down my spine. I sighed. Back to school, again.

I changed and went down stairs. I ate my cereal with my dad in silence. Until my dad asked, "Is there something bothering you?"

"Um… well… no. Nothing, other than none of my homework is done!" I yelled.

And my friend for life hates my guts, I added silently.

"Well you don't have to be so rude..." I stopped listening after that. Rude…The exact word that started Claire's and my conflict. I started listening again.

"...you should never be rude to anyone. Are you listening? Are you like that to your friends?"

I opened my mouth to say no, but nothing came out. Instead, I silently said, Yes.

A thought pushed itself into my brain, No one will ever like me again, no one.

PART 8

"Are you almost done getting ready for school? It's time to leave," my dad reminded me.

"Ready!" I called. We drove in silence. The whole way. It felt like ages before I finally got out of the car. The only word that came out of either of our mouths was, "Bye-bye."

I dragged my feet up to the line. By the time I got there, we were going in.

When we got to the class room, I got unpacked and sat down without a word. I suddenly felt very claustrophobic. In this small class room… with all these kids… and the teachers…

I shook myself. That's silly. It was such an uneasy feeling. I never, ever, wanted to feel like that again.

A few days passed. Lonely, frustrating, days. I'd lost track of time. One day I only spoke when the teacher called on me. One day I didn't say a word at all.

One day I heard my dad whispering to my mom, "She seems so… distant… I'm worried."

I never really thought straight after that. Too tired to worry, too tired to care. Everyone had forgotten me, even my teachers. Except my parents. I was like a ghost, an empty shell. From the real Lara; who lived god knows how long ago.

PART 9

Another month passed, I was getting tired of this, the same old routine, every day. No longer did emotion fill me, no anger, sadness, happiness, or joy. Not even a single thought filled my brain.

I was in school. It was almost lunch, though I was not hungry. Claire and Rachel stood behind me, though I didn't care. I don't know why I even noticed anymore.

"Nobody likes you." Rachel taunted in my ear, "You're all alone. No one has ever, ever liked you. You're all alone."

"Th-that's not true."

I looked around. Who said that, was it me? Yes, it was me. My brain had fought back without me. I disapproved.

"It's not true!" I squeaked. This time, more under my own control.

"Rachel, you're wrong," someone whispered. It wasn't me, so who was it? Claire looked sternly at Rachel, and Rachel looked stunned back at Claire. Was it Claire?

It was! It was Claire!

It wasn't someone. It wasn't me. It was really Claire.

PART 10

Color and emotion and feeling flooded back into my body. I felt like I had died and been brought back to life. I felt more alive than I had ever felt before in my whole life!

"You're wrong!" I pressed. Everyone looked at me like I was insane, but Rachel's and my eyes were locked.

"Lara, I'm not wrong that we're going to gym," the teacher responded casually. I didn't listen.

"Rachel, that's not true, and nobody, is gonna' say otherwise!" I growled.

"It's not true, Rachel." Claire whispered again, as if she didn't know everyone was already looking at us.

"Let's go." The teacher decided. I still didn't budge. "Let's GO."

Claire, who had let Rachel in front of her, said, "How about you go to the back of the line, where you belong." Rachel stepped back out of the line, then the line moved on without her.

* * *

The next morning, the teacher asked Claire and I if we could take the books to the library. So we headed into the hallway, walking beside each other. I stumbled and lost one of my books. Claire picked it up and put it in her pile.

"Why are you carrying it?" I asked.

"Isn't that what friends are for?"

Tidbits

Felix Riley
6th Grade

It was night, 12:30 am exactly. You could go on about, "Hey, 12:30 am is morning!" but you and I both know that it is more like night than day. I was supposed to be asleep 4 hours ago, yet I could not sleep. It was much too quiet this night, no wind, no rain, no noise at all, only darkness.

We all have experienced this time at least once, maybe when you're lying in bed alone when everyone else is asleep, or maybe when you're just staying up in the middle of the night alone and you have the television turned off. This time we call the witching hour, when anything at all is free to roam on this earth. I was quite lonely, and a teensy bit scared, so I tried to come up with ways to pass the time and hopefully finally get me to sleep.

I had the quick and--I admit--stupid idea that maybe, an imaginary friend would help me feel better. I immediately felt less lonely when I saw those two, glowing red eyes appear in the corner of my room. He skittered with those insect like legs across my pitch black room and I got to see his entire form. He looked kind of like a giant ant with a sausage like body covered with messy, mahogany colored fur. He had a very large, yellow pair of mandibles, antennae emerging off of his face like a mustache, 10 sets of tiny, bat-like wings, and 6 bony, lanky legs. He introduced himself as tidbit, nothing more. He said Mr. Tidbit was already taken, so that's why he was one of the few imaginary friends who don't have Mr. in front of his name.

I already liked this guy, he was strange. Who else would even mention that, only he would. In fact, there are a lot of things only he would do. Many, many things.

Every night, he would come, the same, strange little creature, appearing in the corner of the room. Every night he started to feel more and more real. Those eyes started to glow brighter and brighter each night. He became so real to me, that he was more than just an imaginary friend, he was right there, in the room. I could feel the fur on his back. I could now smell what was the scent of apples. My eyes would hurt after staring into the eyes so long, they were so bright. They emitted heat as well, a faint, warm heat, like that of a heater.

One night, he came late. It was just like the first night, dark, quiet, and lonely. He finally came at 12:30 am exactly. He seemed especially happy this particular night, and dirty. "Where were you?" I asked. "I was outside, digging." He said with an almost sly tone of voice. "I just dug the deepest hole. Want to see it?" "Why not?" I asked, "I have nothing better to do." He led the way to the door and down the stairs into the kitchen, trotting with his mandibles high in the air.

We marched out of the front door, which was surprisingly unlocked, and he led me to the hole. "Here it is." He said sounding quite proud, "the hole I was digging all this time." I peered down, and he wasn't lying, it was deep. I couldn't see the bottom. "So, um, what's it for?" I asked him with great curiosity.

"My friends." He said, and he started to laugh, first softly, then growing louder. It soon became a very loud, almost menacing laugh. He then pushed me, and I started to fall. Luckily, the walls were dirt, so I could catch hold of it. I looked up, saw tidbit with a very large, evil grin, then he flew off, his wings creating the noise of 1000 hornets. I lost my grip finally, and I fell.

I fell and fell, and I fell some more. It seemed like an eternity, and, finally, I saw light. It was strange, why would there be light at the bottom of a pit? I didn't care; I knew I was going to die.

Well, I didn't, it surprisingly was another hole, after I fell through the hole, gravity seemed to reverse and I landed safely on the ground. I looked around. It looked exactly the same as where I was before. My house stood in front of me. It was day now, unlike before. I entered my house, calling for my parents. "MOM, DAD!!!!" I shouted at the top of my lungs. I got no answer.

MOM, DAD?" I shouted again. Still I got no answer. I went back outside, and I searched for anyone at all. Nobody at all was there, a lonely world. I sat down on the concrete, and I cried. I felt scared, and alone. All of the scary things I had ever heard or seen popped into my mind, especially Tidbit. That sinister grin I witnessed just before I fell was burned in the back of my brain. I cried for so long, and as I cried, I heard that voice, that slobbery, wet voice.

"Hello," he said slowly, as if he wanted me to absorb his haunting voice. "Why?" I asked him. "Why would you do this?"

"I have been lonely for so long" he started off. "I was so tired of being lonely, lonely in this ghost world, only able to wander earth very late at night. I was so desperately lonely, and now, I have found someone to take my place." He smiled, and quickly started to morph into me. He now looked exactly like me. He laughed exactly like he did before, and disappeared down the hole.

"What do you mean by friends?!" I shouted down the hole.

"You'll see!" he shouted back up as he disappeared into the darkness. I thought. I cried again, this time for only five minutes. I fell asleep. I had a dream, and I found out who his friends were. The shadows, they surrounded me. Every time I fell asleep, they were there. I hated it, so desperately. Every night, at 12: 30, the hole opened up. I went down the hole every night. Wandering, searching for someone to take my place, my place in the darkness.

The Unbelievable Journey

Michelle Rebecca Shavnya
4th Grade

Kristina Salvador almost never went outside. All day she sat in her little room hidden from others. She didn't even go to school.

Her stepmother, Rebecca, tried to force Kristina go outside. Kristina cried and refused to do so, because her mother used to warn her that wild dangerous animals like bears were everywhere. Now that she was dead, Rebecca had come to be the new mother in the household.

"I don't want to go," Kristina cried loudly.

"You must," Rebecca said. "Your mother was crazy. You need friends, life, and being out of your room."

"I don't need friends," Kristina said.

Rebecca was tired. She just looked at Kristina strictly, and said, "C'mon. Let's go."

Kristina did not put her shoes on. Rebecca thought that was weird, so she told Kristina to do it immediately.

"What shoes?" Kristina said. "My mother only allowed me to wear bare feet or socks."

"Oh, well, well. Those days are done and over with. I, Rebecca, am going to make you put them on right now."

Kristina looked strangely. She actually wore a light shirt but no pants. Rebecca opened the door and got out her lunch bag. She carried it into her beige Mustang and told Kristina to get on the backseat. "Please, Kris, I don't want to be mean. Just go with me to town," Rebecca said.

Left with no choice, Kristina put on the clothes that Rebecca offered and reluctantly stepped out of the house. Then she slowly got into the car as if it was something scary. In her mind, she was still hearing her mother say how scary it was out there.

After they had driven for about ten minutes, Kristina asked, "Can we go home?"

Instead of answering this question, Rebecca stopped the car and said, "Please go outside into the woods, dear, and do something for me."

"No, no, no!" Kristina was screaming. "Bring me home and get me my room and my toys and my books and please tell me no more about cars and going outside!"

Rebecca never expected this violent outburst. "There is a nice clean stream nearby. Please go there, it is only a hundred yards away, and get some water. Here," she said, handing Kristina an empty bottle, and trying not to be mean and stay calm.

"No, I won't," Kristina said hesitating.

"Yes." Rebecca raised her eyebrows. "Do it."

"Whatever," Kristina said.

Rebecca unlocked the door and Kristina cautiously got out. She crossed a narrow pavement and hit a hardly visible unmarked trail in the woods. She shivered, so she pulled her cloak over. But soon she began to feel strange in clothes and took her warm jacket off. She went farther and farther away from the car, until she realized that there was no stream close to the road at all.

She then returned back but didn't see the car anymore. "Oh maybe it's over there," she whispered quietly. She looked to the left. Nothing. She looked ahead. Nothing. Finally, she looked back. Nothing, just like before.

She ran over rocks and across small streams until, in about five minutes, she saw a car. She was relieved to find it so soon, but as she walked closer, she got nervous. It appeared to be a large grey boulder rather than Rebecca's car.

Kristina knew that this was not real. She was pretending. She was at home, having a weird dream. In order to feel safer, she climbed a flat rock and tried to sleep peacefully.

A little later she "woke up" and found out that she had never been sleeping. In front of her there was the same boulder, she was still sitting on a flat rock, and it still smelled like spring just as it did minutes ago.

Kristina looked at the wild place. Mostly it was overgrown bushes, a lot of mud, and thousands of trees. Obviously, it was nothing like her house, so she knew immediately that something was wrong with this place and she knew the word: Lost.

The word had made her mind go blank completely. The

word meant gone from the familiar world and being eaten by animals. She walked around in circles, feeling creepy. She thought nature was scary.

Kristina let out a high-pitched cry and then yelled for help. Her heart beat fast and she felt herself breathing quicker than normal. She felt as if someone was going to come and get her. The wind blew sharply into her face, but she left her cloak on a rock somewhere when looking for the water, so she was cold now.

She spotted a bush of blackberries in a distance. She loved them, and she was hungry, so she paced over to the big bush. When she came there, she saw there were various bushes, so she picked up some berries and ate them. They tasted juicy and delicious.

"If only I could get found," she said to herself. "But I won't." She began to feel sick to her stomach after eating a few berries.

She began to cry a little, even though she knew it was useless. As nightfall came, Kristina tried to yell for help again. Her teeth were chattering and she shivered terribly. She needed her cloak dreadfully, but it was probably blown away by the wind somewhere far away.

She thought about the book on houses she had read. She recalled that in some poor countries people make teepees and other kinds of primitive homes. Therefore, she began her great journey of survival in the wilderness. She found about seven five-foot-tall sticks. She tried to fix them in the ground using a stick as a shovel but the idea failed.

After about twenty minutes of her fruitless efforts, and the sun setting completely, Kristina just put a few dozens of sticks on top of the dirt upright, and they stayed, for a minute, two minutes, until she finally crawled inside and got some sleep.

Night was far worse. It seemed as if Kristina had gotten frostbite. She found out that she had somehow lost her shoes too. The howling winds raced around the teepee nonstop like angry monsters. Kristina put her arms around her stomach and cried, as she never had before.

She screamed for help as loud as she could, but she knew

there would be no help at all. None would ever come.

Kristina touched her skin and said something bad. She would die and vanish. She did not know how to survive.

Suddenly, the winds stopped and all was peaceful for a few minutes. Then, they erupted again, with more force and damage. Kristina's stupid little hut fell to the ground but Kristina did not let out any tears. She was too tired and fell into a light sleep. That was Kristina's first day and first night in the woods, the girl who never ever went outside.

In the morning, she wasn't even hungry. There were no ponds, no berries, and even if there was a pond, Kristina couldn't fish and couldn't make a fire. Mom never taught her.

Kristina walked for ages. She walked the same path for about three hours until her stomach rumbled and she felt scared again. The sky turned dark again, promising rain, thunder, and lightning.

She went on. Maybe this trail would end and everything would be all right. However, she'd walked for so long, and the trail was the same, quiet and with no footsteps, as if no one had ever been here.

The rain poured down in torrents. There was no shelter or trees big enough to hide under. Kristina's legs were bare, and they hurt. She had a light shirt on only.

The rain was cold, mucky, and disgusting. Kristina felt it on her legs. She was feeling sick again. Through the muddy rain, she walked on and on. Her legs got dirtier, browner, like dull leaves.

Kristina could bear it no longer. She screamed of fear until she had reached her limit and stopped; she just felt nauseous all of a sudden and threw up.

Kristina was very petrified. No one was here and now she got sick. When she ever threw up at home, she was advised to drink water. But there was no drinking water here.

Finally, she found a little puddle of fresh rainwater and cupped it in her hands. She knew it was dirty, but she had to drink something or else she would get dehydrated, since she had not had a drink for almost a full day.

The water tasted like mud totally, but it was surely better than nothing. It was cold and a little refreshing.

Kristina's legs ached as she walked across a large stream, stepping on rocks. One was so slippery that Kristina couldn't hold her balance. For about ten seconds, she tried to get upright but instead was rushed by the sweeping current down the deep stream. She listened to the drone of thunder overhead. She saw a giant spark of lightning and knew she had to run somewhere.

Her hair was soaking wet and so were her underwear and shirt. If someone looked at her, she would have looked as if she was a wild animal living in the woods.

Somehow, using her sticky hands and almost numb legs, she managed to get to the bank. That was the hardest thing Kristina had ever experienced.

She was shivering again and so bad that she couldn't walk. The wind, thunder, rain, and lightning kept going, stronger and stronger, as if it was battling Kristina and saying "See? That's what you get after eleven years of staying locked in your room."

For the first time in her life, Kristina felt dumb and miserable. Her mother was an idiot and she was too. She was not going to make it out of these woods unless someone sent for her.

In about ten minutes of impossible sprinting, Kristina heard a rattling noise -- a helicopter! Kristina ran out into a field, into the open, and through the rain, she began to limp. She saw a red helicopter faintly circling miles away and she took her shirt off and waved it like a flag.

Unfortunately, soon the helicopter was out of view, its loud noise fading away into the thunder and rain. She was too late, and she felt angry at the people in the helicopter.

"HELP! I'M LOST!" Kristina yelled. In about five minutes, the rattling sound disappeared and she lost her hope of being rescued. Kristina had never felt so tired before. The nausea was returning; she tried to run and put her shirt back on at the same time.

The rain was not so bad anymore, but it was still dripping. Kristina's hair was just horribly wet. Kristina had a new feeling. A feeling of fear, but a different kind. She felt unsafe, treacherous.

Kristina touched her hair. It was muddy and wet. So wet, she thought, that she had gotten about five tons of it on her ruined, dark brown, long and ugly hair.

She had been probably walking for at least six hours when she saw a small river. She was anxious about falling again, so she used two sticks to cross another wide brook. She made it successfully and went on, while feeling as if she was hiking for an eternity.

It became dark and Kristina thought that she should probably just lie down and sleep and get ready for a hard day of work, when she realized something – she had never met a wolf, deer, bear, or any wild animal in the woods during these two days. Her mother was a liar.

Kristina watched the orange, yellow, and red glows of sunset. It was amazing but she couldn't fall asleep. She felt the wind was screaming again, and she pictured it saying, "Now look. You were so stupid and now you'll never find you stepmother again."

Kristina did feel bad for not going outside for years. She wondered if she was not that smart as others or something like that. She used to be a weirdo, but not anymore. She had lived in the woods with no food. But then again, she remembered, life might fake it. She could be close to death.

Next morning Kristina had a feeling that she woke up late. Despite the fatigue and frustration, she got up and instantly got walking again. She had new energy and the day seemed fine. Maybe it would be sunny after all.

But it wasn't. However, a sign ahead said "Shortcut to Livingsville". Kristina took the route. It could take another day to get to the place, but she was going. She wasn't losing hope.

She was so soaked yesterday that she was still a little wet. She looked at her toes and feet and they looked as if brown paint was smashed everywhere. In a puddle, Kristina saw reflection of her face. She had some red spots and countless scrapes.

Now she looked older than she was, and sick. Probably because this was her first experience of being outside in the woods for two and a half days.

Kristina's hours passed by not that bad. She speed-walked along the road, which was becoming a little wider. There were only occasional squirrels or rarely a small stream, but the rain was gone leaving only that mucky dirt behind.

As Kristina began getting into some fields with cottages, she felt in her heart that she had arrived somewhere. But it was not the place where her stepmother had dropped her off, obviously; she was in a different town. Kristina ran quickly and wanted to close her eyes in disbelief; suddenly she saw a man making a fire. She decided to ask him for help.

She walked up and felt embarrassed. She thought she looked like a girl monster. "Ca…can you help me?" she stammered.

"Hello, wild girl," the man said, smiling. "What's your name?"

"Kristina. I am ugly, right?" Kristina said.

"Yes, perhaps. Child, I cannot see you well. Come up closer. You look…very…sick."

"I know. Can I call up my stepmother? Do you have a cell-phone with you?" Kristina said.

"Yes, yes," The man dug into his pocket and got out a shiny phone. Trembling, Kristina pressed the numbers.

When Rebecca started speaking, Kristina handed the phone over to the man. She was too weak to think and talk clearly. Her arms were tingly and her legs ached as if she'd been hit with something heavy a thousand times.

The man finished his conversation with Rebecca in a minute or two. Then he turned to Kristina, "Your step-mom is going to be here in about twenty minutes. She's taking you to a doctor."

"No," Kristina said. "I'm fine."

"But I'm not. Until I make sure you are in safe conditions…"

"Sure, sure," Kristina said. "Thanks for everything. I need to rest now and have something to eat."

"Wait a second. It looks like you have walked in the wilderness for quite a long time. Can you tell me about your adventure?" the man asked.

"I had a nice mother but she thought it was unsafe to go outside and one day I had a new step-mother Rebecca after my mom died. Rebecca wanted me to find out about the world. Once I began hiking, I faced so many troubles, from no food to being carried down a stream. And now… now I have a different feeling about this world, this wonderful, big wide world."

"Kristina, you are amazing. You risked your health and possibly your entire life, and now look: you finished your arduous journey and now you are a completely different person."

Kristina smiled. "Thanks. I always thought that my abilities were very limited, but I don't anymore, of course."

The man smiled back and said, "Kristina, you have so much left to explore and you have ample time left to see the wonders of the world. Your journey has just begun."

Fire Arrow

Natalie Simpson
5th Grade

Slowly, the man crept along the battlement. He wore a dark cloak with its hood pulled up to hide his pale face, dark hair, and piercing black eyes. He carried a coiled rope, and he had an empty pouch and a sword hanging from his belt. Carefully, he tied the rope around a protruding piece of stone in the wall.

Glancing around to make sure he wasn't being watched, he hastily climbed down to the ground. When he reached the earth, relieved he had made it safely, he turned and started along the narrow path to the river. It was a dark, cold fall night, and the leaves, whispering in the breath of the wind, made strange sounds. Their eerie shadows were cast on the frozen ground.

The man hurried along the path, and, before long, he could hear the river's rushing. Soon, he had reached it and stood on its bank, spray showering his face. Wasting no time, he commenced his dark magic. He said the words of power and evil, directing them into the river. When he had finished, there was a wave of black fire in the water, and then a stone, as dark as a cloudy night, appeared at the ground near his feet. Grabbing it, he shoved it into the pouch at his waist before turning and running into the forest.

The man moved quickly along the winding path. Sheets of rain began to fall, and a cold, howling wind started, so he wrapped himself tightly in his cloak. Leaves, shaken loose by the storm, whirled in a blizzard around him. As the weather worsened, he moved faster, racing through the woods and hardly looking where he was going.

Suddenly he tripped over a rock and went sprawling on the ground. The pouch on his belt hit the rock's sharp edge, and its strings broke. He rolled off the pointy stone, groaning, and stood up without realizing that the pouch was lying at his feet. Fortunately, as he started to hurry along the path again, his foot kicked something, and when he bent down to see what it was, he recognized the pouch that held the stone. He hastily picked up the pouch and retied its strings around his belt before resuming his dash down the path.

Soon, the man emerged from the meager protection of the woods into a large, grassy field. Despite his hood, the wind savagely beat the rain against his face. The long grasses danced wildly in the storm. He sprinted to the center of the field. He bent over and dropped the stone from the pouch into a small hole. Then a second wave of dark fire, like the one he had seen at the river, appeared in it. The black fire burned brightly for a moment before vanishing.

The storm grew worse, the wind pounding against the man even harder and driving bigger waves of rain against his back. He turned and ran across the field into the forest on the far side, plunging into the trees. He rushed along the path, hoping to get back to the castle before anyone noticed his absence. The trail was slick because of the rain, so he slipped several times, making his cloak filthy, and the chilling wind froze him to the bone.

At last, he struggled out of the woods. He was on the far side of the castle from where he had started, so he cautiously walked around the perimeter. When he reached his destination, he wearily climbed up the rope. Slowly, the man pulled himself over the top of the wall. As he moved to reenter the castle, he heard raised voices, and he knew that his absence had not gone as unnoticed as he had hoped. The man began to sneak down the hall when he heard quiet footsteps, and a soft, deadly voice whispered, "Malas." He turned suddenly. "You did it?"

Malas nodded. "Yes, Captain," he answered. The captain was a tall man with short brown hair and light blue eyes.

"Good. You'll have to go back tomorrow morning, when the magic is ready. Then head to the cliffs and find the indentation in the rock at the edge of the largest overhang. I'll tell the others you're on business for me." Malas nodded again, and the captain hurried away down the hall. Malas tiredly made his way to his room. As he walked slowly down the hallway past the flickering torches, he did not notice a tall girl with long blond hair and luminous green eyes slip out of the shadows where she had hidden, hearing every word they had said.

* * *

Lady Leona, leader of her father's lands while he fought in the North, hurried out of the castle early the next morning. She carried a sword, a bow, a quiver of arrows, and a knife. Quietly, she saddled her horse and rode out to a large field on the edge of her father's land. There she took cover in a bush, by a hole that spilled the sensation of evil magic. Several minutes later, Malas rode into view, silhouetted by the rising sun. He hurried to the hole and pulled a black stone out from deep inside, quickly tucking it into a pouch at his waist. Leona laid an arrow on her bowstring before leaping out of her cover.

"Halt!" she shouted. "What do you think you're doing, Guardsman Malas?"

Upon seeing her, Malas had pulled out his sword. Now he sheathed it. "Nothing, Lady," he said quickly. "The captain assigned me to patrol the border of your father's lands today." Leona lowered her bow as he spoke, but kept the arrow on the string. She slowly advanced until she was standing in front of Malas.

"Really? Why would he put a new man like you on patrol? You should be at the castle on guard, learning about your job, not on patrol!" Malas was new to his job as a castle guardsman. He had arrived several days earlier and had been hired by the Captain of the Guard. "And why are you here? Looking into a hole doesn't seem like something someone on patrol would do."

"I… well… I… um…" stammered Malas. "I… thought I saw something here."

"What did you pick up?" Leona demanded. "I saw you pick something up and put it in that pouch," she added.

He hesitated, uncertain, before an idea occurred to him. He pulled a bright, silver coin from his pocket. "This," he said. "I saw this. The sunlight reflected off of it."

Leona stared suspiciously at him. "Give me that pouch," she commanded.

"What? No!" shouted Malas, his right hand going to his sword hilt and his left hand moving to protectively cover the pouch. Suddenly Leona dropped her bow and charged at Malas. She knocked him to the ground and hurriedly untied the pouch from his belt.

As Malas struggled to get up, Leona whispered a spell to immobilize him. In the several minutes she had with Malas frozen, Leona examined the stone. It was black, darker than anything she had seen before.

The rock was cold and heavy in her hand. It was extremely powerful. She knew that the stone could only be destroyed by magical fire, which was hard to make because the process was long and required many intricate spells. As Leona replaced the stone in its pouch, Malas overcame her spell. He snatched the pouch out of her hands and then kicked her, hard. She reeled backwards, momentarily stunned. When she sat up, all that was left of Malas was the fading sound of his horse's hooves on the rocky ground. Leona swung herself into the saddle and set off in pursuit.

*　　*　　*

As soon as he had kicked Leona and grabbed the pouch and the stone, Malas leaped on his horse and rode off. At least she hasn't seen my face clearly, he thought. That would make it possible for him to disappear into the crowds on the road. That was a benefit of being new to the castle. Malas had stayed discreet, so Leona didn't know what he looked like.

He guided his horse to the main road in the direction of the sea. He merged with the crowd, keeping the hood of his cloak up and laying his ready bow on the saddle in front of him. Satisfied that he had blended in, Malas settled in the saddle and prepared for a hard journey. He traveled like this until the sun sank below the horizon, when he stopped to camp for the night before continuing on the next day.

By that time, he was sure that Leona didn't know where he was, and he was also certain that she had no idea where he was going. Satisfied that he had evaded his pursuer, Malas settled down to sleep. He knew that there was an inn at the next town, so he looked forward to the luxury of a bed. The next morning, Malas ate quickly before continuing his journey.

* * *

Leona sat in the tree, watching the passersby on the road below her. There, she thought suddenly, that's him. Her bright green eyes were fixated on a hooded man who rode a midnight black stallion. A quiver of arrows was strapped to his back, and his bow lay across the saddle in front of him. A sword hung from his belt.

Despite his inconspicuous appearance, he stood out in the crowd to Leona because of the pouch that was tied to his belt. Black magic radiated from it. Leona had ridden all yesterday and last night to get ahead of Malas. Now she would follow him the rest of the way to the cliffs. Nimbly, Leona climbed down the tree to her horse, which waited patiently in the dense brush beside the path. She mounted quickly and hurried to join the crowd rushing along the road. She easily found Malas in the crowd by following the aura of dark magic to its source.

Leona trailed him for the rest of the day. Finally, he stopped at a small town and entered the inn. She found him inside, being led to his room by a servant. Leona walked up casually to the innkeeper, brushing a stray strand of her blond hair out of her face. "Sir, I'd like a room for tonight. How much does one cost here?" she inquired.

"It costs two silver coins fer a night 'ere," the innkeeper answered.

"I'll take it," said Leona, handing the man his money. He led her to her room. As she entered it, she saw Malas come out of the room across the hall and head downstairs. The hood of his cloak was down, so Leona could finally see his face, which she had never seen clearly before. His pale skin contrasted sharply with his dark hair and black eyes. Surprisingly, the pouch was not tied to his waist. As he walked past, she stepped quickly into her room. The innkeeper quietly left as Leona dropped her bag on the bed and began to rummage in it. She pulled out a knife, which she belted to her waist.

Then she silently left the room, walked across the hall, and entered Malas's room. She didn't see the pouch anywhere, but she felt its dark magic. Leona quickly scanned the room, trying to trace the feeling of black magic to its source. Suddenly she found it. Tucked into a shadowed corner was a small box that reeked of evil. Malas must have left the pouch in the box, protected by spells, thinking that it would be safer here than with him.

Leona picked up the box. It was made of dark wood, and it had a golden clasp. A silver lock hung from the clasp, holding the box tightly shut. Leona was about to call upon her magic to shatter the lock when she realized that she couldn't break it without alerting Malas to her presence. She sat on the floor beside the box, thinking. Suddenly an idea occurred to her. She grabbed the knife at her waist and slid it into the lock. The spells she had carefully put on the knife protected it from Malas's enchantments on the box. Leona used the knife as a lock pick, and after several minutes of twisting, the lock gently popped open.

Leona lifted the box's lid and smiled with satisfaction as she saw the pouch inside. Quickly, she pulled it out. Untying the pouch's strings, she reached into it and grabbed for the stone inside. Waves of powerful evil rolled off it. Leona was about to pocket the stone when she heard heavy steps on the staircase. She quickly replaced the stone in the pouch, dropped it into the box, refastened the lock, and slipped out of Malas's room.

Leona returned to her room. She decided to finish making magical fire. Ever since she had learned how powerful the stone was, she had worked on making the fire, so it was almost finished. For the rest of the night, she carefully completed her enchantments. As the sun began to rise over the horizon, she trapped the fire in a spelled bag. All that she needed was real fire to activate the magic fire and destroy the stone.

Malas left the inn that morning. Leona followed him, though from what she'd overhead the captain say, she knew where he was going, a tall cliff of dark stone that hung over the ocean. As they neared their destination, Leona rode ahead, reaching the cliff before Malas. There, she prepared her magical fire in the small indentation in the rock on the rim of the cliff. She disguised it with a spell so that Malas wouldn't be able to tell that it was there.

As she finished, Malas came into view. He dismounted and walked over to the indentation on the cliff. Leona quickly ducked behind a nearby rock and began to prepare a regular fire. Smiling evilly, Malas pulled the stone out of the pouch and dropped it into the groove in the rock.

Instantly, everything changed. The sunny, pleasant day was destroyed by a ferocious storm. The wind screamed, driving hard waves against the rocks below the cliff. Dark clouds that were an evil greenish black rolled in, sweeping away the sunlight. Rain poured down, soaking everything. Leona crouched over her fire, shielding it from the rain. She seized her bow, pulled an arrow out of her quiver, and waited.

Suddenly, the storm ended. The wind slowed and the rain stopped. The clouds, however, remained just as imposing. This was her chance! Leona put the end of the arrow in the fire. It caught quickly, blazing brightly in the uncertain darkness. She put the arrow on the string, drew back, aimed, and fired.

Her arrow hit the stone and the magical fire, which accepted the flames. It blazed fiercely, consuming the stone. As the stone was destroyed, the clouds broke up and vanished. Leona triumphantly emerged from the rocks. As Malas saw her, he turned and ran to his horse before mounting and galloping back into the forest. Leona dashed to her horse, climbed on, and raced after him.

* * *

Malas rushed away, anger coursing through him. Leona had foiled his plans yet again! Plans for revenge flew through his mind. He hurried back along the road, where people were nervously discussing the storm. Malas decided to journey back to the castle and escape with the captain. He was sure that Leona wouldn't think to look for him there.

Two days later, Malas returned to the castle. "Guardsman Malas! Where have you been?" inquired the guard at the drawbridge.

"On business for the captain," Malas replied. "I'm going in to report to him now."

He turned and started to walk inside when the sentry called after him, "And report to Lady Leona as well. She just got back, and she wants to see you." Malas gasped, shocked, then hid his reaction and nodded before walking to the captain's room.

"You didn't do it," said the captain fiercely as Malas entered. "Why?"

"It was Leona," he replied. "She followed me and destroyed the stone with magical fire. I came back because I thought we could leave together."

"We'll leave tomorrow. I've got work in the capital, so I need to go there, but you can head up north." Malas nodded and then moved towards the door when a quiet voice said, "Actually, you'll both be going to the capital."

* * *

Leona slid out of the shadows where she had hidden. Her sword was drawn and ready. "Soldiers!" she yelled. A group of warriors ran into the room. "Secure these men for a journey to the capital. I'll join you when it's time to leave." She hurried out of the room and ran outside. She carried a pouch of magical fire like the one she had used to destroy the stone.

She sprinted to the river, where she gathered some branches and made a fire. She used the flames to activate some of the magical fire. The rest of it she kept safely contained in the pouch. Leona threw the magical fire into the river. She watched, satisfied, as it burned brightly in the stream. A layer of murky blackness seemed to slide off the water, leaving it crystal clear. Once the magical fire had done its job, Leona doused her regular fire and dashed into the forest.

She ran through the trees, occasionally grabbing branches as kindling. Finally, she arrived in the field. The tall grasses wove and dipped in the gentle breeze. Leona slowed down and walked to the hole. She cleared an area around it and prepared another fire using the branches she had gotten from the woods. Leona opened the pouch and poured the rest of her magical fire into the hole. She used the stick to transfer the flames into the hole, and then she stamped out the fire to avoid it spreading among the grasses. However, she still held the stick she had used to transfer the fire.

The magical fire caught, and then black flames began to seep out of the sides of the hole. The magical fire began to suck the black fire down the hole. At first, the magical fire engulfed the black flames, but then it wavered and the black flames grew stronger. Leona leaned over the hole and dropped the blazing stick she held into it. For a moment, nothing happened, but then Leona's magical fire blazed stronger and prevailed, consuming the black fire. Once all of the darkness was gone, Leona stood up, triumphant, and headed back to the castle.

Canyon Daydream

Kate Soulliere
7th Grade

There is a place where the sky is so blue it stains your fingertips if you reach high enough. Your sanity lies broken on the sand and at night your eyes are prominent in the dark, iridescent under the ghostly promise of moonlight. When you speak your voice tumbles down the cliffs and disappears into the silence and the red rocks crumble in your hands. Your thoughts turn somersaults over themselves and spin ringing pirouettes in the planetarium of your skull, and your breath is the only sound that can escape past your lips.

If you walk far enough you can feel every bone aching in your feet and taste the monotony of your desperation. You can paint pictures in the sand and the blindness of the sun will fill the empty spaces and it is beautiful… but if you stare for too long you might just shrivel up into red dust and blow away and you won't be home in time for supper, no.

There is one law in the canyons. Keep moving. Keep moving, keep moving, because the water moves and the sand moves and the wind moves and if you stand in one place for too long you may just be left behind. You can feel these words, unspoken, sinking in your veins, burning, urgent, screaming in your body, keep moving, keep moving, for if you stop you may never start again.

Your solitary bones begin to crumble. The entire place is burning up, so hot, so deathly hot that you expect it to melt into a chalky red paste at any moment but it doesn't because it is too dry and motionless. Your calendar is scratched into the canyon walls and each day is marked by one word, dying, dying, and so tomorrow and yesterday are one and the same, each moment passes through the dryness in your throat, the yellow heat sinking in your skin. You would cry but you have no water to spare and you are so tired, so tired. Your ragged breath burns shriveled lips, cracking, shattering like the time you threw a rock at the kitchen window and the translucent cracks spread slowly like a spider web made of glass.

You are crumbling away in these canyon walls and your heartbeats become uneven and unmeasured but you keep moving because it is the only thing you remember how to do. You keep moving until your skull almost breaks into a thousand pieces and your body is a slave to your diminishing sanity that screams to every muscle, every drop of blood, keep moving, keep moving. Your heartbeat reverberates in your head and you begin to count it thumping-- one, two, three, four, five, until you don't have enough fingers and toes and you keep moving.

You mumble to yourself because there is no one else to talk to and you reminisce over your childhood, specifically, the August nights you spent catching fireflies in the dark and the way it looked when their tiny neon abdomens went streaking through the sky like one thousand tiny shooting stars and you called it magic until someone told you otherwise. You open your eyes now, and see them flashing in the sky but when you try to catch one in your fingers it simply disappears and your fists clench and unclench, tying and untying these knots of your flesh. At this moment you would rather drown than spend another minute wandering among these canyon walls, and so you try to flood your lungs with too much sunlight and just when you think you may have found escape you take another breath.

And you scream.

You scream at this merciless desert and you scream at the pounding in your skull, you scream at the fireflies that aren't there and the cracks in your shriveled tongue. You scream at the sun and you scream at the absent rain and you scream because you have stopped moving and you are lying on your back and you don't think you can ever find a way up again. You scream because this can't be the end, it can't, forever has come too soon and there is no way to send it back. You scream because you don't want to die trapped between these canyon walls.

Wide eyes staring into yours and you feel your cheeks redden. She asks why you are moaning softly and your mumbled response is hidden beneath your breath. Not ragged breath. Not desperate breath. Normal, hydrated, canyon-day-hike breath, tinted with mint bubblegum and hours of talking around a campfire the night before. Frustrated now, she asks again what's up and should she get help and if it's time to turn around. "We've been hiking long enough, don't you think?"

You look to the sky for help and find only a raven meandering drunkenly under the deep afternoon blue. You fidget with your hands. Not cracked and shriveled hands. Smooth, moist hands, with an insubstantial white scar from an accident with the spatula one month back. Embarrassed, you speak in a murmur that is just barely audible in the silent afternoon air.

"It was just a daydream. Don't worry about it. How did you hear that, anyway? You never listen to me."

She shrugs, rolls her eyes.

"You are the weirdest sister on this planet. How the heck did I end up related to a lunatic like you, anyway?"

You ignore her. She ignores you. You collaboratively succumb to the silence that can only reside between these canyon walls. You begin to slip back into your daydream.

You keep moving.

Half and Half

By Lindsey Spolidoro
5th Grade

Chapter 1
A Sudden Feeling

It was a hot summer day in Iowa. All around me were growing corn fields. You could tell that I was a country girl who grew up on a farm. My jeans were gray and dusty from walking through the continuous corn fields that stretched on and on. I felt the sweat on the back of my neck and my long hair sticking to my face. I heard the dinner horn calling to all of the farmers letting them know that it was time to eat, so I headed home.

After lunch I met up with my friend Chrissa at our special tree just like we always do on Wednesdays. She got there first. We always raced. Chrissa always won.

"I really have to work on running faster," I said.

"Oh yes, you do," Chrissa joked. Usually what we would do was to go to the park and play soccer. That's not what Chrissa wanted to do, she told me she wanted to talk about something important. By the excited look on her face, I could tell that it was something good.

We started walking.

"Guess what!" Chrissa started, "I'm going to get a puppy for my birthday!"

"Oh my gosh, that's awesome! What kind of dog are you going to get? What are you going to name him?" I asked.

"I want to name him Scort and I think it's going to be a golden retriever," she replied.

"Finally! We have an answer to those mice eating all the corn in the fields. The mice won't ever know he's coming because of the color of his fur. But there's one thing that I'm kind of curious about."

"And what's that?"

"Why would you name him Scort? I mean, it's a good name, but what made you think of Scort?"

"Oh you know me, always thinking of crazy, original things." It's true, Chrissa is very original. She always wears blinding outfits where if you looked at her you would feel like someone was shining a flashlight in your eyes. She also comes up with strange nicknames for people. She always calls me Tripper even though my real name is Zoey. It's probably because I'm too aggressive in sports and that I'm known for my red cards in soccer. Sometimes in serious matters she'll call me Zoe.

The next Wednesday after lunch I met up with Chrissa at our tree and this time someone, or should I say something, was with her.

"Oh my gosh, he's so cute!" I exclaimed. I was staring at a tiny golden retriever about the size of a loaf of bread with big brown eyes. A quick mouse scurried across our feet. Chrissa screamed and Scort jumped out of her hands and chased the mouse. For some reason I had a sudden urge to get on all fours and chase the mouse with Scort.

Chapter 2
Connection

I went to bed that night wondering what had happened earlier that day. It was making my head spin. Finally with a slight headache, I went to sleep. I woke up to a huge storm. I could hear the tornado sirens going off in the distance. My mom came crashing into my room urging me to get into the basement.

When the tornado siren goes off my mom gets really scared. I was only half awake, so I tripped on the stairs and I let out a low bark. I slowed myself down and stopped.

"Was that a bark?" my Mom asked.

"I don't know," I answered. I honestly had no idea what had happened or why I had barked.

Then I looked out the window. There was a full moon. I had to howl; I was trying to hold it in but I couldn't. "Aooooooo!"

My mom turned around. "Are you feeling OK?" and then she walked away.

When we finally got to the basement my leg started to hurt badly. It was throbbing. I had a sudden image flash into my head: It was a dog and his right leg was covered in blood. What was that about?

Chapter 3
Coincidental?

After the storm my leg didn't hurt as bad, but it was a little sore. "I must be going crazy," I thought. I needed to take a walk. So I did. The air was refreshing. At least it was until I got to the corn fields. Then I saw Chrissa.

Her face was wet and her eyes were red. Was she crying? Chrissa usually never cried. "Chrissa! Are you okay?" I asked.

"No! Scort ran away and I can't find him," she replied. We both started searching for Scort.

Then I saw something. It was really small and lying in a heap. "Chrissa, I found him!" I exclaimed. We started running to the little puppy, my heart pounding, my mind racing. I was urging myself to run faster.

Lying on the side of the road was Scort with a huge gash on his right leg. Chrissa started sobbing again but I realized something: it was his right leg that was cut and my right leg was hurting. Was it just a coincidence?

Chapter 4
Convincing My Parents

The next morning Chrissa called. "Scort is going to the doctor to get his leg fixed. They said it might be broken!" she cried.

"Don't worry; everything is going to be okay," I reassured her. I was thinking about Scort's leg and my leg and wondering if there was some sort of a connection.

Then I remembered something. That flash that I had in the basement on the night of the storm. The dog was tiny, a golden retriever, and it was his right leg that was hurt! Was it Scort?

In the end I realized that I had to tell my parents. "I hope they'll believe me," I said to myself. I went downstairs. They were in the living room on the couch reading books. "You guys, I need to tell you something," I said. I told them everything, from when Chrissa announced that she was getting a puppy, to wondering if it was a coincidence with Scort's leg and the picture flashing in my head.

My parents looked at each other nervously and then burst out laughing.

"You know what? I might as well be talking to a wall. At least it wouldn't laugh in my face!" I said. That made them stop laughing. They started to apologize but I stomped out of the room before they could finish.

So much for that idea, I thought. Next I should probably tell Chrissa. "I hope she believes me." I thought to myself. If she does she'll help me convince my parents and then we'll figure out what's wrong.

Chapter 5
Convincing My Friend

When I told my parents about the recent events they didn't believe me. I think it was because I wasn't prepared. This time I prepared a speech. It included the whole story, even with witnesses.

I went down the stairs into the office and called Chrissa. "Chrissa, meet me at the tree; is Scort home?" I asked.

"Yep, we picked him up yesterday. His leg is all fixed up and he looks better," she replied.

"Good. Will you bring him?" I asked.

"Sure," she answered.

I ran out the door. It was a little windy. I started to jog. Then I realized that I was going faster than I had ever gone before. Wow, I might even make it to the tree before Chrissa. When I rounded the corner about forty feet from the tree I saw that Chrissa still wasn't there.

That made me go even faster knowing that she could come zooming around the trees and beat me there. But then something unexpected happened. Just as I was about to touch the tree, Chrissa who was holding Scort, jumped out from behind it. I yelped. Then I ran into the tree.

"Oh my gosh. I am so sorry. I didn't mean to make you do that. Are you okay?" she exclaimed.

"You know what? I've been better." I replied rubbing the bump on my head. "Anyway," I laughed, "I have something to tell you." I read her my speech.

"So it's kind of like you're half and half!" and then she dissolved into giggles.

"What? I'm not kidding!" I reasoned. "Besides, I have a witness. You."

"Me? How!" she exclaimed.

"You just heard me. Remember? Right before I ran into the tree, I yelped."

"Oh yeah, you're right," she said.

"So you believe me?" I asked.

"Of course. If that's what you think is going on then I'll believe you. You haven't lied to me before so I know that I can trust you."

"Ok, good. Now all we have to do is convince my parents," I said skeptically.

Chapter 6
Close Calls

Chrissa tied Scort to our "special" tree so that we could think about what to add on to the plan. "Here's an idea," Chrissa began, "I'll be there so that you can call me up for a witness just like they do in real trials."

"Oh yeah, that would be cool. Oh, that reminds me. My mom heard me bark when I fell down the stairs and howl when I saw the moon," I said.

"Wha-" she started.

"What? Like you don't fall down the stairs every once in a while?" I interrupted.

Thirty minutes later, we finished the plan.

Chrissa untied Scort from the tree and put on his leash. He limped along slowly. "Ugh. He's taking forever."
Chrissa complained.

"Let's pick him up and run with him," I said.

It seemed like we'd been running for hours when we reached the train tracks. When we got to the railroad crossing a train was 200 feet away. I turned around to tell Chrissa to wait but I saw her run up ahead of me sprinting with Scort in her arms.
"Chrissa, NO!" I screamed.

Chapter 7
Convincing My Parents #2

I started to run after her. The train was getting closer, 100 feet and Chrissa was halfway across the tracks. I was on the tracks when it was 50 feet away. As I stepped off the track I felt a huge whoosh. I closed my eyes. I was too afraid to open them.

"Zoe, come on; let's go!" Chrissa exclaimed. She was talking to me, so I must be alive. I turned around and saw the train racing past me. I gulped as I realized how close to death I actually was.

We continued toward my house and when we got there, we found out my parents weren't home. "Oh, I forgot. My parents are at bingo today. Let's get our bikes and go find them." We had an extra bike for Chrissa and it had a basket for Scort. We set off to the Bingo-Rama.

It was starting to get dark so we picked up the pace. I had a sudden feeling come over me. It was as if something was watching me. "Chrissa, one second. I need to look at something," I said. I stopped my bike and hopped off.

As soon as I hopped off, some of the corn stalks started moving. Then I saw two red, mean eyes staring out at me. Suddenly a fox jumped out at me. Before I knew it I was barking and had charged at him on all fours. Chrissa grabbed my arm and I snapped back to reality. We got on our bikes and pedaled away as fast as we could.

I didn't even bother to look back when we got in the Bingo-Rama; I was too scared. I found my mom and my dad sitting next to each other. As quietly as I could, I got their attention and ushered them outside. Chrissa was waiting. I read my speech and waited for their reaction.

"Ok, look; I just don't think that it's very realistic," my dad said.

"That is why we have witnesses. First: I fell down the stairs and I barked. Mom heard me." I argued.

"Yeah, but-" Mom started.

"Second: I howled at the moon. Mom heard me."This time nobody interrupted. "Third: Before I ran into a tree I yelped. Chrissa heard me," I said.

"It's true," Chrissa nodded.

"Fourth: Today I saw a fox and I barked and raced after it. Chrissa heard me. Do you believe me now?" I asked.

"Well, I guess," Mom said.

"If she believes it, I believe it," Dad said.

"What now?" Chrissa asked. That's something I hadn't thought of before.

"We need to go see a doctor," Mom said.

"Everybody get in the car. Put your bikes in the trunk," Dad said.

Chapter 8
Professional Help

When we got to the hospital, I read my speech again. The doctors had no idea what to do. So they sent us to the lab to get some tests done. When we got there I convinced them too. They asked my parents to see my birth certificate.

I noticed that my mom and dad had a surprised look on their faces. My mom pulled it out of her purse and handed it to the lead scientist named Dr. Franklin. He looked at it and raised his eyebrows. Then he went into some sort of room with the other scientists. I could hear their hushed voices.

What was going on here? Dr. Franklin came back out and motioned for my mom and my dad to go into the room. Did something bad happen? They finally came back out and my mom and my dad approached me. "Zoe, we have something to tell you. We aren't your real parents," my mom said.

Chapter 9
Confessions

"When we were on our honeymoon in Ontario, Canada we went into a forest to take pictures. While we were there, we encountered a pack of wolves that was caring for a baby. We couldn't just leave the poor baby so we decided to bring her back to Iowa and name her Zoey," my mom explained. For a moment I was too shocked to talk.

"Wait. So you're telling me that I was adopted from a pack of wolves?!" I demanded.

My mom nodded.

"And you never told me?!" I asked in disbelief.

"I'm sorry," my mom apologized.

"Pardon me," Dr. Franklin interrupted, "Did you say wolves?" My mom nodded again. "Does she have some sort of scar?" the doctor asked.

"Yes, why?" my mom asked.

"Will you show me?" My mom seemed to hesitate but she finally agreed. She rolled up one of my sleeves. There were two light pink circles on my bicep.

"You said those were birthmarks, not scars!" I yelled. "That's another thing that I need to tell you. When I was trying to get you away from the wolves I had to grab you. One of the wolves tried to bite my hand but he got your arm instead," my mom confessed.

Dr. Franklin stroked his chin and said, "My hypothesis is that there was something in the teeth of that wolf that went into your body which makes you act like an animal when you are frightened or in pain." I could feel my jaw drop.

"I would like to take some of the liquid out of the scars, examine it, and test it. If a test I have in mind comes back negative we will put the liquid back in and continue testing. If the tests are positive then we take out the rest of the scar-liquid and give you a tranquilizer. All I need is for the parents to sign some paperwork.

Chapter 10
Cure, Curing

While my parents were filling out the paperwork I had the chance to observe my surroundings. The place was full of doors with a window to the right of each door. The curtains were drawn and the hallway seemed to stretch on and on and on. Then my parents came to me and they each took one of my hands. At least I wasn't the only one who was worried.

Is it going to hurt? Will they put me to sleep? Are there going to be a lot of doctors? Will my mom and my dad be with me? Is there going to be blood? All sorts of questions buzzed around in my head.

We walked into the last door of what seemed like a couple hundred doors. Inside there were cabinets, a counter with tools, three chairs, and a bed. The doctor helped me into the bed. Then he took out a needle.

"This will help you go to sleep," he explained.

"I hope the sleep won't be permanent," I thought to myself. My mom and dad sat down and the scientist came over to me. He injected the shot into my arm and it hurt. BADLY.

Then somehow my eyelids started to get heavy. I realized that I was falling asleep. I struggled to stay awake but the blackness was coming over me. Dear God, please let everything be okay! The next thing I knew, everything was black.

Chapter 11
Cured!

When I woke up, I tried to get out of bed but when I moved my arm I felt a sharp pain. I didn't dare to look at my arm. I just wanted to find out whether the results were good or bad. Then I heard the door open and my dad came in.

"How are you feeling?" he asked me.

"My arm hurts badly," I moaned.

"I'm going to get Dr. Franklin," he said.

After a couple minutes the doctor came in along with Dad, Mom, and Chrissa. "The results were what I thought they would be, you tested positive for wolf tracks in your blood," he said. "So here is your medication. Take it once in the morning and once at night for 7 days. I recommend taking pain medicine for your arm. It might hurt a little."

"A little?" I asked. "Yeah, right!" I looked at my arm. As soon as I saw it I almost passed out. My arm was a mix of red, purple, blue, and gray. Oh, gross. Chrissa, my mom, and my dad helped me out of the bed.

After a few days I got to go home. I wasn't half and half anymore. Everything returned to normal. Until the next full moon.

The REAL Reason

Hannah Taylor
3rd Grade

Hey! Are you tired of all the chores, responsibilities, and manners your parents tell you to do or have every day?

Well, I know your troubles.

But listen to me and – whoa! What was that?

OK. I can't tell you in person the real reason why they make you do all these things, so you'll just have to read this book instead.

TOP SECRET

Clean your room:
Fake Reason: To make it organized
Real Reason: If toys go together or touch the floor too much, they will come alive. They will try to chase you, and when they catch you, they will eat you UP! So clean your room kids!

Don't play with your food
Fake Reason: To have good manners
Real Reason: For years, your parents have been keeping a secret from you: food moves. And when you move it, it starts playing with you, maybe trashing your house, causing your parents to get angry. "No TV for a week," they'll say.

Eat your vegetables
Fake Reason: To keep you healthy
Real Reason: Long ago, vegetables roamed the earth. The cave men had an idea: they ate them. So eat your vegetables, so they don't eat you!

Remember, don't tell your parents. This is the REAL reason!

Tom & Maggie Help The Homeless In India

Puja Vengadasalam
4th Grade

One fine summer morning in August, Maggie went to the mailbox. She found a letter that was different looking inside. She opened it and ran to Tom as fast as she could. "Look here, Tom! The Indian superstar Raja sent us a letter. He liked the art work and scrapbook we made for him. Now, he wants to meet us. He even sent us two open airline tickets so we can go to India," Maggie said.

"Wow, that's great!" Tom replied, and added, "India, here we come!"

Within two days, Tom and Maggie had finished their packing and were off to the airport. As they boarded the plane, they said together, "Bombay, here we come!" After a long twenty two hours flight, they reached Bombay, India.

"Uh, I feel dizzy," Maggie said. Tom smiled as he moved on, lugging their two suitcases.

"It's hot here. Let's go for some ice cream," Tom said. Maggie nodded her head and ran up to the ice cream stand.

"Look at those beautiful dresses- I wish I had one! I think they call it a saree," Maggie said as she caught up with her friend.

"Yup, you are right," Tom said as he paid for the ice cream cones. When they were half way done, they spied two kids about nine and eleven, wearing torn dresses and asking travelers for food and money. Tom and Maggie felt very sorry for them and gave them their ice cream. Tom and Maggie watched them as they rapidly finished off the ice cream. Tom asked, "What are your names, and what happened to you two?"

"I am Piya," the tall girl said softly. "And this is my little brother, Ravi," she added, pointing at the small little boy next to her.

"We are very poor and don't have either food or money," Ravi said shyly.

"Don't you have parents?" asked Tom. "No, our parents

died three years back," Piya answered in a sad voice.

"Will you be our friends?," Maggie asked, trying not to cry.

"Sure, let's be friends. And yes, we will be here tomorrow," Ravi and Piya replied.

As Maggie and Tom checked into their room in the hotel opposite the airport, they were very quiet. Both of them were thinking. After a long time, Maggie said, "I feel sorry for Piya and Ravi. They don't have anything. We must do something to help our homeless new friends."

"But we do not know anybody here..., and we are here only for about a week," Maggie added in a voice that sounded like she had given up.

Then suddenly Tom got an idea. "I know what we can do. We can have a walk-a-thon like we did in school. It could be dedicated to finding a home for Piya and Ravi," said Tom.

Maggie replied, "Good idea, but who will pay for it? Who do we ask for sponsorship?".

"Let's ask Raja, the Indian superstar to sponsor us," Tom said proudly.

"Fantastic. Let's ask him tomorrow when we meet him," Maggie said before she dozed off.

Next morning, a loud honk woke them up. When Maggie and Tom rushed to the patio, they found a long, shiny black car that had come to pick them up. Brother and sister rushed downstairs after putting on some clothes. They jumped into the car and it zoomed off. Maggie and Tom saw beautiful sights of Bombay on the way to meet Raja. All of a sudden, Tom spied a giant cut out. "Look! Isn't that Raja in his latest film?"

"Yes, it is Sir," the chauffeur in the black suit said.

"It says 'Oh Zindagi(Life), Releasing Aug 15, Don't miss this'!" Maggie exclaimed. Soon they reached The Gateway of India where they were going to meet Raja. Overlooking the Arabian Sea, the monument had a 26 meters high arch. It was absolutely breathtaking!

Right under the central dome stood Raja. Raja was the handsomest man they had ever seen. He was tall and glamorous. "Hello! You are Tom and Maggie, right?," Raja said.

"Yes," they replied, awestruck. "I loved the stuff you sent me," Raja said kindly.

"We both are big fans of yours. We watch all your movies. Thank you so much for meeting us". Tom said happily before adding "We need your help."

"Go ahead- tell me what it is," Raja replied.

"Can you help us raise money for our walk-a-thon to help Piya and Ravi?," Maggie asked nervously.

"Who are Piya and Ravi?" Raja questioned curiously. "Piya and Ravi are our two homeless friends- we met them yesterday. We want to raise money for them through a walk-a-thon," Tom replied.

"That's wonderful. I will get the permission and arrange the sponsorship. You get ready for the walkathon," Raja said. Tom and Maggie jumped with joy. They would have some good news to tell their friends when they met them at noon.

The next few days were hectic. The duo went to local schools recruiting kids to join them in the walkathon. The response was overwhelming. Every evening, Tom and Maggie would go to the Gateway monument and practice making 25 laps in preparation for the event. The D-day finally arrived. By 9 am of August 15, India's Independence Day, a big crowd had gathered. When Raja came over, the crowd began to clap.

Raja waved the flag- and the walk began. It was long and hard but the sight of their two needy friends kept them going. As Tom and Maggie accompanied by school kids from India completed the last lap, they saw the Mayor of Mumbai standing by to cheer them. Raja and other sponsors had donated 250,000 rupees to sponsor Tom and Maggie's walk. The duo were happy to give away the money to the Mayor, who would find a home for Piya and Ravi and others like them.

It was time to go back home. Tom and Maggie knew they were going to miss India very much-but school was going to restart soon. They boarded the plane, promising their Indian friends that they would keep in touch.

A fortnight after their return, Tom and Maggie found a big box at their doorstep -it was from Piya and Ravi. When Maggie opened the box, she found a saree from Piya inside. There was a present for Tom too. It was a DVD of Raja's latest movie release, a gift from Ravi. "Cool, let's go in and watch it," Tom said excitedly as they both went indoors clutching to their hearts the precious gifts from their Indian friends.

RUNAWAY

Matthew Walton
5th Grade

One hot summers day when LeSean was feeding Reagan, his Golden Retriever, his little brother, Ray Ray, came bursting through the door and shouted, "There are new neighbors moving in right now in the house next door."

"Did you see any boys?" asked LeSean hoping Ray Ray would say there were boys his age.

"All I saw was an older lady and a girl," Ray Ray said disappointedly. "Maybe the boy will come later." Ray Ray walked out and LeSean went back to feeding Reagan.

As Reagan ate his breakfast, LeSean went to his desk and wrote his paper about the "The Alamo" for this history class. LeSean just finished his paper when his friend Allen, who lived down the street, knocked on his door. He knew it was Allen because he knocked five times in a special order.

LeSean opened the door and let Allen in. Allen said, "I tried to call you but you didn't answer."

"Oh, sorry I was doing my paper in my room and I didn't hear the phone ring," said LeSean.

"Well I came to ask if you wanted to hike in the woods on the road to Cherrytown," said Allen.

"We'll have to take Ray Ray because my mom and dad

aren't home and we'll take Reagan for his nose," said LeSean

"That's okay," said Allen.

"I'll get Reagan's leash and a water bottle. You go get Ray Ray," said LeSean.

The two boys met up at the front door. Then they set out for their hike. Once they reached the top of the hill that marked the outskirts of Cherrytown. They then turned left into Sheerwood Forest.

LeSean picked up a stick and used it as a walking stick.

Allen, LeSean, and Ray Ray all listened to the birds high up in the trees. They watched rabbits run right in front of them. "What a beautiful day it is, thought LeSean, everything is peaceful."

LeSean then saw a man approaching them holding a gun and what looked like rabbits and squirrels.

"How are you boys today?" asked the man.

"Good," they all said at once.

The man kept on walking and LeSean noticed the rabbits and squirrels looked flat. He also noticed the man tried to hide the animals from them. LeSean tried to push the thought out of his head, but he couldn't. Something about that man bothered him.

They kept walking until Reagan stopped, sat down and looked at LeSean, then back at a spot in the leaves. LeSean had taught Reagan what to do if he saw, heard or smelt something bad. He would sit on the ground.

LeSean didn't want to mess with this so he walked to where Reagan sat and moved his stick on the ground in front of Reagan.

"What are you doing?" asked Ray Ray.

"Trying to see what Reagan hears," said LeSean.

Reagan heard whistling in front of them. He heard wind going through metal. LeSean brought the stick forward when SNAP. Leaves flew and LeSean, Ray Ray, Allen and Reagan saw a Foot-Hold-Trap.

Ray Ray asked, "What is that?"

"It's a Foot-Hold-Trap, to trap animals by their feet when they walk on it. They're illegal at this time of year," said LeSean.

They stared at it with big eyes. There was silence for a moment. Then Allen said, "What if there's more of them here?"

"We have to walk back carefully. Reagan in the lead, me second, Ray Ray third and Allen you watch behind us," said LeSean.

They made it back to the road without finding any more traps. LeSean was still wondering about the man and his animals. When they got home LeSean told Mrs. McCoy, his mom, about the man, the animals he was carrying and the trap.

"I don't want you hiking in those woods anymore," she said. "That was too close."

"Do you think that trap belonged to the man?" asked LeSean. "He didn't look nice at all."

"We can't tell the police until we know the facts," said Mrs. McCoy.

During all of this Reagan walked up and sat right by LeSean's leg. "Hi Reagan," LeSean said. Then it popped into his head what he hadn't told Mrs. Mc Coy.

"Mom," he said. "I didn't tell you how we knew the trap was there. Reagan heard it and smelt it. Then he sat and stopped to tell us there's something there."

"Wow, that's amazing," said Mrs. McCoy. "You're lucky he was with you. He's a very smart dog."

With that, Mr. McCoy said, "Time for bed." Everyone said their goodnights and went to bed.

LeSean went to bed that night with a thousand questions going through his mind.

* * *

Brandon was in his truck driving to the Trap and Bait store. He was worried the kids he saw earlier were smart enough to know he was trapping out of season.

He arrived at the store sweating from thinking what would happen if he were caught.

He walked in with his box of pelts and set them on the front desk. Brandon's best friend, Tim, was working his night shift.

"Hey, Brandon," he said his voice crackling from smoking.

"I've got some pelts for you," said Brandon. "Five squirrels and seven rabbits. How much can I get?"

"The best I can give you is fifty dollars," said Tim.

"That was more than what I was expecting, so, deal," said Brandon.

The two men shook hands.

* * *

LeSean woke the next morning to find Reagan lying on top of him. "Reagan," LeSean coughed sleepily. "I can't breathe."

Reagan got off and walked downstairs. He sat by his food bowl waiting for LeSean to come feed him.

LeSean came down, poured Reagan's food then poured his. They sat and ate in silence, for they were the only ones up in the house. LeSean thought about what they would do today. He thought they would take a walk, come inside and eat lunch and later run around outside.

When they got done eating Ray Ray was walking down the stairs. "Ray Ray," LeSean said. "Remember to tell Mom and Dad that Reagan and I went on a walk, OK."

"OK," said Ray Ray.

LeSean and Reagan walked outside and began their walk. They walked two miles then turned around and went back.

When LeSean and Reagan got back it was 12:00 P.M. Reagan sat by LeSean's leg as LeSean ate his lunch.

When LeSean finished eating, he called Allen and asked if he wanted to come over and shoot baskets. Five minutes later LeSean and Allen were playing HORSE at LeSean's basketball hoop.

LeSean won the first game, Allen won the second one and they were playing to see who was the champ. LeSean won the last game as they finished, Allen's mom called and said Allen had to come home.

The two boys said good-bye. Allen rode his bike home and LeSean went inside. He rested a little while and then decided to play with Reagan in the yard.

LeSean and Reagan walked out into Reagan's yard. His

yard had silver chain link fencing around it. His yard was about 50 feet by 35 feet. His fencing was very short, about short enough for Reagan to be able to jump over it.

They played with Reagan's favorite toy, the big blue Jolly ball. LeSean threw it to one end of the yard Reagan chased it and brought it back to LeSean. They did this about fifty times. After throw number fifty Reagan and LeSean were very tired so they started to walk back to the door.

LeSean heard gunfire in the distance. I wonder what that was about, thought LeSean, it isn't hunting season here.

He wanted to get Reagan inside because Reagan didn't like gunfire. LeSean walked faster afraid Reagan would start running around scared.

LeSean saw a man on the other side of the road hunting deer. That was legal this time of year. He heard the gun being cocked. Then it fired, again. Reagan heard it and ran like a golden streak running toward the woods behind the house.

LeSean ran as fast as he could run into the house and yelled, "The man I saw was hunting and fired a shot, Reagan was scared and now he ran away."

Ray Ray started to cry but Mr. and Mrs. McCoy dashed with LeSean outside to look for Reagan. They searched for three hours but no sign of Reagan was found.

* * *

Reagan heard the gunfire and he bolted toward the fence. He ran as fast as he could and jumped the fence. He ran toward the woods without even looking back to see where his house was.

He ran and ran and ran jumping dead trees and dodging live ones. He ran for what seemed like hours. It was dark by the time Reagan stopped.

His stomach was growling as he lay down. He spotted a squirrel and pounced. He enjoyed the fresh meat.

That night Reagan found a hollow tree and slept in it. He had never slept in the wild before. Reagan slept dreaming of LeSean and his warm bed. He thought about the day, how it started peacefully and then turned to a nightmare.

*   *   *

The next morning LeSean got up and looked for Reagan in his room. Then he remembered yesterday and how Reagan had ran away.

He walked downstairs and ate breakfast quickly. No one was up so LeSean took a piece of paper and wrote, “I’m looking for Reagan.”

He walked outside and ran straight for the woods. He walked all around where he thought Reagan was but Reagan was in a different place.

*   *   *

Reagan kept walking looking for his way back. Reagan walked across a road he had seen before but didn’t know when. He then heard the familiar sound of wind going through metal. Reagan then heard rustling in the bushes in front of him. Then he heard rustling in the bushes behind him. Then everything happened so quickly.

A man jumped out in front of him and threw a net that covered Reagan and cut into his skin. Then a boy that Reagan couldn’t see very well jumped from behind him.

The boy yelled, “You won’t take my dog, not as long as I’m here.”

Reagan recognized the voice. It was LeSean. LeSean threw dust in the man’s face. Then he ran to Reagan and cut the net and freed him.

“ The cops are coming,” said LeSean with a grin on his face. “You’ll get caught and go to prison.”

“Not if they don’t find me,” said Brandon.

Brandon put his fist up and pretended to fight with LeSean.

Reagan charged at Brandon as fast as he could and nailed him in the leg. Brandon went flying and Reagan rolling. Reagan rolled into something that caught hold of his back and stung up his back.

Reagan let out a yelp as LeSean heard sirens. He rushed over and was kneeling down when something hit his head and yelled. Everything was black.

*   *   *

LeSean woke up in the hospital feeling drowsy.

"You woke up. You've been knocked out for quite a while," said Mrs. McCoy.

"What happened?" LeSean asked.

"You found the man that we saw in the woods," said Ray Ray. "He is in jail now."

"Where's Reagan?" asked LeSean. "Is he at home?"

"Reagan's at the vet being treated for cuts and maybe hypothermia," said Mr. McCoy.

When LeSean was released from the hospital and they got Reagan back from the vet, LeSean hugged Reagan so hard Reagan couldn't breathe.

"Don't ever run away again, no matter how scared you are!" said LeSean with tears in his eyes. I was worried and sad. I wouldn't let anything happen to you."

Reagan replied with a loud "woof".

Bullied

Alexis Witcher
6th Grade

I ran through the courtyard heart pounding, but I was not fast enough. Quickly they surrounded me. One by one their words struck me like knives. I was weak. I pushed through and ran home. They didn't bother to follow me.

When I came to our front door, I threw my stuff down and took off through the woods. I climbed up the old rope ladder and thrust myself into my tree house. The smell of honeysuckle drifted through the light spring air, but even that was not enough to calm my nerves. I started to cry.

I thought to myself, Why me? Why do those bullies pick on me? Ever since third grade when Jake became popular, he stopped being my friend. Now he thinks l'm weird because l'm different. We used to play in this tree house together. lf it wasn't for his good looks and money he would just be one of us, the nerds. I wish he was on ugly beast! Ha! Then nobody would pay any attention to him.

"Kayla, come home. lt's time to eatl" I heard my mom's voice calling after me. As I walked through the front door, I saw chicken and rice on the table, "How was school today?" my mom questioned.

"Great!" I answered back. I hadn't told my mom about the bullies yet. I didn't want to tell her because since my dad left us, she had to work two shifts. She didn't have time to worry about me. The rest of dinner was silent. I was exhausted, so I went straight to bed after dinner. As my head hit the soft, comforting pillow I quickly dozed off.

My eyes slowly opened as the warm sun shone in my face. I was late! I rushed to get ready, throwing on an old t-shirt and shorts. I quickly grabbed my bike and pedaled toward the school. As I entered the school, the tardy bell rang. I had made it! When I took my seat, I noticed that Jake wasn't there. Was I going to get bullied today?The rest of the day I was stuck with the same question. When the last bell of the day rang, I gathered my books and made my way quickly to the bike rack. That's when I saw them. The bullies without their leader made their way toward me.

Hoping I would get away, I untied my bike and hopped on. As I pedaled off and started towards the woods, I saw shadows following from behind. I looked back. Trevor and Megan were close behind, throwing rocks to slow me down.

As I turned back to look in front of me, a hooded figure jumped out. I ran into it and fell, crashing to the ground. The last thing I remember was the crowd of bullies running away in horror. As my head weakly fell to the cement, l was out.

About 5:00 that evening, my mom woke me up. "Are you sick?" my mom asked worriedly. Confused, I asked my mom what had happened. She wasn't sure. She had been working overtime and came home to find me asleep. What did happen? Did I dream it or was it real?

The next morning, l woke up fairly early. Walking down the stairs l called out, "Mom! Mom, are you home?" No answer. For breakfast I had my favorite, Lucky Charms. Then I stuck a note to the fridge that said, "Went out. Be back in a bit."

Today was the day that I was going to fix up my tree house. I grabbed a hammer, nails, paint, and a paintbrush. I set out excitedly, lugging my heavy materials in my big gray backpack. Through the woods I walked, when I heard a mysterious sound of crunching leaves behind me. Was I being followed?

Determined to face my fear, I turned around, only to see trees and vegetation. I turned back, alarmed to see a hooded figure before me. lt was the figure I saw in my dream.

"Don't be scared," said a familiar voice. "lt's me, Jake."

"Jake, you scared me to death!" I replied. "Why are you dressed like that, and why are you following me?"

"Let's go somewhere and Ican explain everything," Jake replied. I led him to my tree house where we could talk. He started, "When I woke up yesterday, I ran downstairs smelling Gracie's homemade sausage. When I walked into the kitchen, she chased me out of the house with a steak knife. She acted like I was a strangerl As I looked back through a window, I saw my reflection. I looked horriblel I looked like thisl"

He pulled off his hood, and he was not exaggerating. He looked like a troll! He had big pointy ears, bulging eyes, long fangs, and wild hair. I gasped. "Now I have nowhere to stay," Jake admitted.

"Why did you jump out in front of me yesterday?" I asked.

"l wasn't trying to harm you. ln fact, I was trying to stand up to them for you! Watching my friends bully you made me realize how bad I have been, and I'm sorry. After you hit your head, I brought you home. lf I had a chance to be normal again, I would stop bullying and apologize to everyone that I harmed."

"No, l'm sorry! I think I am the reason you turned into this ugly beast," I apologized.

"Why do you think that?" asked Jake.

"Because the other day I was tired of you bullying me and I wished you into an ugly beast."

Jake looked puzzled, "How did your wish come true and how can I change back?"

"l don't know, but we will figure out a way. ln the meantime, you will sleep here in the tree house and I will come back with food for you in the morning. Then we will figure this out."

I ran home, mind racing. I stayed up all night, the scenes of the day playing over and over in my head. When morning finally came, I went straight to the tree house. Jake was awake.

" l've been thinking," Jake said. "lf you wished me a beast because I was a bully, maybe I would turn back into myself again if I changed."

"Good idea! Lefs try it," I responded.

"But how?" Jake asked.

"Apologize to everyone you bullied."

"People can't see me like this!" exclaimed Jake.

"People don't care what you look like. They care about your actions. lf you apologize, they will be so grateful." Jake agreed ,

"Ok,l will try it. I need to apologize to Amber, Ryan, Tyler and Haley."

"We will hold a meeting in the tree house this afternoon. I will send a text to each of them saying to meet me in the woods behind my house at 3:00."

That afternoon, we all met . On our way to the tree house, I explained about meeting Jake and how he wanted to apologize for bullying each of them.

"I don't need an apology from him," Ryan argued. "He won't mean it anyway!"

"Don't be like the bullies!" I pleaded. "Jake has really changed and wants you to accept his apology."

As I finished my sentence, we approached the old wood tree house. Jake peeked his head out the window. His eyes, as blue as the sky, saw right through me. I didn't care about the scars or dirt that covered him. His fanged toothed grin took me back to a place of comfort. It was the grin I've missed since third grade. Jake's grin.

"What is that thing?" Amber shrieked.

"Don't be alarmed. It's just me, Jake," he answered back.

"I am not going up there with him !" Amber whispered to Haley.

"Yes, you are!" I pushed her toward the ladder as I overheard their conversation,

Once everyone got into the tree house, Jake greeted them. Then one by one he started to apologize.

"Haley, I just wanted to say I'm sorry for teasing you because of your height."

"It's ok, but it really hurt my feelings. Hearing you apologize makes me feel better. Thank you."

Then the tree house began to shake. The children screamed in shock. When shaking stopped,

"Jake, your ears are back to normal!" Haley screamed in delight.

Jake went on, "Tyler. Dude, I'm sorry for taking your money every day." Jake pulled out fifty dollars and handed it to Tyler.

"Thanks Dude, I need this tomorrow for lunch money," he said, laughing.

Once again, the tree house shook. As it stopped, Tyler called out, "Your eyes, they changed back."

I looked at Jake. His big blue eyes shined again.

"Next, Amber, I should not have picked on you, calling you a stuck up brat and embarrassing you in front of everyone," Jake said.

"Thank you for apologizing. I was really hurt..." Amber was interrupted by the shaking again.

Jake's teeth had straightened and whitened as perfect as before. "Last but not least, Ryan, I should have never physically hurt you in any way. I thought it was cool," Jake hung his head.

"l have scars and bruises from you! I never thought you would use violence against me. We used to be best friends!" exclaimed Ryan.

"Let's get back to the way we used to be," begged Jake.

"Deal!" They agreed.

After the tree house shook for a momeirt, take was back to normal. Even though Jake looked the same, he had changed on the inside. Soon, our school year was coming to ajn end. I knew we were going to have the best summer of our lives. We had all become the best of frierlds, and the boy I had a crush on when I was in the third grade, now had a crush on me.

The First Loser

Emmy Wood
6th Grade

Chapter 1

"Hilary?" Mrs. Gallagher asked.

Great. History will repeat itself, just like how the Great Depression repeats itself in modern times. Except instead of stock market issues, I'm dealing with reading my writing project out loud. Just like last semester.

You can hear Chloe and her stupid cheerleader friends snickering from the back of the classroom. Of course, this is the only class that at least half of them aren't failing. I hate them more than anything, except maybe Justin Beiber.

"Hilary," Mrs. Gallagher said again, a little annoyed. "Please come up to the front so you can read your story to the class."

I'm not anyone special, don't worry. Reading our stories is part of our huge grade for English. But I hate reading aloud. People can be really judgmental.

As I slowly slumped out of my seat, and walked with heavy steps to the front of the class, I could feel at least 20 pairs of eyeballs on my back. At least 20, maybe more. I knew for a fact that 5 of them belonged to Chloe and her friends, and 1 belonged to my best friend, Trinity. If only they couldn't see me. "Here you go, honey," Mrs. Gallagher said, handing me my story.

Honey? REALLY?!! I'm glad no one else heard that. I took the neat little packet from her hands, and looked at Trinity for sympathy. All she gave me in return was an encouraging nod.

So I started, because obviously I couldn't do anything better, like jump out a window. Again. (Word to the wise: never do something considered "ill-advised" to administrative adults while in school. Especially when they happen to be visiting the classroom.)

"Have you ever thought about what's underneath your feet? If you are thinking dirt, you're completely wrong, because I'm talking about the Earth's Mantle. The mantle is made of the same elements as the Sun, which makes it extremely hot. Scientists have found many rock types in the Mantle, and sometimes even diamonds!! Most of the rock is carried up to…."

BRIIIIINNNNNNNNGGGGG!!!!! The term "saved by the bell" just got a whole new level of appreciation to me. LUNCH HAS ARRIVED!!!!!!

"Nice job, geek," I hear Chloe hiss.

"You did awesome!!" Trinity said, suddenly appearing at my side. "I don't understand why you were nervous; you knew it practically by heart! If only I had the time to memorize my essay!! Butnooo, mydadsaidthatIhadtopracticemytrumpet, and…"

That's all I could hear. Trinity can go on and on about anything and everything that comes up. I can never keep up. On average, the most I can manage is a murmur of agreement or dis-agreement, which I can decide by the tone of her voice.

When we enter the cafeteria and all you can hear is a big huge droning, because everyone is talking at once. "I'll save you a seat," I think I heard Trinity say, but I really couldn't tell from the noise. She always saves the seats, because she always packs her lunch and I always buy mine. When I get to the line, it is pretty short because A) buying was deemed totally uncool by Chloe in the 3rd grade and B) its Taco Thursday, which translates to: Ground-up-leftovers-from-Meatloaf-Monday Thursday.

Usually I just stick to the cheese pizza. That way, I know I'm not eating horse meat.

Speaking of gross meaty things, here comes the football team. The only thing they seem to care about is themselves. Don't be fooled by their "I love my girlfriend" act. (BTW, the only people the football team will date are cheerleaders)

You know, most girls who go to my school have a crush on the stereotype jock, but of course, I'm not a stereotype girl. Hon-estly, they're a little too sweaty/ego avid/ muscle head for me.

So anyway, they all come up to the lunch line (Chloe's rules only apply to girls), and each order like 6 tacos. So gross and they eat like pigs. Thank goodness I'm already halfway to our table!

Since Chloe always sits indoors, Trinity and I and all our

friends sneak outside to avoid the drama. I was 5 feet from the door to outside, and I feel a tap on my shoulder. I turn around, although I know I shouldn't.

"Hi, Hilary!!!" says a completely over-enthusiastic voice. I recognize it immediately. I look below my eye level. Found her.

"Hey, Sharon" I said, a little less enthusiastic then she. I would be a little friendlier, if she wasn't my little cousin.

"Where are you sitting?" she asked.

"I don't know," I said, trying to came up with an excuse. "I think I'm going to go to Mr. Turner's and make up for an Algebra test."

"Oh," she said, looking slightly disappointed. I don't know why, because she used to hate my guts up until this school year.

"Is that Sue over there?" I said, trying to distract her. "You should go see if she wants to eat with you!"

"Ok!" she said. I blinked, and when I looked down again, she just was already in front of Sue. Gosh, she's fast.

I finally made it to the outside seating area. The great outdoors seem to only appeal to the emo, artist, emo artist, and theatre geek populace in our school. Believe me; me and my friends stand out more than you'd think. But we all have two things in common: A) Chloe Jones hates our guts, and B) we hate hers back.

When I reached our table, a discussion had already begun. It goes like this:

Lizzie: "What do you mean you don't know who Jonas Salk is?"
Trinity: "Who is he? Geez, it's no big deal!"
Lizzie: "Of course it is! He's probably the reason you're still alive!"
Hilary: "Sorry to interrupt your incredibly important conversation about Mr. Salt, but we have a more important topic to discuss."
Trinity: "Which is?"
Hilary: "I don't know, I just want to be on the same page as you two!"
Lizzie: "How about we talk about extracurricular activities?"
Hilary and Trinity: "Extra-what?"
Lizzie (rolls her eyes): "After school clubs!"

Hilary: "You know Chloe is going to be president of every club, right?"

That pretty much ended our discussion on extracurricular activities. So I started eating, and Lizzie and Trinity kept talking about some Salt guy, or Salk, as Lizzie tells me, and that summed up my lunch.

After lunch, my day droned on and on until it was over. When I got off the bus and into my house, my mom had left a note taped to the fridge:

"Sorry I can't be home tonight, I had a meeting at last-minute. I left some lasagna in the microwave for you to eat. Night sweetheart!!! -Mom"

Yum, week-old Stouffer's. After I ate, I checked the online school calendar. Tomorrow was the day when the whole school "voted" on our new president of the US. Hooray. It's pretty pointless, because no one at our school can vote.

The next morning, I woke up and hit snooze. Five minutes later, I decided to get out of bed for the day. I went to brush my teeth, and got dressed. Ten minutes later I was at the bus stop.

As usual, my day was a drag. When we went to the gym to vote, I picked a random guy without reading any names. I'm not into politics. Then my day carried on. Well, it could be worse. Malcolm in the Middle could not have been invented. Then I would officially feel bad for myself.

Chapter 2

My week dragged on. And then next week started. (Nothing interesting happened, so I'm skipping ahead.) By Friday, I was bored out of my mind. So after school, I turned on the TV. My mom left on the stinking news. I'm too lazy to reach for the remote, so I just watch. I mean, it's not the end of the world.

Then the news women said that the presidential election was tonight (I don't get why she did, because most people who watch the news know that already) and to tune in tomorrow to see the results.

Then a story came on about some old lady gone missing from her retirement home. It was so boring that I think I fell asleep, because when I woke up, a completely different show was on. So I went to eat dinner, which was good because Mom ordered in Chinese takeout. Then I went to bed.

When I woke up the next morning, and decided to turn on the TV, knowing that the news was on. The newswoman was on again, and I turned it on in the nick of time, because she was about to announce who won the presidential election.

"Congratulations to our new president-elect, William Davis!"

Omigod. That's my father's name. Not to mention that the picture on the screen looked exactly like him.

My father is the new president. Well, president-elect. He left me and my mother when I was five. I mean, I knew he lived in Washington D.C., and that the he was a politician, but I was thinking more of like low-level Senator, not PRESIDENT.

"MMMMOOOOOOMMMMMMM!!!!!!! GET DOWN HERE!!!!!" I heard her running down the stairs.

"Everything okay, honey?" Ack! Not that "honey" thing again. It's bad enough my teacher used it.

"You tell me!" and I show her the TV.

Her face went completely white. It was almost like she was a vampire or something. I've only seen her like this a couple times before. First she gets all white, and then she starts stuttering. "Bu- I di- this-"etc.

Then her face turns red, and everything comes out at once. "*TheonlyreasonIdidn'ttellyouisbecauseIhonestlydidn'tthinkhe'd wintheprimaries,andIdidn'ttellyoubecauseIthought:Wellwhatarethe chancesofhimactuallywinning?I'msurprisedyoudidn'tnoticewithall thebillboardsandschoolassembliesandstuff,butIguessyouactually listentomewhenitcomestopolitics...*"

Then I have to calm her down. "Okay Mom, you gotta slow down and tell me from the beginning. Deep breaths now, deeeeeep breaths," I say, irritated.

In, out, in, out, I show her, getting more agitated with each breath. "Oooookaay. Can you tell what happened now?" I ask.

"Yes. So one day, your dad called me. I picked up, and he

explained to me that he was going to run for President. I was like, 'Yeah, good luck with that!' Then he told me he was serious, and that he wanted you to help with the campaigns. And I was all, 'No way! Hilary is our daughter, not your personal commercial advertisement!'"

Oh, by the way, my mom talks like a teenager. She dresses like one too. Sharon's wardrobe is older than hers!

At that point, I was felt so mad and betrayed that I went up to my room, locked the door, and slumped onto my bed. Just to think, you know? I do this a lot, because it calms me down, and helps me find the best solution to the problem I'm trying to solve. Of course, I couldn't think of anything. It's pretty hard with these circumstances.

After a while, I picked up the phone to call Trinity (of course not my cell phone, because I don't have one). But as I went to dial her number, I thought of a better idea. Mom wouldn't like it. Well it's not like I like any of her "great ideas" anyway.

So instead I dialed my dad's number. I hope it's still the same, since he changed jobs and everything. I paused for a moment, because I haven't called my dad in ages. It didn't help that my mom wouldn't let me. Remembering why I was calling in the first place, I punched in the last digit and pushed call.

It was really weird, because he picked up on the first ring. He must be really desperate or something. "Hello?" he asked.

I froze. I honestly thought I wouldn't make it this far, because I usually chicken out by step one. "Hi, Dad, this is Hilary." The air in the room he was in must have brightened dramatically, because he seemed very happy all of a sudden. "Hilary! I'm so glad you called!"

"I'm glad I called, too," I said, not being able to think of anything else. "Congratulations!" I added at the last minute.

"Thank you! So how are you?" He said.

"Good, thanks. I'm sorry I haven't called you any earlier," I say. Seriously, I don't know where any of this is coming from.

"That's quite alright. I've missed you, you know."

"I've missed you too," I say.

"We should get together sometime. Just you and me— oh,

and the secret service," he jokes.

" That sounds great! Maybe we could do it sometime this week," I say. Then I add with a sweet voice, "Only if your schedule opens up, though. I don't want to get in the way of your work."

"Thank you for being so considerate. When I usually schedule meetings with important ambassadors, they only seem to care about their schedule," he said.

"That sounds so frustrating. I feel bad for you, Daddy." Gosh, where is this coming from?

Our conversation went on. We are meeting this Wednesday after school at a local coffee shop my dad really likes. My mom doesn't know, I will tell her I went with Lizzie to science club. Dad doesn't know that Mom doesn't know. But it will work out. When I think about it, I've never done anything like this. I guess I've been a kinda maybe goody two- shoes. Never really got in trouble, or been yelled at. Maybe that's why Chloe hates me. Maybe I'll have to change that.

Chapter 3

Finally! Wednesday is here! It's last block, with only 10 minutes left in class. The clock is taunting me, going all tick, pause. Tock, pause. It's extremely annoying. Hah! Now only 9 minutes left! Gosh, I need to find something to do.

Just then, Chloe decides to walk into the library and destroy my concentration on the clock. "Geez, you're so lame that the clock is the only one that listens to you? I told ya she was lame, didn't I, Bobbi?"

Bobbi quickly nods her head and goes back to staring at the shelves of books like she's never seen such madness. Told ya they were dumb, didn't I?

"Whatevs, Chloe," I say, putting as little emotion into my words as possible. "I'm surprised you even know what a library is, much less how to find one."

Chloe scoffed. She was obviously surprised that someone, especially me, had made her eat her own words. Then she sauntered towards the door, her "friends" rambling behind her. It was really entertaining to watch the 5 wannabees try to squeeze through the door all at once, which failed. They all wanted to be right behind Chloe, so they would be considered her right-hand man.

Then, when I least expected it, BRIINNNNNG!! School was out for the day. It took me a second or so to realize, Oh! School is out for the day!! I finally get to meet my dad! Well, in person.

When I got outside, the first thing I saw were 3 huge black SUVs in the carpool line. I was just standing there staring, and then a front window from the middle car rolled down and a huge beefy man was inside. He started to beckon me over, and then it hit me. This is the secret service! I was just planning to take the public bus, but obviously that's not what my dad had in mind.

On the way there, I tried to look out the windows. I couldn't see anything on the outside, probably because they use bulletproof glass on these things. But I could hear outside. It didn't take a genius to get that my trip to the coffee shop had completely stopped local traffic.

When we finally got to the "coffee shop" it was not at all what I expected. I was thinking Starbucks, or Caribou Coffee, or someplace like that. Of course Dad was thinking extremely high-end really-fancy café. I looked down at my clothes. I was wearing a pair of skinny jeans that I wore the knees out of two months ago, with grass stains and everything, and a tee that says "Hello, my name is Inigo Montoya. You killed my father, prepare to die." Don't you just love the Princess Bride?

So I reached for my Abercrombie hoodie. It was better than my old tee-shirt. The jeans won't be a big deal. But as I walked in, I still felt extremely out of place. Respectable men and women were all making small talk, and a couple stared at me with a smirk that highly resembles Chloe's. Maybe it's a rich people thing?

As soon as I thought my fate was most likely going to involve shriveling up on the plush carpet, my dad called out "Hilary! I'm sitting over here!"

It was weird how polite it sounded, even though he was kind of yelling in a typically quiet environment. I guess that's something a president-elect has to master. I know I never will be able to.

"Coming, Dad," I said, trying to sound as casual about it as possible. It didn't help. Most of the Fancy-pants diners were gaping and murmuring under their breath. And I knew what they must be thinking.

"This girl is going to be the First Daughter? The one dressed like a hobo?!"

Okay, so maybe not hobo, maybe homeless person, but still. You get my point. So I practically skipped to my dad's table, mentally kicking up dirt at the rich individuals. So we both ordered, and then we made small talk. It went like this:

Dad: It's so nice to finally see you in person!
Hilary: Same to you! It's extremely lovely to see you in life-size instead of TV sized. (Thinking: Lovely? Really?)
Dad: (Laughs) Yes. We should do this more often.
Hilary: Oh, we definitely should. (Beams in a Daddy's girl kind of way)
Dad: Oh! That reminds me. There's a big charity gala for Wildlife Conservation Society. It will be loads of fun, and I need a plus-one. (Does funny eyebrow dance and fake nudges me) You interested?
Hilary: (just realizing how cool some dads can be): Sounds awesome! I've always loved the WCS! (Although have only vaguely heard of it until just now)
Dad: Great! I'll give you a copy of the Evite (Hilary thinking: Evite? I used that last year for my birthday party).
Hilary: Awesome.

The food comes, and we eat. After we finish, Dad pays the bill and escorts me to the parking lot. On the way out, I noted with satisfaction that the rich diners were all gaping at me. Like they would if they just found out I was Lady Gaga or something. Maybe it's a rich people thing.

So Dad went to his house in a separate troop of SUVs, and the three black cars directed me home. I quickly realized my mom might notice if I came out of a huge gang of super-vans, so I told them to park a block away from my house.

As I went in, I glanced around. I made a good call hoofing it down the street, because my mom was obviously home. You could hear the TV droning in the background, and the pantry door was open. Someone had obviously helped themselves to the Pretzel Crisps.

So I went up to my room to start my homework. It was pretty straightforward for homework. Math worksheet, then comprehension questions for English. Then I studied for my science test on gravity. Then I watched the ASDF movies on YouTube (my favorite) and updated my status on the Facebook page I have that my Mom doesn't know about. After that I checked Amazon for any deals on cell phones that I could afford to pay for myself and was unsuccessful (maybe because my budget is $15, but that's just me).

Just as I was logging out, Mom called me down for dinner. We ordered in pizza with cheesy bread. After our, um, meal, I guess you could call it, we watched Jeopardy and went to bed. We were both tired, so it wasn't difficult.

Chapter 4

A couple days passed, and then I remembered: What was I supposed to wear for that Gala this weekend? I haven't exactly been in to dresses since age 6. But I knew exactly who to go to for help.

"Trinity, can you help me with something?"

Explained to her the whole anecdote, and told her I needed to find a cheap but decent dress for Saturday. When she had processed everything, she tried to think of a solution. You could see the gears turning in her head.

"Will you help me study for my huge English test this week?" she asked, knowing that I absorbed Vocab words like a sponge.

"Sure, whatever. So how will I find a dress in time?" I said, getting impatient.

"You can borrow one of my recital dresses! We're practically the same size!"

"That's good," I said. "What about shoes?"

"I know for a fact that you and Lizzie have the some foot size," she replied. "Remember the pair she got last year for the Science Geek Association dance?"

"You know she'd kill you if she heard you saying that," I said. "It was Science Genius Association, right?"

"Same diff," she said with a smile.

By the time it was all said and done, I had a turquoise knee-length dress, a pair of gold-strap semi-high heels, and not exactly a professional hair stylist, who was still awesome at French-braids.

"Ow! You're pulling my hair!" I shouted as Trinity twisted my hair into a respectable knot. We were in her bedroom, and my mom thought "sleepover" while it was really "stay for dinner, go to a party and come back". It worked because Trinity's parents went to Fenwick Island for the weekend, and left her 17 year-old brother in charge. He didn't care if we set fire to the kitchen as long as we left him and his precious Xbox 360 alone.

"Sorry! I'm almost done!" she said, sounding was if she were trying to wrestle a monkey or something. "Your hair is really stubborn!"

The name tag on the inside of the dress started to itch, the one that said: Property of Trinity F. Hilary D. We put that there just in case I had to take the dress off and someone found it. Not that the chances of that are at all likely, but hey, better safe than sorry!

Just then, we heard a car pull up. "That's probably your ride!" she exclaimed, sounding both excited and nervous at the same time. I was actually pretty calm. It surprised me a lot, which made up for all the excited-ness I was missing out on.

When we got to the porch, my ride turned out to be a limo. A Limo!! And it wasn't a cheap limo either. The limo was at least 10 feet long, with a huge moon roof. I couldn't wait to see the inside! Trinity squealed, and on the inside I did the same. But on the outside I was still pretty calm.

Suddenly the back window rolled down. "Are you coming,

honey?" my dad asked. Then I heard a faint giggle, which definitely didn't belong to my dad.

Trinity literally pushed me down the steps. I shakily walked to the car, mainly because I wasn't used to high-heels. When I got into the car, I waved to Trinity. She waved back. She really should come with me to one of these things sometime. But as soon as the chauffeur opened the door, I heard a familiar voice that I didn't expect to hear at all.

"Ready to go, sweetie?" my mom said.

Uh-oh. This is bad.

Chapter 5

So basically what happened was this:

Mom: yesterday, your father called to check in on you. But of course, you weren't home, so I picked up the phone. Long story short ending, both me and your father are very disappointed that you lied to both of us.
Hilary: Bu-
Dad: We are serious. There will be punishment for this. What is it that we agreed on again? (Looking at Mom)
Mom: Grounded for three weeks.
Hilary: BU-
Dad: ... Starting tomorrow.
Hilary: Really? So I can go to the Gala?!
Mom & Dad (irritated): Fine.
Mom: But I'm coming, too.
Dad & Hilary (upset): Really?
Mom: Yes. That is final (Dad & Hilary groan).

Well, Mom did end up coming. Not that it was more fun with her. Thank goodness my mom didn't stalk me the entire time (like she did once at Pump It Up. Don't ask). The whole time, she was talking to a lady who looked suspiciously like Martha Stewart. But maybe that's just me.

I met a couple of nice representatives (and their nice, maybe-kinda-cute sons). Right before dinner was served, my dad announced that I was his daughter. The guys here took it surprisingly well compared to some people I've seen (not to point any fingers, but think money bags at a café).

And after like five courses, I felt like I was gonna hurl. So despite my entire brain urging, I did. And when I came out of the girls' bathroom (which was very nice, by the way), they had started dancing. The thing was, it reminded me way too much of the ballroom scene in Cinderella. And honestly, I don't feel like losing both my dinner and a shoe on the same night.

But I ended up dancing with my Dad, a couple of boys my age, and pretty much every male representative at the place. I mean, I guess it was fun. Dad says that if I think this is awesome, I should go to the Inaugurational ball. Yay. At least Mom will help me pick out a dress this time.

So I guess that's all. I mean, so far. There'll always be more to the story, no matter what. Whether it's an Epilogue, or 30 years later, or a high school reunion, whatever. But my point is:

The End.

Group 3

8-12th Grade

Serpent and Sky

Julia M. Allen
9th Grade

She placed the fruit in my hands, caressing the tips of my fingers as she slid her angelic ones away.

"Eat it," she pleaded. The serpent at her feet hissed in agreement.

I looked down at the fruit. A generous stem shot from its top, while the bottom was rounded and luscious with juice. It was from the forbidden tree He counseled us not to take from, but from the purple entrails surrounding her lips I could tell Eve had already eaten some of its wonder I had examined countless times. It appeared safe enough. Eve hadn't mutated into a grotesque monster or fallen dead, and that snake seemed to enjoy it.

When God placed me in the garden, He said I could eat from any of the trees except the center one He called the Tree of Knowledge. Among the trees in the garden flowered scarlet apples and sweet peaches, though the center tree bore thick, violet creations. Its branches infinitely frayed from its sturdy trunk and weaved through one another. God told me I would die if I were to eat its fruit.

That night, my dreams took form of the tree's lengthening arms which extended toward me, calling with their shrilling voices while embellished with delicate leaves. When I woke, my woman, Eve, stood before me. Though even her beauty did not match the Tree of Knowledge's, whose visits in my sleep intensified when she slept beside me. I would wake from my slumber in the middle of the night and become agitated with her prickly legs intertwined around mine.

Day after day passed. The moon chased away the hot sun to reveal a landscape of individual, minuscule lights. How many of them existed? I would try to count them but lose my place every time only to find an altered arrangement the next night. Some lights were more visible than others. Eve insisted it was futile to stare at them; she fixed her attention on the larger light that fluctuated between a slight sliver and one full, rounded circle.

After countless days of restlessness, I visited The Tree while Eve was tending to some roses. Its fruit was always in bloom unlike the other trees which went through rotations of growth and death. Maybe if I ate from The Tree of Knowledge I could know how many tiny lights were situated above me. After hours of longing for its taste on my tongue, I trailed away. I wished to live more than to know the total sum of my sparkling companions.

Though when Eve held out the fruit to me, a lust overcame my soul, shattering the sanity I had straddled. I would know each piece of luminescence in the sky by name and understand how close they were to my body.

"Alright," I answered her, looking out to the horizon as I took a hefty bite. Surprising bitterness attacked my senses and stained my mouth. A red drop of blood trickled off Eve's thigh, and a thunder sounded from above higher than my beloved lights that were all hidden with the night. The Tree's fruit shriveled to the ground, as did my tears when we exited the garden.

Years have passed since I resided in the garden; much has changed. Eve toils every 28 days and only rests from the cycle when she is with child.

Serpents do not walk as they used to; they slither, hissing in anguish, unable to reach the fruit they once devoured.

And to this day, I am unanswered about the stars. They whimper for me, and I for them. Though they followed me from my garden, we will be perpetually separated.

Eastern Redbud

Emma Berman
12th Grade

On my sixteenth birthday, I met with the witch of the town. My employer granted me a day off from my duties as a maid at the Howell manner. I journeyed into town and ascended the shaky steps to the witch's little cottage.

"What is it that you want, little girl," inquired the green-skinned woman. She grabbed my chin with her withered hands and scratched the skin encouragingly with curdled fingernails.

I chuckled nervously. "My mother says that if I do not marry soon, it will be too late and I will not be able to find a suitable husband."

The witch sighed and put a grimy hand to her forehead. "How does this pertain to me, child?"

I gulped and went on. "I want to ensure that this does not happen to me. Do you have a spell that can ensure that I will not turn into an unmarried old woman?"

"Gah!" the witch cried and flung her arms in the air. "What is so wrong with being an unmarried woman? I have never been married, and things worked out perfectly for me!"

I blushed. "Sorry to offend you. While your choice of lifestyle seems," I paused, "thoroughly lovely and fulfilling, that is not how I want to live." I withdrew ten golden medallions from my coat pocket. "Will this be enough to cover the cost?"

While the witch cackled in agreement, I was too pleased to notice the sinister glimmer in her black eyes. I watched over her shoulder as the witch brewed me a red, lumpy potion. She dipped a vile into her cauldron and handed me the steaming mixture.

As I left the ghoulish cottage, my head in the clouds with my prince charming, the witch called out to me.

"My magic is not without limitations," she screeched. "There is, in fact, a thing that can break the spell!"

Having what I wanted, I ignored the old witch. I had no reason to break my marriage spell.

That night while my mother slept, I crept from my bed to

drink the potion underneath the moon. I toasted my drink with the glamorous lake and sucked down the repulsive concoction. Immediately after I drank it, I felt a strange tingling in my toes and fingertips. My body became long and thin, and I watched my skin turn brown and hard.

"Help!" I tried to shriek, but my voice was muffled by the leaves that were growing from my tongue.

Within mere minutes, my maidenly body had morphed into that of an Eastern Redwood tree. I stood, paralyzed by both shock and by my expansive root system, in the very spot where I had drunk the witch's potion.

Why would she do this to me? I wondered. Why would she scam a paying customer? That is when I realized, I had offended the evil witch by insisting that I did not want to be like her. I also did not say exactly that I needed a man to marry. I only said that I did not want to turn into an old unmarried woman.

How could I be so stupid? The witch did, in fact, obey my request. As I thought of how handsomely I had paid her, my branches began to sway and howl with fury.

Unable to move, I named this spot by the lake my new home and surrendered to my life as topiary. I watched the years passed by, my only indicators of time being my thickening waist and the gradual lining of the skin of the Howells.

Many lazy generations passed, and I remained an Eastern Redbud among the perennials of the Howell home.

The Howell's threw magnificent parties on the lawn behind their home. I, an inherently invited guest, watched the frivolities from my mulchy perch and reflected on my deepening loneliness.

Then, Benjamin Howell was born.

Benjamin was a little blue-eyed boy, and was much different than any of the other Howells.

He, unlike his brothers, was kind to the forest animals. Instead of distributing cruel traps around the Howell manner, Benjamin spent his time filling bird feeders and sketching Tundra Swans in his little book.

The boy set out on little adventures every Sunday afternoon, hiking deeper into the woods each week. Benjamin's journeying was much hindered by his insistence on stopping to examine each flower he passed.

I loved Benjamin with all of the fibers of my pith.

Benjamin came to visit me many times in a week. He would often carry with him a book or his guitar, and he would read aloud to me or play sweet songs. Occasionally, Benjamin carried nothing at all and he would sit and peer out onto the lake or sleep in the soft bed of grasses that lived among my trunk.

In these times, I would admire the angular planes of his young face. Benjamin was a magnificent beauty; his plump lips and brown eyes were so reminiscent of those that belonged to his ancestors that lived in the Victorian house while I still worked as a maid. I loved Benjamin with all of the fibers of my pith.

During the winter, I was the worst version of myself. Bereft of the only vanity I could afford- my blossoms- and weakened by the chill, I felt the wear of the years in my branches. I was so tired, so enervated. Benjamin hardly came outside during the frozen months, and he was the only reason I strived to live.

While the yearly Christmas Eve parties would linger late into the night, I would watch with longing and try to make peace with the cold snow that nested on my achy branches.

As each spring flourished, the Howell children would emerge from their stagnant house. They shed their scarves and rediscovered how to play. My beautiful Benjamin grew transformed more drastically every year. With each ring that formed in my belly, Benjamin grew inches taller. He spent his time outside with his brothers as they played boyish games of pirates and Vikings. Occasionally, he would pick a handful of wildflowers to bring to his mother.

Before I knew it, little Benjamin was brimming on manhood. He took his mother out for Sunday strolls, and was going away to college in only a year.

On one particular Sunday stroll, Benjamin and Mrs. Howell wandered through the manner's gardens.

"Don't you think it would be spectacular if we had more hydrangeas?" Mrs. Howell asked her son. "I think that they would look fabulous by the lake."

She walked up to me. "This tree, for instance, could easily be uprooted and replaced with a bed of flowers. What do you think?"

Benjamin ran up to me and grabbed me by the trunk. "I do not think that is a good idea at all, Mother!" he exclaimed. "I must insist, for I truly love this tree!"

As soon as the words escaped his lips, my body started to tingle. My flowers fell to the ground and my roots shrunk and formed two distinct legs. My trunk turned into a waist.

My girlish looks were restored, complete with my long, blonde hair and the nightgown had worn the night some hundreds of years ago when I drank the witch's potion.

Realizing that his hands were suddenly grasping the waist of a woman, not the trunk of a tree, Benjamin took a gentlemanly step back and lowered his head in an attempt to conceal his reddened cheeks.

"I am sorry to frighten you!" I exclaimed with my stale, out of practice voice. "I am Eloise."

With much explaining, the Howells came to understand my story. They invited me to live in their house as neither as their maid nor their indoor plant, but as a guest.

As I was settling into my new room, a room I had swept many times before, I heard a knock on my door. It was Benjamin.

"May I come in?" he asked.

"Of course," I said, embarrassed to be granting him admission into a room of his own house.

"Is the reason I loved the Redwood tree so much is because I was sensing your spirit, and because I knew deep down that the tree loved me too?"

I smiled. "I had been watching over you since you were a boy. I have loved you for your whole life."

With that, Benjamin wrapped his arms around my waist we kissed with a passion that had been cooped up for centuries.

I felt a rousing sensation on my skin that was much reminiscent of the flowering of the early spring. This was, I understood, because I was experiencing a bloom that I had dreamt of since my initial girlhood: the blooming of a tender heart.

Glass Like Greatness

Dani Blum
10th Grade

It's times like this I wonder how I got roped into this.

And then I remind myself: Oh. Right. I signed up for this. Voluntarily.

I know I'm lucky to have a summer job, and that I should thank my lucky stars or whatever that I worked up the nerve to apply. "You had direction," my parents would say later, nodding their heads so I wouldn't notice they were thinking, for once. "Not many kids your age have that," they'd repeat. That's their go-to response whenever they ask me what I want to do with my life and I shrug. "Not many kids have focus," they say. "You need to stand out." Like I should plan out my life if only so I can be one of the few who do.

They're not very accurate, anyway. Everyone I know works during the summer, that's why it's so hard to find a job. But grown-ups like to think that adolescence is like a disease or something. No matter what else I am, the fact that I'm sixteen always defines me.

The truth is that while I could use some extra spending money, and a job looks better on a college application than "bummed around the summer before junior year, waiting for school to start so it could finish", the main reason I applied for the job was Opal Kingsbury.

My parents aren't exactly fans of Opal, so I kept this hidden from them. But once I found out Opal was spending the summer at Disney, it didn't take much to get me to apply.

Opal is the kind of person that things happen around. Not that anything of importance—anything real—ever does happen in small, suburban Florida, but if it did, it would happen to Opal. And if nothing does happen, after a few weeks of having nothing more exciting than Macy Lamane's new haircut to talk about, Opal makes something happen. Or at least, as close to something as she can get. It was Opal who led the first-ever sophomore class prank, outdoing the seniors by releasing rabbits in the girls' bathrooms.

Opal would organize infamously epic games of Truth or Fare at parties—the kind of parties I'm too scared to go to—and manage to be wilder than anyone else and the only one sober. Opal never drinks; she claims she doesn't want to miss out on anything while she's plastered ("The only thing that happens is that people get plastered," I tried to tell her once), but I suspect she just wants to save that experience. There are a long list of contenders to top the "Craziest Things Opal's Done" list, and I figure she wants to guarantee there's a boundary left to be pushed.

I balance Opal out. I think that's why we're friends. I tag along with her—joining the Mock Trial team with her, taking a minor part in the musical she's the lead in, accompanying her to a few birthday parties every once in a while. But I draw the line somewhere. I cover for Opal when she's late for Mock Trial tournaments after spending quality time with the opposing council; I stay at the back of the stage with the freshmen; and I never, ever stay out later than 9:30.

"Honey," Opal tells me. "You've got to live a little. More than you do."

The thing is that just because I don't go around trying to make things happen doesn't mean I don't want them to. I've gone through my life waiting for some Greatness to hit, until I realized I'm not going to find it here. The whole "we're-bored-so-let's-go-to-the-same-crazy-party-we-go-to-every-weekend" thing doesn't seem that great to me. I don't think Greatness, or at least the kind I'm looking for, can be found in a bottle of warm beer in Jay Marshall's basement.

But Opal gets to me sometimes. She has this way of coaxing me into her plans, before I balk at the last second. Still, Disney sounded pretty safe. Maybe I could actually stick with her all the way this time.

"Besides," she had said when she brought up the idea. "You can be Cinderella. She was my fave when I was tiny."

"Why don't you just be her?" I said. I had already decided to apply, but I didn't want her to know she could win that easily. I didn't like the idea of Cinderella, though. Being the center of every little girl's fantasies for eight weeks seemed…stressful. I had plenty of that in my life already, thank you very much.

"Honey," she said. "Look at me. I don't think society has progressed quite that far." Opal's black, which, I hated to admit it, made her chances of playing a white princess slim to none. Dangit, Disney.

They chose her to be Minnie, which she loved. ("You're a rodent," I tried to explain, but she shrugged me off.) It turned out we didn't even had a say in which character we wanted to be, but they took one look at me (followed by several more looks at the background check we had to submit) and told me I'd be Cinderella. Not that I'm pretty or anything, but being tall and blonde and reasonably thin was good enough.

They were kind of desperate, too. I was surprised. People applied, but not enough to prevent me and Opal from getting hired, which was the case for a lot of kids I knew. Why hire a high school kid when you can get a 25-year-old? It seems like nowhere, from the mall to the local restaurant, was sacred.

No one ever thinks about being a Disney character, though. Like I guess the idea of being a waitress crosses your mind, but playing dress up for a squealing crowd of six-year-olds who complain if your signature's not princessy enough? Not what I'd call a dream job.

So it turned out that most of our coworkers are also teenagers. Which was pretty lucky for me, because if some mob of college grads had swopped in and taken all our jobs, Opal would have been the one to find some shard of Greatness, and I never would have met Chase Arlington.

This is not a summer about Chase, any more than this will be a summer about Opal, or even me. This is a summer about Cinderella, and having the glass slipper fit, every single day.

I'm not the Cinderella they use in the performance at 4. That's the big leagues. I'm her understudy, though, and sing autographs for her and walk around the muggy park for hours while the lady who plays her (who might actually be a college grad) puts on her makeup or whatever. The funny thing is, I never did get to meet her.

Chase is in a similar position, only he's the other Prince

Charming. Which means that every day from 10 to 2, I walk around with Chase Arlington on my arm.

The first thing I noticed about Chase was that he was uptight. Chase took this job seriously. I do too, to a certain degree, but I'm not above sneaking through the backdoor of Goofy's Lemonade Hut a few times a day. Gus gave me free drinks, which wasn't exactly a park-approved decision, but I considered it employee perks. Florida is hot, and the mass of petticoats don't help. Chase, however, tried to talk me out of it, and threatened to walk away without me.

He'd make up excuses. "I need this job," he'd say.

But he also needed me—you don't come just to see Prince Charming—and I needed to not have heat stroke, so he'd end up waiting outside in the sticky heat. He was trying to prove something about how he was too moral or whatever to take time away from his all-important role as the Stud with the Sword who Signs Autographs, but I always brought him out a drink. Maybe I should have let him swelter in his own stubborn stupidity, but I liked to let him think he was being noble. Though I guess anyone would feel noble in that princely getup.

Chase and I were encouraged to talk as we walked around. The park execs apparently want customers to get a sense of "the real Disney", as Patrick, our supervisor put it. It was with that in mind that Chase and I strolled through the park, chirping away like we were Walt Disney himself. I swear, that man wouldn't stand a chance against the elaborate plots Chase and I created.

Me: Shall we go to the ball tonight?
Chase: Why of course, darling, for we must celebrate Priscilla's engagement.
Me: Oh, what a lark!
Chase: And then I must go hunting and strangle six wild boars with my bare hands.
Me: You do know how to charm a girl!

We'd only do this when there were kids around (with some editing about the boars). You'd be surprised how many adults come to Disney on their own. I guess if I were 43 and single, I'd want a reminder of happily ever after, too. But as Chase gradually got rid of the stick up his butt, we decided we could have a little fun (after Chase spent a good five minutes making sure there were no park officials around).

Chase: Shall we go to the ball and celebrate Priscilla's engagement?
Me: And then six months later we can celebrate her divorce!
Chase: I heard a chipmunk say she and Duke Derek are getting a pre-nup.
Me: So scandalous!

But after trying to be funny and realizing, sadly, that neither of us were, Chase and I started talking. Actually talking. I don't remember there being a conscious decision to start acting real to each other. But after two weeks, on the hottest day of the whole summer, Chase turned to me and said, "You know, it's kind of pathetic how many people come here." It was the first time I heard him without his Prince Charming voice. He was a little higher, a little more uncertain, a little more of who I guess he actually was.

"Tell me about it," I groaned. "My hand is aching from signing autographs."

Chase laughed. "Can we call them autographs if they're not really ours?

"Sure," I said.

"Autographs," he repeated. "I guess this is my one shot to feel what it's like to be famous."

I probably should have paid more attention to that, but it was pushing 100 degrees that day, and I was worrying about what Patrick would do if Cinderella got sweat stains on her ball gown. "It feels like this," I said. "Hand cramps and weird costumes that don't fit the weather. And eight-year-old girls snapping embarrassing photos of you."

I expected him to laugh, but he just shook his head. "That's only the part we see. But I kind of like feeling…" he trailed off.

"Important," I said without thinking.

Chase looked at me. "Yeah," he said. "I guess that's right."

He looked kind of glum about it, and I felt like a twit, so I blurted out, "Well, that's what everyone wants. Like, to feel important and like you matter and everything. Everyone wants that." I didn't know where I was going, but it was hot and I had said something stupid and I rambled on. "Even those people that go down to, like, Ethiopia and build homes for orphans and stuff, they do it so they can feel like they're doing something meaningful."

Chase didn't say anything, so I kept talking. "Everyone worries about that so much that they don't live, though. I mean, my grandma died when I was, like, ten." I didn't know why I was saying this, and to Chase of all people, but , I don't know, I wasn't feeling like Cinderella that day. It was too hot. And after spending these last two weeks talking about balls and trying to fit myself in to this perfect like world, I jumped a the chance of something real. Cinderella melted away.

And without her, all I had was me.

"And I went to her funeral and I just kept thinking, 'where are all the people?'. There were, like, thirty people there, max, and I kept being like, 'Is this really everyone Grandma was important to?' Her obituary wasn't even front page of the local paper. It was in the middle, where no one reads, across from an ad for the consignment shop." I moved to run my hand through my hair before I remembered how it was all coiled up and doused with hairspray, so I let my arm that wasn't resting on Chase's hang there awkwardly.

I was still practically attached to him, walking around the park like it was normal, but I kept my voice down and watched my feet pass one brick at a time. "But when those people went up to speak about her, they said she had changed their lives. They talked about how she was an angel in her last few years, how she never complained, and how inspiring her fight was against the cancer." I bit my lip. I didn't want to tell Chase that I had never really known Grandma; she and Mom had fought a lot. It wasn't until the cancer kicked in that I met her. But she had found Greatness, somehow, and that was enough.

A gaggle of pink-clad girls was coming towards us. "Incoming," I murmured. The tallest one saw us and squealed.

I smiled as best I could. “Good morning,” I called, my voice higher than usual. I gave a royal wave. The girls ran over and flipped through their autograph books furiously. Tigers were less eager to kill their prey. They found their blank pages and shoved them into our faces, the pink sparkly pens they whipped out jabbing me in the nose.

I asked each of their names, scrawled, “With much love, your friend Cinderella”, and passed them to Chase. But he was still caught off guard by our conversation. The first girl he handed the book back to scowled after examining it. “Who’s Chase?” She pouted with miniature lips.

“Um, that’s my nick name!” Chase scrambled. “Here,” He ripped the book out of her hands, scribbled “Prince Charming”, and gave a shaky smile. She looked satisfied.

Chase wasn’t though. “It’s not like being famous, though” he muttered as they walked away. “No one cares about Chase Arlington.”

We had half an hour for break, thank God, although ours was at a different time than Opal’s and everyone else’s. They couldn’t let us all disappear at once. I grabbed my brown paper bag, wondered if my peanut butter sandwich had melted, and went to the small cast trailer.

I walked in. The last person I ever expected to see with a joint, Chase Arlington, was smoking away.

“What the heck?” I said.

Chase whirled around, almost dropped it. The joint hung clumsily between his fingers. Not like I’ve ever smoked—and I shudder to think of the damage a pot arrest would do to my college app—but Chase looked like he was trying to figure out how to hold it.

He was paused, with the joint about to hit his lips.

“Chase!” I scanned the trailer. No one except us, but still… “Put that out right now!” I half-screamed, trying to keep my voice down. “Get rid of it before anyone sees!”

Chase looked up. “Why?” he said, just like a child, like he was just curious.

I ripped the joint out of his fingers, sprinted to the bathroom, and flushed it down the toilet. Then I washed my hands for five minutes. I didn't know if that stuff left traces.

When I went back to the main part, Chase was sitting on his stool, still in his prince outfit., Changing back and forth took too much time, so we ate in our costumes and prayed we didn't spill. I sat down on the stool across from him. "What. The. Heck."

He looked like he had been caught stealing a cookie.

"Seriously, Chase! I thought this mattered to you! You keep saying you need this job! If someone else walked in, you wouldn't just get fired, you'd get arrested, Chase!"

"No one else goes in here," he muttered.

"They could have, Chase! Any one could have! Don't you see…" I swallowed. I was acting like his mother, I knew it, but of all people…

Chase was staring at the floor.

"Chase?" I said softly.

He looked up, straight at me. "It appears," he said. "That I am a prince." Oh boy.

"And this chair," he continued. "Is eating my leg. Becca, why is the chair eating my leg?"

He looked scared all of a sudden. "Becca!" he said. "Make it stop!"

It was then I realized what he had done. Chase Arlington, formerly one of the most goody-goody people I had met, was officially stoned.

"Chase," I said again. He glanced up. "Why were you smoking?"

Chase sat there for a minute. Then he fumbled with the fake sword on his belt. Jesus…He held it up to his face and stared at it.

"I," he said quietly. "Am going to war."

"That's great Chase," I said, trying to be soothing. Maybe I could treat him like the kids I babysat.

"No," he shook his head wildly. "I'm serious! I'm going in the army. I have it all figured out."

I couldn't tell if he was kidding. "I'm enlisting in the fall," he said. He gave the sword an experimental flick. "So they'll drug test me in October," he stabbed the sword through the air. "Which means," he continued. "That my first and last drug usage has to be sometime this week. I calculated!" he added, nodding. "I'm good at math!"

"The army?" I repeated.

"The army," he said gravely. He whacked the chair with the sword. "Cross my heart and hope to…" He trailed off.

I didn't want to think about why he didn't finish. "So you decided to smoke because you could?" I said. I tried to make it sound like it wasn't an accusation.

"My dear Rebecca," he replied. "I could and I wanted to. What other reason is there?" I started to respond but he cut me off. "My brother Robby's in the Marines," he said. "But I get so damn seasick. I can't pay for college, didn't have the scores to get a scholarship, and this has always been a back-up plan. My mom likes the idea of a military man. Honor and glory and all that. My dad was in the army, before he left."

And I'm sure that was honorable, I thought, but I wanted to let Chase finish. I felt like I was taking advantage of him somehow—like I was hearing things meant for someone else, things that only came out because of the weed, but I couldn't feel guilty. Maybe I had only said those things to him because of the heat. Maybe we were supposed to say things like this to a different person, but here we were, stuck together, and for no reason at all we were us. I think there's a moment when a person becomes real. Looking back on anyone who's ever been close to me, it always happens in a conversation, in something they do or say. And after weeks with Prince Charming, I wanted Chase to be real so badly. So I let him talk.

"I'm going into the army," he continued. "And this is my last chance to have a summer job. To do something stupid and call it work. And I thought it was fitting to go to work at the most concentrated center of childhood before I went off to be more adult than I wanted." Chase looked like he was about to cry. "So I apply here after getting rejected a few times, and they tell me I'm going to be Prince Charming."

"And you know what," he said, his voice rising. "It made me want to be stupid Prince Charming. It made me want to matter and save the day and be a freakin' hero., And then I meet you and you tell me how selfish that is, and…" I guess he notices he opening my mouth to protest. "Bec, you were just telling the truth."

Bec? I thought. "It is stupid, it's so stupid, and I know I shouldn't want to be important and all that, even though everyone does. But I don't even have a life full of stuff I've done what I can fall back on. Like if I die—God, Bec, don't look so surprised—if I die in the army, I'll have served my country and all that, but I wouldn't have done anything. I guess I shouldn't care if I'm a hero or whatever, but to die without…" His face scrunched up. He closed his eyes and I was so sure he was going to cry, but he didn't.

"To die without having a life is a tragedy," he said. "And sometimes I wonder if this qualifies as a life. I know that sounds stupid or whatever, but…"

"Chase," I started, but Patrick barged in.

"Did you eat at Goofy's Grill?!" he shouted.

"What? No," I said. Chase didn't look that different, I guess, but still, if Patrick noticed…

But Patrick was too wrapped up in bigger issues. "Don't. There's something wrong with the salad. Lucy and Ray ate it and are sick. The real you!" He explained. "The Cinderella and Prince in the show! I need you to cover for them this afternoon," He glanced at his watch. "In twenty minutes." He rushed out of the trailer.

"Wait!" I shouted. "What do we do?"

His eyes narrowed, he looked stressed out of his mind. "You know the story!" He shouted. "You put on the right freakin' glass slipper!"

Lucy and I are the same shoe size, thank God. I wonder if they planned it that way, me being just a spare Lucy and all. I think Chase is okay. I'm hoping everyone around him is too flustered to pay attention to any more "the stool is eating me" comments.

I have so much makeup on I look like Barbie. You couldn't find a blemish on me, but that doesn't mean I look good. Nicki, who I guess is the resident makeup artist, sprayed a ton of gook on my face to make everything stay, but I can feel it threatening to melt off.

Patrick dashes into my makeshift dressing room and pulls me backstage. It's a huge platform, and I hear the crowd outside. I guess I should fell nervous, but I've become Cinderella so many times that I just slip into her. Everyone running around back stage stops in their step a little to look at me. After all, I'm a princess. I'm important, as important as it gets behind a thin curtain in a theme park in the sticky Florida heat.

Opal runs up to me, still in her mouse shell. "Good luck, Becca!" She squeals and half-hugs me, but I'm Cinderella now. And then someone pushes me on stage. If I'm surprised, I don't show it. I think of the script Patrick slammed into my lap while Nicki was painting my face, but mostly I just play my way through the story I've been acting all summer.

Chase comes on. We dance, and we should be a mess because we don't know how to dance like this, and not together, but somehow it works, and somehow his eyes aren't that bloodshot. And then I'm running from him, letting my shoe fall off and prancing over to the side of the stage.

"I must find her!" Chase declares. He looks straight at me, which he's not supposed to do, but we go with it. "I must," he tells me. He brings the slipper over. For the sake of time, the performance skips over some things, makes the happy ending easier to get to. He kneels and places the glass slipper on my foot. It should feel silly, but it doesn't. "A perfect match!" He shouts.

It's times like this I wonder how I got roped this. How I became the one to fit Prince Charming's shoe. How I was the one to see Chase Arlington become real. And then transform seamlessly into what he never would be.

He takes my hand and we spin around for one last dance. And I swear, we look perfect, like we belong on the top of a cake. Like my shoes aren't all that's made of glass.

Collective Thoughts

Kelsey Bush
10th Grade

She sat down on the floor, methodically laying her dolls in front of her. She lightly petted each dolls' wiry hair, whispering a greeting to each figure. The dolls sat quiet, each waiting in turn to be changed from their sleeping garments to their morning attire. Elise looked over the set of figurines, finally satisfied with her morning ritual, she opened the door of her miniature Colonial Williamsburg style house with a flourish.

Knowing that now was my chance, I stepped out from my hiding spot behind the door. Holding onto the doorframe of the room, I peered into what was once known as her bedroom. Clothing littered the floor, piled high in corners, threatening to topple over. Half naked dolls were shoved in boxes, spilling over. Broken body parts lay askew, between articles of clothing, arms reaching through the debris, as if they were begging for help.

No longer able to see the once pristine floor, I carefully stepped over items, trying to find some purchase for my feet. I kept my hand on the wall to steady myself. Standing behind Elise, unaware of my arrival, I looked her over. Her greasy, dingy hair lay in clumps down her back, pleading to be brushed so birds don't mistake her head for their nest. Her pale skin was so translucent you could notice the blue veins standing out. Skin stretched tight over jutting bones, looking ready to snap at a moment's notice. My heart sunk; irrational thoughts fill my head, but I still feel as though it was somewhat my fault.

Clearing my throat, I attempted to make myself known; I needed to get Elise ready for the day. A bath, her least favorite part of the day, the time where she's away from her dolls'. Unaffected by my subtle noises, she continued whispering to the dolls, moving them from room to room, playing house.

I remember the first doll she ever received, she had ripped off the wrapping so quickly, squealing when she saw the present our parents had bought for her. It was a regular Barbie doll, platinum hair, orange skin tone, and a pearly white smile. Nothing out of the ordinary for a regular seven year old. My parents beamed with pride, as they had finally done something right. Mother preferred to drink rather than to spend time with her children; she also had a heavy hand when someone got in her way. I've done my best when I got old enough to keep Elise from her straying hand.

Father on the other hand is a workaholic and fails to see the actions Mother takes. Had I gotten anything that Christmas? No, but I was happy they were focusing on Elise. But that day, that day changed everything. I saw the excitement in Elise's eyes that day; saw how she carried that doll around every day after it. So was it really that wrong of me to encourage Father that Elise needed another doll? Was it so criminal of me to steal money from Mother just to see that jovial expression of Elise's? Was it truly that wicked of me just to want my sister happy? I'd say not at the time, but in retrospect I have second thoughts.

That one day when I had gone to the supermarket with Elise to get some milk, and we happen to pass the toy section. Elise found the doll section within a matter of seconds, before I even realized she had left my side. She snatched up the nearest doll and held it closely to her chest. Elise screeched at me, telling me she just had to have that doll, she would die without it. I stared bewildered at her, the shock sinking in. A mother in the section next to us shot me a glance of scorn before grabbing her son's hand and leading him out the aisle. But yet I still stared at Elise, unsure of how to say no. I think that was when the obsession started, when Elise fell down the rabbit hole, only rarely coming back to reality.

Junior

Christopher J. Calhoun
11th Grade

They call me Junior. Everyone pronounces it Joon-Ya. My real name is Juquan Abilene, but no one knows that. I'm just a regular ordinary boy, and I'm considered "average" in the family. There's nothin' special about me, except that I can barely read, and I almost fail all of my classes. That's typical in my family.

My granddaddy owned a plantation here in the South years ago. I never met the guy. He died before my time. We live up in the rural valleys of Georgia, in the town that's not even on the map: Mellowfield. We have nice people surroundin' us, and the town crier always gives us sweet potato pies on Sunday afternoons.

There's a chapel on the corner, a small shoppin' center next to it, and farmhouses beside some mobile homes next to the corn fields. Besides that, nothin' else is goin' on here. The dust crosses the town when the wind is high, and the rain pounds down the broken windows we got 'cross the porch. The squirrels like to run around in the cornfields, and eat up the corn seeds we plant. Everywhere you look, there's corn and lots of it. From time to time there may be oats, but that's unlikely to spot.

We go to a schoolyard across town. It's a forty-five minute ride by bus, so I gotta get up extra early just to make it to school. Let me tell you somethin': gettin' up earlier than everybody else is not fun.

I'm sixteen, soon to be seventeen, and I'm barely making it through my junior year in high school. My family lives in a small plantation house owned by our neighbors across the fields. There ain't a single house in front of us, and the graveled road next to us is the only thing noticed. The house ain't big enough for all of us to live in, but there's nothin' we can do about that.

My Mama don't work. She stays home, cookin' and cleanin', and her normal routine is sittin' up in the chairs lookin' at them court shows all day. I got two little sisters and a little brother. Naydeen is the second oldest. She's ten, and in fifth grade. Deja is seven, and she's only in second grade. She's the bad one. She always gets into trouble at her elementary school. She got black hair smeared around her face, and she wears red ribbons everyday she gets from her friends. Naydeen is kinda shy. She puts on a fake smile just to let you know she's happy, but I know she misses her father on the inside.

Speaking of which, our father (we call him Daddy) lives in a different county of Georgia. He don't pay for our child support, and he's been incarcerated for over the years. My Mama don't like talkin' about him, so I never knew what happened between them two. He'll never come back in our lives. I don't have to worry about that.

And then, there's the "other" Junior, my five-year-old brother named Marcus. Mama decided to wait 'til next year to put him in kindergarten. He stays home with Mama during the day, helpin' her clean the house and gather food from our local market, and corn from the fields. He sort of has a job of his own.

Since Mama don't work or do nothin' outside the house, she ain't got much money. She doesn't have a car, so we can't go anywhere but stay here. She used the Volkswagen from a hill-billy across town, but he got tired of her never returnin' the thing, and he almost sued her for it. She didn't like it much. It was an old piece of metal anyway. On the weekends, we have to walk to different places, and we even walk to the chapel on Sunday mornings. I don't mind walkin', but tryin' to walk with two sisters and a brother who won't shut up is hard work.

I'll admit. I'm not the best son around, and I do have difficulties with my Mama. She says I don't respect her enough. How can I respect a woman who doesn't do anything for me? We lucky we even got this house! She insists I go to college, but how am I gonna go to a college with a 1.8 Gpa? That's not happenin'.

There are a lot of things I think Mama has a problem with. She never listens to me, and I'm the one tryin' to care for her kids. These ain't my kids. I shouldn't have to deal with them and put up with them. I find myself helpin' them out with their homework than I do with my own. Mama hardly ever lifts a finger around here, and I'm stuck cleanin' up after her. The worst thing is she always calls me "Junior", and she never says the name she gave me. I don't mind being called that, but I do have a name. She treats Naydeen, Deja, and Marcus like angels, and maybe it's because they're young and still children. When I was growin' up before Naydeen came in the picture, she never treated me like she does with the other three. It does hurt, but I've gotten over that. Life doesn't stop because you want it to. It only stops because your mind wanted it to stop.

Our Grandma lives in Alabama with the rest of our folks. We moved out here right when I was born. We only go to Alabama to visit her for special holidays like Christmas, Easter, Mother's Day, and occasionally on Thanksgiving. She never visits us. She can't stand the atmosphere out here, and she can't do the things now like she did years ago (one of those things includes driving.)

Easter is comin' up soon, but we're too lazy to go visit her. We told her to come here with the rest of the folks, but she already has plans to barbeque with all our cousins, aunts, uncles, and half-cousins. I was kind of sad to find out we weren't going to see her this Easter. I think the main reason is we don't have a car or vehicle this time. Last Christmas, a friend let us borrow his car (he wasn't doing anything that Christmas.) I love seeing my Grandma, and although I only have pictures to remind me of a wonderful woman she is, I know I can go to her for anything. I guess there's next year.

The kids around town call her Miss Abilene. Mama don't like to be referred by her real name, and she'll get the fryin' pan on any of those kids who disrespect her. She was thinking about starting a daycare for the other kids around town when their parents go to work, however she can't do that unless she's licensed from the state, and she definitely not gettin' a license anytime soon. There's a small television in the kitchen. Our house is a two-floored house with a small basement, and since no one goes down in the basement, we only have two floors. Luckily, I have my own room. Naydeen and Deja have to share their rooms, and Marcus has a small bed right across from Mama's room. As for me, I get some privacy.

I try to appreciate my Mama everyday, but it seems like our lives are gettin' worse and worse, and we can't get nothin' done. I love her, but I wish she would see me as her own child, and not some average, ordinary child the world sees me in. I'm sharing this story because I wish I could've gotten the chance to show her how much I care, and that I'm not that little boy down the street that everyone points to and laughs at. I'm more than average, mom.

I'm your son, and I wish I could've told you how much I loved you before you had to go. I wish I could let you know what I have to offer to the world. I wish I could've made you proud. My prayers will always be in your heart.

2. The Big Argument

It all started the Thursday before Easter. Mama was baking the rolls that day, and spreading butter on the mashed potatoes. The cows were mooing from the barnyard, and the school bus was arriving. I wasn't home yet. Naydeen and Deja always get home before me.

Mama heard the bus stoppin' outside of the house. She quickly stopped stirring the collard greens, and ran outside. Deja and Naydeen, both of them wearing a dress, came runnin' out of the bus holding an art project. Mama waved to the bus driver, and he took off.

Naydeen and Deja ran into Mama's arms.

"Naydeen! Deja! I'm so glad you're home! How was school today?"

"Good, mommy!" Deja said.

Good, mommy! I had a good day as usual," Naydeen added.

"Did you do anything special today?" she asked them.

"Yeah!" both girls answered.

"We made pictures of our family in arts and crafts today," Naydeen mentioned, showing Mama the picture.

"I made a vase in my art class. We used glitter and glue and scissors! It was so much fun!" Deja said, showing Mama her picture.

Mama took both pictures in her hands. "This is wonderful," she said, "I'm gonna put these pictures up on the fridge. You both did a wonderful job! Yall should be proud. My girls are doin' something great. Let's hope your big brother can do the same."

The girls laughed. Okay, it's true. I can be a klutz sometimes, but you don't have to rub it in. It just makes me feel bad.

Naydeen and Deja ran inside the house with their art projects, dragging alone their schoolbags. Mama waited outside. She knew I'd be home soon. Marcus ran out, wearing his overalls way too tight.

"Mama! Mama!" he screamed, "when is the food gonna be ready?"

"In a minute, sweetheart," she answered, tussling his hair.

"Whatcha doin' out here, Mama?"

"Waitin' for your brother. He should be home soon."

My bus came bouncing down the gravel street. It's weird, because I don't think this street has a name or anything! The bus approached the house. I got off. "See ya later, Junior," some kids were saying sarcastically. One of them even threw a paper ball at me. I would've retaliated, but I was already at home.

I get off the bus and it turned away, driving off in the pavement. Mama sent Marcus back in the house.

"Hey, Mama," I said, grasping my backpack.

"Hey, Junior. How was your day?"

"It was alright. It was better than most days."

"That's good. Listen, Junior. I got some potatoes on the stove that needs butterin'. Also, the trash needs to be taken out, and them clothes need to be washed by tomorrow. I already did some of Marcus's clothes. I think you can manage the rest. Naydeen and Deja's school clothes can't go in the dryer, so make sure you fold them up. You can do that stuff after dinner."

"But Ma, I got things of my own. I got homework to do, and I have to write up a late paper for my teacher. I have a life of my own. Why didn't you finish the laundry while we were at school? You know darn well you could've finished before we got home. Can't you teach the girls how to do their own laundry? I'm not gonna touch their dirty laundry!"

"Get inside the house, boy," Mama fiercely said, tugging on my arm. She pushed me inside the house, and slammed the door shut.

Marcus wanted to know what was going on, so he peeked

his head out from the living room.

"Go to your room, boy!" Mama ordered him. He quickly vanished.

"Mama, I can't do all of that right now. I need to do my homework," I explained.

Mama slapped me hard across the face. She made a mark on my face, and I was down to the ground. "Listen here, boy," she told me, putting her finger up, "I don't care about nothin' you gotta do. You should've done your late homework yesterday. I need work done around this house, and I can't do it by myself!"

"Maybe if you got up off your butt and do something, the work would be done!"

"Don't talk back to Mama, Junior. I'm only askin' you to do one thing! Now go do what your mother told you to do!"

"I'm always doin' what you tell me to do. You never listen to me! When was the last time you called me by my full name? When was the last time you told me where my father is? You don't even know where he is. You're just selfish, and you only care about yourself!"

Mama scratched her face. "Junior, let's not do this right now," she said, "listen to me this instant. You only get one mother in life and that's it. I deserve the same respect from you as I do from Naydeen, Deja, and Marcus. One day, you're gonna know what it's like to live in the 'real' world, and see things you haven't seen before. You respect me 'til the day I die. Now go to your room and don't think about comin' out 'til dinner is ready."

I gave her a sinister look, and ran up the stairs. I slammed my door shut. Naydeen and Deja came racing down the stairs, wondering what was happening.

"What happened, Ma?" I heard Naydeen ask.

"Junior's havin' a bad day. That's what. He'll snap out of it soon," Mama answered.

She always says that when things go wrong. "Junior's havin' a bad day." To be honest, today was a good day for me.

I ended up doing all the chores she wanted me to do, and I got no study time in. I'm definitely gonna fail these quizzes comin' up, but I've failed before, so I don't really care. After the steak and mashed potato dinner with rolls, I quickly fell asleep. The girls were still up playing dollhouse, and Marcus was with Mama, helpin' her wash the dishes.

"Will our lives get better soon?" he asked her.

"Our lives are fine the way it is. Junior and I got into an argument, that's all. All is well in our family," Mama told him. She was lying.

3. Mama's Last Words

Easter Sunday came quick. Naydeen and Deja got their Easter baskets ready, and Mama gave them some candy. The baskets matched their blue and green dresses. Mama helped Marcus dress into a nice suit. "You children look nice today," she said, all of them standing near the front door, "if only I had a camera to take the picture."

Here I come trotting down the stairs, wearing tight jeans and a sleeveless shirt I found buried in my room. "Where's your suit, honey? I got it prepared just for you," Mama said.

"I didn't wanna wear that old thing. It looks hideous!" I answered.

"You lucky chapel service start in ten minutes, or else you'd be on the floor right now," Mama told me.

"Junior's in trouble!" Marcus laughed.

"Be quiet, Marcus. Don't talk to your brother like that. Come on. We're walking to the chapel this morning. Service is about to begin."

We walked to the chapel. Some of the folks around here gave the kids some candy for their baskets. After service, there was an Easter hunt for the kids at Becky's house across the cornfield. Of course, Mama was there talkin' to some adults, and I sat alone, watching the kids play in their dresses and suits. Mama comes up to me.

"Junior, you're in big trouble. When I tell you to do something, you do it. You don't go upon yourself doing whatever you want to do. You don't have that right."

"I don't got any right in this family. I'm just ordinary to you. Nothing else. I have no special talent to you. I'm just your pet. That's all I am."

"Is that how you feel, Junior? I love you boy. It's just, you make mistakes, and I don't want the other three kids to make those same mistakes. It's okay, Junior. Everything will be all right."

"No it won't, Ma. Our lives are not good and you know it. You said it yourself. One more bill you get and that's it. We're gonna have to move in back with Grandma, and she can't raise all of us. You gotta get a job somewhere."

"Where am I gonna get a job, Junior? It's impossible."

"No it isn't, Ma. You have to try."

Mama turned away from me. "You're still in trouble when we get home. Don't worry about the Sunday dinner. Our neighbors got it covered."

We ate dinner there, and went home. I got yelled at for not wearing the suit she picked out, and I was grounded for the rest of April, and all of May and June. I didn't care. There's nothing to do here anyway.

The next day, Becky comes over early in the morning to take Marcus for a play date at her house with her small children. He'll be there the entire day. Mama waves goodbye to Naydeen and Deja as they're on their way to the bus. I come down the stairs, and she puts her hands on her hips. "What'd I do?" I asked.

"Nothin', Junior. You did nothin'. You'll always be ordinary, and you'll never be the special boy I know you can be. There's somethin' in my heart that tells me you're gonna be special one day. You have to know that, and tell yourself to do somethin' with it. I can't be the one doin' that for you."

"I'm not gonna be special, Mama. I'm not goin' to college, I'm not workin' anywhere, and I'm not certified for anything. I'm just gonna stay home and take care of you. What else do I have goin' for me? You said I'm ordinary and plain, so that's what I am. I'm not that southern boy lookin' for adventure. That's not me, Mama. Why don't you see that? Why don't you love me for who I am?"

"Junior. I love you with all my heart."

"That's why you gave me the spanking. My face is cut."

"You know why too."

"Please, Ma. Save your dramatic story for someone else. I don't wanna hear it. You won't even tell me where Daddy went. He could be dead for all we know, and you think that's okay. It's not okay. I want my Daddy back. At least he gives me things I want, and treats me like I'm somebody."

"Did something happen in school?"

"No. Nothing happened. Why do you care? You never do."

I turned my head away. Mama was about to cry. "Whatever happens, Junior," she said, trying not to cry, "I'll always love you. Can you at least love me back?"

"I don't know," I quickly answered, "I'll have to think about that. There's my bus. I'll answer you when I get home."

I grabbed my schoolbag, and got on the bus. Mama restrained her tears, but a few came dripping down her face. The bus pulled off. Mama was alone at that moment.

I get home before Naydeen and Deja today. I don't know why, but I'm guessin' the bus schedule was a little off today. I open the house door with the key.

"Mama! Mama!" I yell, trying to see where she is. I go in her room. Maybe she's sleep. She wasn't there.

"Mama! Are you in the kitchen? It's me, Junior. I'm home," I called.

She still didn't respond. I ran to the kitchen, and saw her body on the ground.

"MAMA!" I screamed.

I didn't feel her pulse. I could see she was eating a tub of chocolate ice cream while watching some court show. I quickly reached for the phone, and called the Mellowfield ambulance.

"Mama, wake up! Please! Wake up!" I scream.

I turned around to see Naydeen and Deja skipping in the house. They spotted me in the kitchen, and Mama on the ground.

"What happened? Is Mama okay?" Naydeen asked.

"What'd you do this time, Junior?" Deja asked me.

"Mama won't wake up! I got here and she was right here! I swear she was!" I answered.

"I hope she's all right," Deja said.

"She has to be! She's our mom! Who's gonna feed us?"

Naydeen wondered, starting to worry.

The paramedics came in, quickly checking our mother. There was about ten of them, and they put her on a stretcher and into the ambulance.

"Is she okay?" I asked.

"It appears she suffered from a heart attack. Who knows how long she was there. It could've been hours, and she couldn't reach the phone. It was an abrupt heart attack," the paramedic answered.

"Will she be okay?" I wondered.

"I don't know if she'll make it. You kids are coming with us to the hospital!" the paramedic urged, other men grabbing us and putting us in the ambulance with our mom.

"What? She's gonna die?" Deja asked, starting to cry.

They closed the doors on us, and we were left alone with our mom.

"What about Marcus? Where's he gonna go?" Naydeen asked.

"Don't worry. Mama gonna be fine. We'll see her tonight, and she'll live out with all of us," I encouraged them, making them feel better.

Marcus arrived with Becky and her kids to the hospital. I quickly called Grandma to tell her what was going on. She had no choice but to drive down here now.

She was pronounced dead the next hour. All of us started crying. We couldn't believe our mother was gone away from us.

"She had to have been on the ground for over three hours. She wouldn't have made it regardless," a nurse told us.

"What are we gonna do? We ain't got no Ma anymore," Marcus said, crying on Naydeen's shoulder. Deja was crying on my shoulder. I tried not to cry.

"Mama wants us to be strong. That's what we're gonna do," I said.

We buried Mama the next weekend. As for us, we were gonna finish out the school year here with our Grandma watching us, and then we would go and live with our Grandma in Alabama when school is over.

"Don't feel bad, Junior. Your Mama loved each and every one of you children," Grandma told me one day.

"I know, but I wish I could've told her how much I loved her. She'll never know. Do you think I killed her?"

"That's a silly thing to think about, sweetie! I know your mother was hard on you, but she did it because she loved you, and she still does. She knows your heart, and she knows you love her. You don't have to tell her. If you want forgiveness, you pray to God, and ask Him for forgiveness. Mama's in Heaven now, and she's lookin' down, and saying what a wonderful son you are, and the same for the rest of her kids. She loves you, Juquan, and so does the rest of us."

I gave my Grandma a hug, and started crying.

"Thank you, Grandma. I love you too," I said.

"Everything will be fine. I promise you that," Grandma said. Marcus, Naydeen, and Deja come into the kitchen with the rest of us.

"I miss Mama!" Naydeen cried.

"We all do, Naydeen. Your mother will always be in our hearts. She loves each and every one of you. You only get one Mama, but you will always have one God. Remember that for the rest of your life," Grandma said.

"Will we see her again?" Marcus asked.

"Of course, Marcus. She's waiting to see what her children will be. She knows they will be the best," Grandma answered.

"What will happen to the house?" Deja asked.

"It will be auctioned off. We'll get some money for it. Start packing, children. School is almost over, and we have to go back to Alabama soon. I love you all, and don't worry about anything. Mama is in our hearts."

I went to my room, and prayed to God. I know Mama is in my heart, and I know I'm in her heart. I didn't get a chance to tell her how much I loved her, but this made me realize something. I can be whoever I want to be, even when things look bad. I don't have to rely on Mama or Grandma or anyone else. Before, I was always under my Mama. Now, I can discover the world, and become my own person. I prayed for my brother and sisters, and I hope they can be fine without their mother. I think they will be.

I'm definitely going to college now, and I'm taking my mother's advice, and going to try very hard in school during my senior year. There's still time for me to get into a good college, and start my life abroad. It's never too late.

Thank you Mama, for everything you've done. I'll never forget you, and I'll always love you. I want you to know you have the best kids, and we'll all try to not only impress you, but ourselves too.

As for me, I am no longer "Junior."

I am Juquan Thomas Abilene.

Suburban Meltdown

Janaki Chadha
11th Grade

Their stalemate had been going on for about a month when the storm hit. In the false comfort of their $2.5 million house, a "cozy" New England property far too picturesque to be described as a war zone, they idled at separate ends. Avoiding each other at all costs, they fought with glares and silence, both of them well aware that subtlety was far more effective. In a way, perhaps, they were learning how to live without one another. After six years, you couldn't say it would be easy.

It had all crumbled about a month ago, in a painfully typical fashion. She caught the same paranoia that all women get by the fifth or sixth year of marriage, and became convinced that he was cheating on her. The symptoms were the usual; he was being quiet, withdrawn, over-apologetic. Maybe it was the fact that they hadn't had sex in five weeks. So, while he was at work, she rummaged the house for evidence, looking for receipts, letters, anything, really. One night, while he was in the shower, she looked through his Blackberry and there they were, messages from a woman named Emilia. They weren't exactly sexual, or even implicative of anything in particular, but when she asked, or rather, questioned, him about who this "Emilia" person was, he broke down. He had always been a bad liar.

For a few weeks, they flipped back and forth between fighting like animals and trying to make things work. But on a pleasant Monday morning in October, right before he was about to leave for work, she uttered the four sacred words, I want a divorce. After an astoundingly short period of deliberation, he called a lawyer the next day, and they began to work through it with as much cleanness as possible. He had been set to move out that Saturday. But the storm was the worst thing their town had seen in decades. It reduced the otherwise flawless streets to complete destruction. Tree branches and electric cables had fallen everywhere, blocking half the roads in their neighborhood. Power had gone out in a heartbeat, and they were trapped.

On that same Saturday morning, he stood by the window in his pajamas, holding a mug of coffee. Luckily, their stove wasn't the electric kind. The last time he had seen this much snow in October was in the autumn of 1983. He had been a young boy of ten, had all the dreams in the world. He remembered getting a week off from school and playing between the branches and wires like there was no tomorrow. It all only really dawned on him then. He was soon to be divorced and he wasn't even forty.

She stayed upstairs in their bedroom for as long as possible that morning, hoping that if she slept in late enough she wouldn't have to see him before he left. But by around ten, the cold absorbed her and she reluctantly rolled out of bed. She only realized that their power was out when she tried to turn on the heater.

Wrapping herself in about four of those nice, but useless, luxury blankets that they had probably gotten as a wedding present, she stumbled downstairs.

When she entered the kitchen, he kept his back turned towards the counter.

"The roads are all closed. Rob apparently got stuck on Auburn Avenue at, like, seven and hasn't moved since. But I called the CP&L people and they said the power should be back by tonight. I mean, I would've left by now, I just…" he began, glancing back to see her reaction.

"No, no, I, uh, I understand," she replied, her voice stiff.

"I made some coffee, if you want any," he added. She looked him in the eye, her face wary and skeptical, but still took the mug from him with a faint smile. "I'll go light a fire," he said as he left.

So they spent the day at opposite corners of the living room, reading novels and magazines but never once actually speaking. She glanced at him every now and then, admiring his rumpled black hair or the bump on his nose. As night fell, the wait for electricity became more and more tiresome and though they figured it would come in the next few minutes or hours, at least, around six they decided to begin looking for candles and flashlights anyway.

They only found a few, in forgotten corners of coat closets and make-up drawers, so they lit one on the first night, and sat on the same couch in the living room eating packets of Ritz crackers as their dinner. They just chatted at first, in the eerie darkness, talking about how the power company shouldn't have cut so many workers and how much worse the situation was up in Massachusetts. But then he stood up, said he was going to open a wine bottle to "take the edge off". He brought her a glass, too.

Both of them half drunk, they reminisced about the past. She remembered the time they ran off to Thailand, both twenty-two and far too idealistic for their own good. It was one of their many youthful escapades and they wandered the country like the pseudo-hippies they were, enjoying days of adventure, nights of passion. Along with other unkept promises, they swore to each other, then and there, that they wouldn't buy into things.

But on that still Saturday night, they laughed like old times, their carefree, relaxed past selves again, as they unknowingly drifted closer and closer to each other on that beautiful, camel-colored, leather couch. She put her glass down and stared curiously at him in her delirium.

"Were you," she asked, "really that unhappy?" He frowned; staring back into her slightly squinted, teasing eyes.

"What do you mean?" he asked back.

"Well, I mean, you probably slept with that Emilia girl at least a dozen times. Were you really that unhappy?" Her eyes widened, awaiting an answer, and he realized that she wasn't as drunk as she seemed.

"Can we not go over this now?" he asked, turning his head away from her. But she moved closer to him nonetheless, now on her knees.

"Why not? Do you have some…other priorities?" She looked him straight in the eyes, everything else blurred in the darkness.

"No. And I told you it was a one-time thing."

"Oh really? Then why were you texting her?"

"I said, can we just not go over this right now?" He stood up. He was nearly shouting.

"No!" she shouted back, standing up off the couch herself. "Why'd you do it?" she asked again, in almost a whisper, her eyes beginning to well up with tears.

"Because you saw me exactly the way I was afraid of seeing myself. This stupid house. My stupid job. We're sell-outs, Tess."

There was a short pause, and they stared at each other in silence. Out of impulse, she moved closer to him, holding the sides of his face, and kissed him, full of apologies that she was far too much of a coward to say out loud. So they moved with each other, closer to one another, cheeks touching and hair mixing. But soon, they were interrupted by the sharp, unforgiving tune of his phone. He pulled away, panting, and picked it up.

"Uh…yeah, yeah, no, that'd be great. Um, yeah, thanks." He put his phone back in his pocket and looked back down at her. "It was Rob. He said that some of the roads around the area are cleared now and he's going to the Holiday Inn in Greenwich with Paula. I guess I can leave…" he said, but he didn't move.

"Stay," she whispered to him, her eyes wide, all concerns of judgment, reputation completely gone. He smiled. And so they spent a last night together, in a blissful limbo, different people, different dreams, caving into an old, old desire.

Us

Alison Chai
9th Grade

Even when I was born, I barely stood a chance. She was already so much more mature than I, and my presence was unnecessary. Why was I born? It was for her. Long ago, she had said, "I want a sibling," and thus I was created by our parents. Unfortunately it was ten years too late. By the time I had grown up into a child exposed to the world, she had found a second family of friends and no longer needed the extra attention.

"Aaaagh! Get out of my room!" Her fluffy flower pillows came at me and strong hands shoved me out, locking the white wooden door as a final touch. As I stood there, unmoving, I could hear her continue her conversation with her friends as if I had never been there. At that time, all I could hear were snippets of conversation my five-year old mind couldn't understand, but wanted to be a part of, if it meant being with her.

"You're so spoiled." They say that the people who will often tell you the truth about yourself and be most honest with you are your family. Somewhere inside, I already knew that was true. At eight, I was trying to find a hidden meaning to her words. Did it mean she hated me? That she wanted me to change myself if I wanted her to like me? Ok then. I'll do my best to change. Even so, critical words of hers trailed with me throughout my life.

"He's coming over for dinner tonight." Her third "boyfriend" this year. At least it felt like it was the third. They never lasted too long. For a while, they were the subject of her affections, but I always expected her to come back to me, or at least away from him, when either lovebird realized they were better off as friends. What a fool I was to think that she wouldn't eventually find her soul mate.

"You don't want to hang out together?" She looked at me funny. In a small hissy fit, she tromped out of the room. Being twelve was rough, and I made a firm resolution. There would be no need for me to chase after her anymore, after this girl who always shoved me aside and called me mean things. The girl who hurt my feelings the most and left me behind, letting my affections fly away in the wind. She didn't treat me like a human being. I don't know whether it was because she honestly didn't like me or because it was true when Father said she was jealous of me getting more attention as the baby of the family. Yet it didn't give her the right to act that way to me. My decision was that I would stop endlessly loving her and that I would learn to hate her.

But love is a funny thing. No matter how I tried to ignore her, or avoid her, it hurt me so much more than I thought it would have hurt her. I could never be a genuine mean towards her, and any request she asked of me, I did my best to fulfill it anyway. If this was my version of hate, I might as well have called it lovesick. I was terrible at trying to keep her out of my mind.

Now at fifteen, I look back, thinking how the love was never one-sided. To me it may have seemed that way, but to her, I had always been one of her higher priorities. She went out of the way to help me many times when I was in trouble. She'd come home in the middle of the night to help me with an unfinished project. She took me places I needed to go whenever our parents couldn't do it even though she had things to do too. She offered to threaten anyone who would bully me at school. She trusted me and confided many of her feelings toward me that no one else had ever seen. Most importantly, she gave me a reason to live when I wanted to fade away.

I have never heard her say to my face, "I love you." That isn't necessary. Our relationship is odd and questionable. I am a puppy, following her willingly, even if she were to lead me off a cliff. I will never be able to stop loving her. Hate is a word that can't exist in this dictionary. To her, I am an embarrassing childhood toy that others make fun of. Something she will never be able to get rid of and where the true feelings are to be kept secret.

Where will we be in time? I'm sad to know she won't always be here as she heads off to college. We've only really ever talked once about our future. How our promise is that we won't be separated and that we will retain closeness even as we get older and busier with our lives. I know for sure that I'll do my best to keep our relationship mended together. Without realizing it, we have integrated ourselves deeply into each other's' lives and rely on one another in rough times. There's no one better for us to confide to in our darkest times than each other. The difference between us doesn't matter. After all, what are sisters for?

Snow

Bernice Chan
12th Grade

The cold snow pierces your face. It attacks mercilessly, whipping, stinging. It's not even snow anymore; it's ice. You're walking through blizzard, trudging actually. Two long blocks from home. The snow is heavy as it piles up on the fur of your brown boots. There's supposed to be eighteen inches. The harsh winds pelt you with more ice. The hood of your jacket stands no chance against the icy wind.

* * *

Two Days before Christmas 2008- Train Station

I'm with Zee and Charley. We just finished Christmas shopping at Century 21 in Manhattan.

"The snow is so pretty!" I say. It's falling heavily now, all throughout the streets. "It's so beautiful."

I check my phone. Three missed calls from my mom and a new voicemail. I put my phone to my ear as I walk down the stairs to the train station.

"I'm gonna be home late. I'm at the hospital right now. Your grandma fell," her voice is shaky. She's speaking a little too loud and a little too quickly. "Don't go Christmas shopping anymore. Just go home early." I scrunch my eyebrows and replay the message. I quickly speed dial her back. She doesn't pick up. I continue to walk with Charley to the train platform.

Charley starts telling me a story I won't remember. I half smile, pretending to listen. I take a step onto the bumpy yellow line and lean forward to peer into the darkness. Still no light. I step back, trying not to worry. It'll come soon. Charley and I talk about how we almost died running across the street. He laughs at how I slipped earlier because I didn't see the frozen ice on the sidewalk. I playfully hit his shoulder and smile, trying not to think about the voicemail.

* * *

Two Days before Christmas 2008- Home

"Where's mom?" I ask my grandma in Chinese.

She closes the lid to the pot of soup she's making and walks over to me.

"They're in the hospital now. Your grandma passed away today."

I look up at her.

"She's not here anymore," she continues. Her voice is soft. There are small wrinkles next to her eyes.

"Oh," I say.

She looks at me to see if I'm going to cry; maybe she'll need to get me a tissue. I look away from her small figure standing in the doorway. I hear the audience's superficial laughter on TV. She's still watching me, hesitant to leave. I turn away and start watching TV.

*   *   *

The snow is starting to seep through your old boots now. You use your right hand to pull the flimsy brim of your hood closer to your forehead as you use your left to cover as much of your face as possible. It's no use; the little shards of ice slip through the space between your fingers, cutting your face numb.

*   *   *

Two Days Before Christmas 2008- Home

I'm sitting on the edge of my mom's bed. She's telling me how it happened.

"Grandma went out to pick up Jasmine and Dylan from school. There was a heavy blizzard out. And then, I don't know, I guess she fell. Someone found her body and called the police. But by then, it was too late."

Christmas 2008

There are no presents this year. My two youngest cousins are jumping around the house, playing with their stuffed animals.

"Stop," I say to Jasmine.

"I just want to have fun," she says, frowning. She knows grandma died, but I guess she doesn't get it. I walk over to my other cousins who are sitting on the stairs with my aunt.

"I should have taken the day off," my aunt says. "Then I could have picked them up. I was going to but I decided not to." She says those words in a low tone, almost as if to herself. "I should have."

"What about you? Couldn't you have come home early to pick them up?" my cousin asks me. "You live right next to them."

"Yeah…" I say, not wanting to stay long in that conversation. I think about how I went shopping instead.

*   *   *

After Christmas 2008- Walking my dog

I'm walking my dog with my mom at night. It's dark out. The

snow still hasn't melted, pushed off to the side of the sidewalk.

"Let's go this way," my mom says. Her voice is soft. We turn the corner.

"Your grandma was walking here that day." We cross the street, approaching the corner where she fell.

"What's that?" my mom says. She quickly walks closer to a black thing lying on the ledge of the sidewalk.

"Ohmygod."

It's an umbrella. The handle is bent completely at a right angle. The wires are protruding out of the frame. It's my grandma's umbrella.

"Ohmygod." Her voice is weaker now. It's starting to crack. I stand there, looking at the broken black umbrella, hoping it was a car's wheels that caused the metal to break. Not my grandma's fall. My mom sniffles.

* * *

As you listen to the ice pelting the back of your hood, you realize how hard it is to walk through all this fresh, deep snow. That your feet are giving in. That maybe, if you hadn't taken the bus, you wouldn't even have been able to make it home. You think to yourself that if you weren't so young, perhaps you wouldn't even be able to endure this walk home. Maybe you'd collapse and fall in the snow and someone would find your body hours too late.

* * *

Christmas 2010

"Grandpa, this one's for you!" my youngest cousin screams as he scurries to my grandpa with a giant box in his hands. Grandpa smiles. It's his third present. I smile too as he slowly unwraps the Macy's box. The expected "ooo's" and "yay's" erupt from my family as he pulls out a new jacket from the box. We're all cheering now. I smile seeing how happy he is, but for a brief moment, as I'm sitting there, I remember Christmas two years ago. How it was so much different than this one. How the truth is my grandma's absence is lingering in the back of my mind, in the mind of my dad who's clapping now. One of my cousins has gone off to the kitchen. She's sitting at the dinner table by herself, looking at the wall.

And as I sit there and watch my grandpa slip his arm through his new jacket, I can't help but wonder how many more Christmases he'll have left.

* * *

You finally arrive at the foot of your door. You ring the doorbell and see your mom's shadow as she unlocks the door. You tell her how much you hate the snow. You moan now, complaining about how you just had to walk through all that. She tells you to stand in the bathtub as she uses a dustpan to brush off all the ice.

The little pieces of ice that stuck to your face have melted. You can feel your cheeks again. But they burn with cold. You listen to the swift brushing of the dustpan as your mom pats the snow off the fur of your boots. And in that moment, you start to cry. They're small tears at first that blend with the ice water as you wipe it away from your eyes. And then you cry some more. And the tears start coming down quicker.

You cry because the cold snow hurt. Because it was scary walking home, trying to shield your face from the blizzard while making sure you didn't fall. You cry because your grandma died two years ago and she's the first in your family to die. Because you know, from today, how she must have felt while she was walking through the blizzard. You cry maybe because as we're growing up, we realize the snow just isn't as beautiful anymore.

Promise of Spring

Maggie Colson
7th Grade

Kissa gazed at the brightly colored flowers in the walled garden. A bee flew lazily from blossom to blossom, collecting pollen. It landed on Kissa's arm and she flicked it off with her fingernail. Crouching in the dirt, her finger traced the pattern of a sun in the dust.

Amun poked his head through the doorway, a wooden dog clutched tightly in his fist. Under the dog's body was a small, well-concealed handle which, if pulled, made the dog's tiny mouth open. "Will you play with me, Kissa?" Amun asked hopefully.

"What do you want to play?" said Kissa, annoyed at the interruption.

"I want to play 'Hounds and Jackals'!" he shouted joyfully.

"You don't know how to play that," Kissa grumbled. "You're too little."

"I do!"

Kissa sighed. She loved her little seven-year-old brother, but sometimes he bothered her when she wanted to be alone.

"Well then," Amun continued, oblivious to his sister's sullen face, "you can teach me, Kissa."

"All right," Kissa finally agreed reluctantly. She grabbed Amun's hand and led him toward the villa, her father's grand house. Her father, Ammon, was very rich and served in Pharaoh's court.

"Where are you going, Kissa?" Kissa's mother asked as Kissa led Amun by her open bedroom door.

"Amun wants me to teach him how to play 'Hounds and Jackals'," Kissa replied. "May we use Father's gold set?"

"Yes, Kissa, if you are careful," Femi assented. "Thank you for watching Amun," she added as Kissa promised to be careful, running down the hallway to where the games were kept.

With the little table in her hands, Kissa led Amun up to the roof. Sitting cross-legged on the cool, smooth stone, she showed him how to move the little gold pieces around the wooden board.

Amun was fascinated with the figures, shaped like the heads of hounds and jackals but, after playing for a while, he grew bored and sulky.

"I want to play with my clay balls, Kissa," he complained.

"No, Amun," Kissa replied. "It's time for dinner. Hear Mother calling?" Amun listened for a moment, nodded, and bolted downstairs. Kissa followed, carrying the game tightly in both hands, then, after putting it back where it belonged, hurried to the reception hall where the rest of the family was waiting. Kissa slid into her seat between Amun and her sister Mert. Mert and Aloli were twins. They were fourteen and Kissa was ten.

Although they had been born on the same day, Mert and Aloli were as different as could be. Mert was quiet and shy, like the little rabbits Kissa saw in the vineyards. Her name meant 'lover of silence'. Aloli, on the other hand, liked to boss Kissa and Amun, and sometimes, when Mother wasn't around, even Mert.

"Amun, what are you doing?" Kissa whispered sharply, looking down at her brother, who sat on her other side.

Amun grinned and lowered his eyes to his lap. Kissa followed his gaze and tried not to smile as she took the little wooden dog from his grasp. He was stuffing bits of fruit into its open mouth.

Kissa dropped the toy to the floor under her chair. She glanced toward the end of the table where her mother sat next to her father, Ammon. Good. Femi hadn't noticed. She was deep in low conversation with Ammon. Kissa resumed eating.

* * *

The next morning, Mert wakened Kissa before dawn. "What is the matter, Mert?" Kissa asked sleepily, rubbing her eyes. "Is it Hebony?"

Mert nodded. Hebony was the black cow that lived in a stall behind the garden. She was going to have a little calf. Mert beckoned to Kissa and disappeared down the hall. Left alone, Kissa shivered in the early morning air, and then dressed hurriedly. When she reached Hebony's stall, she heard low mooing from within. Kissa was frightened. Perhaps Hebony was going to die... she pushed the door open.

She saw Ptah, the cattleherd, seated on the ground. Hebony was standing calmly in her stall, munching a bunch of sweet, clean hay that Ptah had given her. At first, Kissa did not see the small heap of brown lying on the other side of Ptah and she looked around wildly. Smiling, Ptah moved out of the way, revealing a tiny, perfect calf curled up against his leg. Slowly, so that she would not startle Hebony's sleeping baby, Kissa lowered herself to the ground next to Ptah.

"She's so perfect," she whispered, still staring at the calf. Timidly, she stretched out her hand and touched the calf. Her skin was a dark chocolate color and as soft as velvet. Kissa stroked her back. "What is her name?" she asked, glancing at Ptah.

"She has no name yet, Missy." Ptah's white smiled gleamed in the dusky light.

Kissa looked at him curiously. "No name?"

Ptah nodded, grinning at Kissa. "That's right, Missy." He hummed softly to himself.

Kissa began to grow impatient. "She must have a name," she insisted.

"Well, then," Ptah got up and began pitching more hay into Hebony's manger, "you had better pick one out."

Kissa's eyes widened. "Me?" she asked in disbelief.

Ptah nodded. "Your father told me you could name the next calf." He started to sweep up the dust from the floor.

Kissa turned back to the calf, eyeing her gentle eyes and big, velvety ears. They looked like the soft petals of lotus blossoms that bloomed along the banks of the Nile, reminding Kissa of the promise of spring. "Amisi," she whispered after a long moment of careful consideration, then a little louder, "Amisi."

Ptah looked up, nodding in approval, and then went back to his sweeping. Amisi was the perfect name for the calf. It meant 'flower'.

Suddenly a loud, barking dog startled Kissa's thoughts. "Go away, Bes," she ordered in irritation to the dog, which was sniffing Amisi curiously. When Bes did not obey, Ptah chased him out of the stables with his broom.

"Kisssss–a!" A high voice floated to Kissa's ear. "Kissss–a!"

"Coming, Mother," Kissa shouted, struggling to her feet. Amisi stirred and Kissa gave her a loving look, and then hurried out of the stable.

"Kissa, please go and tell Muminah to draw me a bucket of water," Femi requested.

"Yes, Mother," Kissa obeyed, heading to the reception hall, where the maid was polishing a delicate urn. "Muminah, Mother wants you to get her a bucket of water from the well," Kissa relayed the instruction to Muminah.

Muminah pursed her lips and mumbled under her breath, but not loud enough for Kissa to hear her words. Kissa watched as the maid grumblingly made her way to the well.

Kissa began to head back to the house, but stopped in her tracks as a scream pierced the air. She looked around wildly. Seeing no one in the hall, she rushed outside of the house. The screams seemed to be coming from the well... Kissa saw Muminah standing there, pointing and screaming with her hand clapped over her mouth.

Several other servants came running, and so did Kissa's mother Femi. "What is wrong?" Femi gasped as soon as she reached Muminah, "Are you hurt?"

Muminah did not answer but kept shrieking. "The gods are angry," she mumbled in between screams. Femi grasped her by her shaking shoulders.

"Muminah," she said gently but firmly. "Stop crying and tell me what has happened."

Muminah sniffed. "Look—in the—the well," she finally managed. Kissa ran to the edge of the low stone wall of the well and peered in, and her heartbeat quickened.

"What is it?" Femi was concerned. "Is the well dry?" Kissa shook her head. Femi, with a sigh, got up and made her way to the well herself. She drew in her breath quickly as she, too, looked into the well. "Kissa," she said in an unnatural tone, "Go and fetch your father, as quickly as you can. Quick now!"

Kissa flew along the well-worn path through the village and into the city. Dodging dogs, sheep, and little children that were in her way, she arrived at the gates to the pharaoh's court. Kissa's father, Ammon, was a scribe in the royal court. His job was to list the rich gifts that people brought to Pharaoh. Once, when Kissa was eight, he had taken her to court with him and she had viewed in awe the beautiful and bountiful offerings people brought and gave to Pharaoh. That day, there had been a visitor from Nubia, part of the Egyptian Empire. The dark-skinned Nubian had given Pharaoh the handsome skin of a leopard he had killed, and a trained pet baboon as a gift for the queen. How Kissa had wanted to take that monkey home! She wished Amun could have seen it.

"Hello, Horus," Kissa greeted one of the guards, "My mother has a message for my father. May I go in?"

"Hello, Kissa," Horus opened the gate and Kissa hurried inside in search of her father. Usually when she visited the royal court, she walked slowly to gaze at the paintings and riches, but today she didn't notice them at all. When she neared the heart of the court, she stopped short in dismay. Servants and courtiers were milling about in confusion. Someone shouted. Kissa scanned the area anxiously for her father. Seeing him standing under a great pillar covered in paintings, she gave a sigh of relief and hurried toward him.

"What's going on?" She shouted to be heard over the noise. Her father put an arm around her.

"All the water has been turned to blood!" Her father yelled back. "There isn't a drop of clean water to be found anywhere. Even the Nile is blood."

Kissa stared at him in shock. No clean water anywhere?

"Why have you come?" Her father's voice broke into her thoughts. Suddenly she remembered Mother's message.

"The well is filled with blood!" She blurted, and then felt foolish. Her father already knew that. He had just told her that there wasn't any clean water.

* * *

That evening at dinner Kissa listened to her parents' conversation—when she wasn't telling Amun to wipe his fingers, or not to stuff his mouth because he might choke.

"He says it is a sign from his god," Her father's voice was sarcastic. "But our own magicians did the same thing."

"What did they do?" Mert was listening intently.

"Turned their staffs into snakes," Ammon told her.

"But, Father," Amun's small voice broke in, "Aaron's snake ate all the other snakes. Ptah told me." To Kissa, he added, "That must have been a very fat snake!" Kissa giggled.

Father glanced at him then continued his conversation with his wife. "Anyway, I think that man, Moses, is crazy to even think that Pharaoh would 'let his people go'," There was contempt in Ammon's voice. Femi murmured something in reply, but she spoke so low that Kissa could not hear what she had said.

* * *

The next day, Kissa woke up, hopped out of bed with a yawn, quickly got dressed, and went downstairs. It was early and everyone else was still sleeping, so she slipped outside and into Hebony's stall. She leaned up against the sides of the stall and watched Amisi sleeping in silence.

The next thing she knew, the gate of Hebony's stall was opened and light came streaming in. Ptah walked in swinging the milking pail. He gave a start when he saw Kissa already there. He looked amused and said, "Go run inside. Your mother will be wondering where you are." He bent down and placed the milk pail on the ground. "Run along now," he ordered teasingly, and Kissa went back to the house.

"My goodness, Kissa, where have you been?" her mother exclaimed.

"I went outside to see Amisi," Kissa replied. "Everyone was still asleep."

"Well," Femi sighed. "You've already dirtied your dress. Go upstairs and put on a clean one."

Guiltily Kissa examined the dirty hem. "I'm sorry. I didn't

mean to."

"I'm sure you didn't. Go upstairs and change now, Kissa; breakfast is waiting."

* * *

After breakfast, Kissa asked her mother timidly, "May I go outside now?"

"I suppose," Femi said, "Just as long as you don't get dirty again."

Joyfully Kissa skipped outside into the sunshine. She went over to the cattle pen where the cows were kept during the day. Kneeling in the soft dirt by the pens, she grabbed a handy stick and traced two cows in the dust, a big one and a little one.

"Look, Amisi," she spoke softly to the calf, who had ventured over to her on wobbly legs. "This is you and this—" She stopped talking as a little movement in the dirt before her caught her eye. She looked down and saw a large frog.

"Hello," she greeted it, stretching out her hand cautiously. When it made no attempt to move, she picked it up and held it in her cupped palm. Another frog hopped into sight. "Why, this must be your wife! And these must be your children!"

Kissa was amazed. She had never seen so many frogs before, or such large ones! "You have a very big family," she complimented the frog that was still held captive in her hand. She viewed all the hopping creatures doubtfully. "Perhaps some of them are just friends, not all family," she said at length, then fell to catching as many as she could and depositing them in an old clay jar she had found. No matter how many she popped into the jar, there were still more to be caught! "Why," she finally stopped in exhaustion, "it must be a whole city!"

"Kissa!" Aloli's shout roused Kissa from her thoughts. Rising, Kissa put her hand to her forehead to shade the glare of the hot sun. Then she gasped. As far as she could see across the shimmering dust, frogs covered the earth. "Come inside! Mother wants you!"

*   *   *

The next few days were miserable. Although the water was no longer blood and was therefore drinkable, the frogs were an even bigger problem. "I like frogs alright," she remarked to Muminah as she watched her setting the table. "Just not in my soup!" She giggled as Muminah used a wide broom to try to sweep the frogs off the table, for they had invaded the insides of buildings as well as outside.

"Run along, Kissa," Muminah mumbled. "You're more of a bother than these frogs." Kissa frowned at Muminah then went outside to find Zivah. Zivah was a new Hebrew servant. Kissa liked it when Zivah would tell her and Amun stories or sing one of her Hebrew songs. She wasn't grumpy at all like Muminah.

*   *   *

Although they were now gone, the dead frogs were piled up along the riverbank and the odor was intolerable. Kissa still itched from invisible little flea bites, for after the frogs had died, the Egyptians were plagued with the annoying bugs, until, they, too had gone. Now, there were the flies—loud, buzzing things that always seemed to find their way into your cup or bowl. Kissa could hear the steady buzz of their wings and she wondered how much longer they would be around.

She didn't have to wait long. A few days later, the flies were gone and she skipped outside to visit Amisi. She was growing so big so fast that Kissa could hardly recognize her as the tiny calf she was at birth, although her ears were still as soft and as velvety as lotus blossoms between Kissa's fingers.

"Hello, girl," She crooned to the growing calf. "I bet you're hot." She glanced around the stall. Amisi had been kept in the stall, instead of the cattle pens, because she had been sick recently, and was not yet recovered. Night was falling and Ptah walked by the stall.

"Kissa," he asked, "Will you bring Hebony back over

here?"

Kissa nodded. One of her favorite chores was helping with the cattle, although Kissa wasn't sure that her mother would approve if she knew. "All right, Ptah." She jumped up and ran toward the cattle pens.

"Thank you." Ptah walked toward the servants' quarters, located on the east side of the villa. Kissa continued toward the pens. She stopped short with a scream that brought Ptah running.

"What is it, now—" He stopped as he, too, saw the cattle lying on the ground, dead. "Not that," he moaned. "Not the cattle!"

Hebony was dead, too, lying amid the other cattle. Fear gripped Kissa's heart. How would Amisi survive without her mother? She began running back to the stall, and a new thought occurred to her. It might not matter.... Her fears were confirmed when she reached Amisi's stall.

She stood in the doorway until Ptah's shadow loomed over her. "Come away, Kissa," he said quietly. "She is gone."

Kissa spun around and ran. She was not in control of her feet...they just kept running...she couldn't stop until—finally she reached the river and knelt on the bank. Splashing away salty tears, the cool water felt good on her hot face. Her shoulders heaved softly, but she made no noise.

After she had washed her face, she started collecting the flowers that floated on the surface of the river. She waded out until she was standing knee deep in the chilly water, but she didn't even feel the cold. Her body was numb and she swallowed hard to keep the tears from flowing freely again.

When she returned to the villa, Ptah and two other servants had dug a grave for the cattle. As they lowered the cattle into the deep pits, Ptah drew Kissa aside. "Look over here," He led her a short distance away from the graves, showing her a smaller hole. "For Hebony, and Amisi," he whispered. Kissa managed a weak smile. "Thank you," she whispered back. When the two bodies had been lowered into the hole, Kissa threw her bundle on top of them. Before he filled the grave with dirt, Ptah leaned over to see what she had thrown—a bouquet of lotus blossoms.

*   *   *

A week later, Kissa made a face at her reflection in the pot of water. The boils had left ugly scars, and they had been painful, too. Pretty Aloli had been the most upset at the disease. She did not want her face and skin to be marred. Kissa did not care very much, now that they were done hurting. She didn't really mind how she looked.

She felt bored. Amun had a fever, and her cousin, Jamila, was away for the month on a trip, so she had no one to play with or talk to. Ptah had taken the cattle to a pasture far away, and Zivah was busy caring for Amun.

She looked up in curiosity as a tiny noise like raindrops sounded on the roof of the villa. "It's raining," she called to her mother in another room. But then, the sound just kept getting louder, and louder, until Kissa covered her ears with her hands, and lay her head on the low table.

"It's hail," her mother corrected. "Hear it on the roof?"

Kissa nodded dutifully, but inwardly, she wondered how anyone could not hear it. The noise sounded like a thousand camels, marching on the roof overhead.

A few hours later, it was still hailing, and Kissa was even more bored. On top of having no one to play with, she now had to stay in the house all day! She went into the guest room where Amun had been moved when he fell sick. Zivah was there, bending over his forehead with a cool cloth. Her hair was tied up, but little wispy curls escaped and framed her hot, sweaty forehead. She jumped when Kissa pushed the door open.

"You must not come in here, Miss," she gasped. "It's contagious. I'm afraid you'll have to leave." She herded Kissa toward the door. "Your little brother will be all right in no time at all."

Kissa sulked in a corner of her bedroom.

*   *   *

"Kissa, time for bed," Femi called. "The sun's already set."

Kissa sighed. "I don't want to go," she said.

"Go, Kissa," her father ordered in a voice that Kissa didn't dare argue with, but instead went dutifully to her room.

Swallowing hard, she flung the covers back and stepped away. Five grasshoppers jumped out. After making sure that there weren't any more locusts under the covers, Kissa got into bed slowly. Even though it was a hot night, she pulled the blankets over her head in an attempt to keep the locusts out. Last night, all that was kept out, though, was the fresh air.

The next morning, Kissa awoke with a yawn and a happy heart. There were no locusts to be seen anywhere! "Mother," she shouted joyfully as she ran to her mother's room. "The locusts are gone!"

That morning, Amun was feeling much better and even sat with the family at the table as Zivah served breakfast. After lunch, Kissa whispered something in Zivah's ear, then, receiving a positive answer to her question, ran down the hall.

"Amun," she told him joyfully as she entered the guest room, holding something behind her back. "We can play 'Hounds and Jackals'! Zivah said so." Amun greeted this distraction with enthusiasm. He, too, had missed his playmate and was tired of being sick.

"Your turn, Kissa," he said after moving one of his smooth wooden pieces. Suddenly he shouted as total blackness fell over the room. He grabbed Kissa's hand. "Is the sun god angry?" he asked fearfully. Kissa was too scared to answer. Shouts of confusion and sounds of toppling chairs from other rooms reached their ears. The darkness was thick and choking. Kissa could feel it surrounding her like a hot, clammy blanket.

"Kissa!" Femi's frenzied calls reached her ears.

"In my bedroom, Mother!" She yelled back in a frightened voice.

"Where is Amun?"

"He is here, too." Kissa dared not move in the pitch blackness, but instead held Amun's hand tightly. They both sat cross-legged in the bed.

"Do not move, Kissa," Femi ordered. Her voice sounded

closer now. "I am coming. Just stay where you are."

"Oh, Kissa, I'm scared," Amun whispered. "I don't like the dark." Kissa didn't like the dark, either, but she tried to sound positive, so that Amun would not be more scared than he already was.

Femi reached them at last, and Mert and Aloli were behind her. They all sat on the bed. "How will Father get home?" Kissa wanted to know. She felt better with Mother sitting next to her.

"He will have to stay at the palace until—until the darkness has passed," was the only answer she received.

* * *

"Father!" Amun's cry woke Kissa from a sound sleep. She rubbed her eyes, letting them adjust to the light—light! Sunlight was streaming into the room, and Father was home! Kissa's fear melted as she hugged her tall father.

"I missed you, Father," Kissa told him as he hugged her mother and sisters.

* * *

At midnight the next day, Kissa sat bolt upright in bed, wakened by a nightmare. She slid her feet out of bed and shivered as they hit the cold floor. Amun sat up in bed as she passed him.

"What are you doing?" he asked softly.

"Getting a drink of water," she whispered back.

"Get one for me, too, please," he said, then lay back down. Kissa tiptoed from the room and down the hall. When she reached the reception hall, she found the pot of water and grasped the dipper. She drank some water then refilled it and carried it back to her room for Amun, walking slowly so that it wouldn't spill. She paused in the doorway.

"Amun," she called quietly, then a little louder, "Amun!" No answer. Giggling to herself, she set the dipper on his nightstand and walked over to his bed. She stood over him with her hands on her hips, waiting for him to roll over and laugh.

His covers were thrown off and lay at the foot of his bed.

Moonlight bathed his face and cast shadows on the floor. She reached over and poked his side. "Wake up, Amun; I got you your water!" Still Amun did not move.

Kissa began to grow worried. "Wake up, Amun! Wake up." Her heart was beating faster. "Amun," she whispered, "please wake up." She jumped as the bedroom door opened with a squeak. Zivah stood in the doorway.

"I am just checking on my patient," she whispered with a wink. "And what are you doing out of bed?"

"He won't wake up," Kissa sobbed with tears in her voice.

Zivah flew to the bedside and put her ear to his chest. A sad look crossed her face.

"Oh, Kissa," she murmured. "It is true." She slid onto Kissa's bed and sat down next to her. "I didn't think it would really happen," she wiped a tear from her cheek. "I didn't believe it was true, and now it is too late. I should have warned you." Her voice was sorrowful. "At least you could have said—goodbye."

Kissa was frightened. Say goodbye? "What is true?" she asked, puzzled at Zivah's words. "What are you talking about?"

Zivah sighed. "Moses said so, but I didn't believe."

"Said what?"

Zivah ignored her interruption and went on, "There was no blood on the door..."

Kissa was really scared now. "Blood on the door? What blood? What for?"

Zivah shook her head, laughing weakly a little. "The blood of a perfect lamb had to be sprinkled on the door, or else..." Her voice grew quiet and she glanced at Amun, "or else the angel of death would not pass over the house." A hush fell over the room. Zivah closed her eyes. "Every firstborn son will die," she said as if she were quoting something she had heard, "if the blood of a lamb is not on the door."

Kissa felt her heart constrict. Every firstborn son would.... die? Amun was her mother's first son...her only son... She tugged on Zivah's sleeve.

"Is—is my brother going to—to die?" she asked.

Zivah said softly, "He is gone, dear."

*   *   *

Kissa ran until she had no breath left in her body, blindly, dodging branches and trying not to run into thorns. She ran until she could not run another step. Then she dropped to the uneven ground and buried her face in her hands. Her mother would miss her, but for once she didn't care.

"Why are you crying?" The voice was gentle and kind. Kissa looked up in surprise at the old man before her. By now the morning light was streaming over the hills.

"My—my brother is—is dead!" She sobbed. The man took her hand, which was wet with tears, and led her to a large, flat rock. "Who—are—you?" She hiccupped.

"My name is Moses," said the old man. He had long, white hair and a white beard. Suddenly, anger flared up in Kissa.

"You killed my calf," she accused. She had stopped crying. "And—and you killed my brother!"

Moses looked at her sympathetically. "I did not kill anyone—only once, a long, long time ago." A sad look passed over his weathered face as he remembered. "But I certainly did not kill your brother."

Kissa was at a loss of words. "But—but Zivah said you told them that they had to have blood." Her words were a confused jumble, but Moses understood.

"The blood was a sign," he told her, "for the angel of death to pass over the houses of the Hebrews."

"Zivah said something like that," Kissa told him, sniffing. "But why did you want things to die?"

"I did not want your brother to die." Moses told her kindly. "It was the will of God, that the Hebrews could be free. They are tired of being slaves to Pharaoh. The death of the firstborn sons softened Pharaoh's heart."

Kissa was thinking hard. "My brother died so that the Hebrews could be free?"

Moses nodded. "Something like that."

"I—have to go home now. My mother will be wanting me."

She jumped down off the rock and started to walk home, rubbing her eyes.

* * *

A year had passed. Even though Kissa still missed her brother, she felt a little bit better knowing that Amun's death, along with many others, allowed the Hebrews to be free from Pharaoh's harsh treatment. Zivah was gone now; she had left with her mother-in-law, walking in the shimmering heat in the long line of people leaving Egypt.

Kissa scanned the valley. The fresh, new springtime air blew in a gentle breeze across her face. The Nile flowed lazily, winding like a silvery blue snake around the cities below. She walked down to the bank of the river that flowed close to her home. After searching for awhile, she found what she was looking for. Again, she started the long walk home, a budding lotus blossom cradled gently in her hands.

Egyptian Names and Meanings
Kissa - sister of twins
Amun - hidden one
Ammon - hidden one
Femi - love
Mert - lover of silence
Aloli - grapes
Ptah - opener
Muminah - pious
Amisi - flower
Hebony – black
Zivah (Hebrew) - divine

Dominic

Megan Corbett
10th Grade

"It's a funny thing, death. It's like a sea monster waiting for the most innocent of ships to sail by, and out a deadly tentacle flies and snatches the ship into its clutches, never to be seen again." The legions of black-clad mourners listening to my every word nod and sniffle at my wavering voice. "But this? This is a death that could've been harpooned and dragged to shore; a death that could have been prevented," the tears are streaming down my face, "Dominic did not deserve to die. Nobody deserves to die, but least of all Dominic. And he took his own life. Think about that. He tried telling you, and not a single person in this room listened but me. Would you like to know a secret? He saw things in his dreams. Torturous things, like monsters and pain and ghosts, but at the end of the day he was more afraid of you people. You cry, you mourn, and you sob and shake as you contemplate the beautiful life that was lost today, but why decide that now? Why decide that his life was beautiful after he ended it? People need reminders, not eulogies."

My words echoed around the now silent church as the stunned audience waited for what I would say next. What would I say next, I wondered? I could feel the silence embrace me, calm me. A curtain had fallen over the room, hushing, muffling all sound. I took a breath and started again.

"I miss him, you know? It's terrifying, the thought of spending the rest of my life without him. I've been told that when someone dies there is a hole in your life, well I can tell you right now that is not true in the least. What they call a hole is actually a gaping chasm, this huge tear the size of the Grand Canyon shredding the very fiber of your being. And it's so much worse with someone like Dominic. He was the type of person you wanted to hug forever. Being with him never felt like "being with him". It just felt like being alone- with company.

He used to say that the sunset was jealous of my smile. He

used to bring me flowers out of the blue. His used to tell me that his favorite days with me were in March, because of his favorite Charles Dickens quote. 'It was one of those March days where the sun shines hot and the wind blows cold: when it's summer in the light and winter in the shade.' He used to do this. He used to do that. How could we let this happen?

Look around you. Go ahead, look. This hallowed hall we all sit in is filled to the brim. There are people crowded onto pews, standing shoulder to shoulder in the balcony. All of us, every single one, believed in Dominic. We saw someone special, someone with all the potential in the world and the ability to reach the stars. That's the problem, isn't it? We only saw with our eyes. We didn't really see him."

I took a shaky breathe, and then I couldn't help but laugh, much to the surprise of my enraptured listeners. "He wrote a note. To bid adieu to us mere mortals left behind. And the first line was him telling me not to rant and rave about how miserable I'll be without him; he told me not to take it out on you, the innocent bystanders. Now riddle me this, how can I not? How can I not lash out at the people who were supposed to be there, to help him when he was struggling? I don't blame any of you people. I blame myself. He was, is, the love of my life. He is my one and only, as corny as it sounds. Without him, the world feels like it's turning backwards. The grass is crimson, the sky is violet; nothing makes sense to me.

He killed himself. I had to find him sprawled on his back, completely motionless, with an empty bottle of pills in his hand. Devastation doesn't begin to describe what I felt. I am now devoid of all emotions except love and anger. I love him so very much. So much that it hurts. But I am so angry for not being able to tell. He was constantly reminding me that I knew him better than anyone, and now it seems as if I never knew him at all." I close my eyes, and grace the congregation with a smile.

"Would you like to hear a story?" There are a few uncertain looks, several heads bobbing up and down, nodding their decision.

"Once upon a time," I saw the knowing grins on the faces in the audience who had heard this before, "there was a boy and there was a girl. They met one day in the middle of the woods and had no idea that one day they would be so important to each other."

I close my eyes as I speak, wrapping my arms around myself, hugging each precious memory as it becomes a thought, then flows out of my mouth. "It was June twenty-seventh, 2010. I had escaped into the woods behind my house to avoid giving the wretched new neighbors one of my mother's heinous homemade casseroles. I lay on the damp ground, staring at the puffy cotton ball clouds lazily swimming through the sky above, becoming one with the peace and serenity of the forest. Or at least I was, until the scrawniest, pip-squeakiest, most annoying little fourteen year old popped out of the bushes and triumphantly proclaimed that the cloud I was looking at was shaped like a manatee munching on a head of lettuce in the San Diego Zoo. Needless to say, I brushed that off and very cleverly replied with 'I think it looks like a cotton ball'. Golden stuff; I should really get paid for the things I think of in the presence of my true love." Laughter enveloped me in a sweet embrace.

"Three months later, I found him again, chasing a lady bug through my backyard, complaining that it kept flying away as he was trying to count its spots. Two weeks after that, I saw him lying on his roof, looking at the stars. And the night after that, I was up there with him. The Big Dipper, Draco the Dragon, Orion's Belt, he knew every constellation, his personal favorite being Equuleus. 'The pony'. Three weeks after that he asked me on a date, and I accepted. Little did I know that Dominic's version of a date was breaking into a junkyard, having an epic one on one lightsaber duel and then getting chased out by the night watchman." Appreciative chuckles and disapproving titters peppered me as I paused momentarily.

"Obviously, that was the night I starting falling in love with the weirdest, sweetest, most insane boy I'd ever met. And almost two years later I stand before you, smiling. I exhausted my supply of tears as soon as I found out that he would never again look into my eyes and tell me that his love for me was like diarrhea. Explosive and uncontrollable." More laughter from the audience, and as I scanned the assembled faces I saw tears in a few eyes. "I'm sure many of you know and perhaps feel the same way, but I've never cried as hard as I did over his death. It was the worst kind of crying, too. It's when your lips start to shake and tears build up quickly and spill out, like a dam collapsed. It all comes flooding out, and no matter what you do you can't stop it. You're bent over or crouched trying to suck it in and not make noise, but it hurts too much to hold it in. You've been so shattered that you yelp and then comes the loss of breath, which in my opinion is the worst part because not only are you sobbing helplessly, but you're also angry at yourself for not being able to breathe properly. You're just a mess when you think about your loss; you're inconsolable when you look over at that wooden box and imagine him slowly decomposing in it for the rest of eternity. He will be six feet under and you will be sitting next to a patch of grass, conversing with a rock and futilely trying to convince yourself that he can hear you."

I survey the scene before me. Scan the crowd, the sunlight streaming through the stained glass windows, leading my eyes to the casket and the beautiful boy inside of it, frozen in time. Never aging, never going grey, never getting to experience his wedding, or the birth of his first child.

"What an inconsolable ache," I whisper, almost to myself. I caress that cold face with a shaking hand; gently brush his hair out of his eyes for the last time. Leaning down, I kiss his forehead and in that moment I swear I could hear his laughter, his voice. I could feel his lips on my lips, his arms around my waist, his fingers laced through mine. In a final moment, all that I felt while speaking to those solemn faceless people rushes towards me and his lifeless body, lying there, immobilized by the only solution he saw to a seemingly endless sea of pain.

I stand and stare at him for God knows how long, thinking of how fleeting your life actually is. One day you're cuddled up on the couch with the one you love, the next you're in an ocean of people in all black, paying their respects and saying goodbye. Life is so short. So keep your heart strong, and love long, and be sure you tell the people you love that you love them while you still have the chance.

The Grand Scheme

Madeleine Davison
8th Grade

"Hey Mom, I need some money!" I call down the stairs, hoping. Crossed fingers she'll loan me some...but no such luck.

"Vince, you just blew forty bucks on a gum-ball machine last week. You are not borrowing any more from me until you can pay me back for that. In fact, I think you will owe me fifty if it's not paid by the end of this week. Not a chance."

"Pleeeeease!" I beg. I'm the youngest, so sometimes this has worked in the past. Not this time. My mom is unyielding.

"Go clean your room, young man," She shouts, "Or you're not going to that game tonight!"

I go to my room. But there's no way I'm cleaning it. I mean, hey, it's my room! If I want it messy, I'm the only one who has to live with the consequences. I guess every now and then a dirty sock or two ends up outside the door in the hall but really, it's not like my mom doesn't have time to stoop down and pick it up as she walks past. She basically has all the time in the world! Me, I have to budget. Time and money. I call my buddy Kate. She's a complete nerd-head; she'll know what to do.

"Hey Kate, what's up?"

"Homework, which is what you should be up to, Vincent De Luca." I should've known.

"Well I am kind of in a big jam here--"

"Let me guess... Homework, your room, or money." The girl knows me way too well.

"Well, see, it's actually--"

"All three." My point exactly.

"Well, yeah you could say that..."

"Spit it out. I need to finish my Pre-Calc homework, and then I've got an extra credit paper to write by next week and I'm not even done with the rough draft. I have no time for your petty complaints."

"Hey! They're not petty! I owe my mom forty smackers for the gum-ball thing and she keeps bugging me to pay up. Problem is--"

"You have no money, I know, now get on with it! Do you want a loan, or are you asking for fundraising ideas? I don't have time for chitchat." Sharp as a knife, that one.

"You wouldn't happen to have forty bucks lyin' about the place you could spot me..."

"I most certainly do not. My money goes directly to my college fund. Vincent, you have been my friend since preschool. If it wasn't for that, I don't know what I'd do with you. You are absolutely incorrigible." I know better than to ask what incorrigible means.

"Um, yeah, whatever, see ya later."

"Goodbye and good luck with your mom." She hangs up.

I consider who to ask next. There's Dan, who is more like me. If he could help me, he would, because he gets into the same kind of trouble as me and he knows he needs to be able to count on his buds to bail him out, but the problem is he probably doesn't have any money either.

Then there's Nick. Nick is a jock. He's playing in the football game today. Trouble with him is, he probably can't count to forty and I'd end up with fourteen dollars or something. Not a good thing. Man, I just need to bum a couple twenties off someone--who'd have thought it'd be so hard?

* * *

The next day at school, I'm walking to class with Dan and Nick when I see the "Queen Bees." Loads of guys in our class have the hots for one or all of them, but they only go out with kids like Nick or Tyler Clarence, the basketball stud. This is why it's advantageous to hang with Nick. We get to see the cute girls up close a little more often than other guys do.

"Oh my God, did you see the thing that girl was wearing?!" It's Ashley, the richest (and cutest) one of them.

"Oh my gosh yes! That was so awful!" This is Britney, her second-in-command.

"I know!!! Oh, and did you hear? Justine is totally crushing on Blake. She passed a note to Diane Wilson at lunch today and it said 'I love Blake S.'!!! I can not believe it!" The speaker this time is blonde cheerleader Kelsey. She is practically bouncing off the walls with excitement.

"No way!" Ashley has obviously not heard this juicy piece of news. Kelsey looks satisfied that she's provided the clique with some new talking material.

"Yes way! And the best part is, when Blake heard, he smiled and blushed a little! Isn't that, like, so cute?!"

"Aww! Yeah, that's adorable!" Ashley gushes. I notice that Britney hasn't been exactly contributing much to the discussion since Blake was mentioned. Maybe she likes him, too... And then the thought strikes me. It is the single most brilliant idea I have ever had.

All through class that day, it occupies my whole brain and I completely forget the assignments for the day, so I have to copy from Dan's assignment book.

At home, I race to the computer and sit there. Five seconds into my plan and I'm already stuck. I have no idea how to make a new website. Dang it, I'm gonna have to call Kate again. She's going to be really annoyed with me.

"Um, hey Kate. I have a question."

"What is it? I have homework, you know."

"I know. So do I. I need to figure out how to make a website."

"Why?" Oh, great. There's no way in heck I can tell her my real reason, so I'll have to come up with a whopper, and quick.

"Um...It's for tech ed. It's our, uh, homework for this, um, semester." Great. Good thing I'm not usually all that articulate or she might suspect something. Actually, she probably already does.

"Mmmhmm..." She definitely smells a rat. Great.

"I'm serious. It's this project. Just tell me already!"

"Well...Ok, fine. Log in to Internet Explorer..." She explains to me the way to make a website. That's why I love Kate (as a friend!). She can't resist showing how much she knows. I follow her advice and soon I have a little website going, with a blog. It's very simple and to the point: "Find out all the juiciest happenings at Woodland Middle. Membership $5." Then I need to figure out how people could pay me. I decide that PayPal would be the best way to make this happen, so I sign up for a PayPal account in my mom's name. Perfect. My mom will never notice the per-purchase fee on her credit card bill, it's so small.

Then I call Dan.

"Hey Dan, what's up?"

"Hi Vince; nothin' much. How 'bout you?"

"Well, a bunch, actually. I need your help. I'm in need of a business partner for a top-secret cash cow I have planned. See, I made this website, and I was thinkin, we can listen up on other people's secrets, see, then we make a, like, a code name for each person, or we could have, say, a number for them, and if you pay five bucks, you get to see the list of secrets with the numbers of people. Then, for an extra, oh, I dunno, dollar, along with A SECRET OF THEIR OWN you get to see who's who, like they say 'I wanna see who number 586 is,' so they pay up, write 'I have a crush on Ginny Warrens,' and I tell them, '586 is Fiona MacArthur.' So they can see, ok, Fiona likes 435, and 672 likes her. Then they give me another buck, and another secret to find out who they are...see what I mean? It adds up. Plus then my secret pool keeps expanding. But I need an equal-shares business partner, and I want that to be you. But you've gotta swear secrecy. I can't have anyone finding out it's me."

"Ok. I got it. And sure, I'll be in on it, long as you promise me equal shares no matter what."

"I promise. And you've gotta promise secrecy or this isn't gonna work."

"I promise."

"Cross your heart?"

"And hope to die."

"Then it's a deal."

"Deal."

And with that, Woodland World of Gossip is born.

* * *

At first, business goes slowly. Only two membership applications come that week, but I hand Mom my share of the cash, and she's mollified (and naive!) enough to give me an extension on the deadline. Meanwhile, I sneak around, hungrily looking for extra secrets. It is truly astounding what you can find out when you listen. That Wednesday afternoon I post:

Post #1
Hey everyone! Did you hear? There's a new blog post in town! Here we record all the best, juiciest gossip in Woodland Middle. To find out who any of the following code names refer to, send $1 to the address at the bottom of the page, and WWG will respond asap.

Today's Gossip

Who knew? It's true! 1021192 DOES like 212119! They are now an item...how cute!

Word is that 1121217, who is NOT single, is secretly in love with 1011116!!! Uh-Oh...

And how about this? While 212119 is happy with 1020192, 218919 is not so happy...seems like they liked 212119 themselves... Drama alert!

And last but not least, breaking news is-- heartbreak in WM. 131186 will likely break up with fling 181194 tomorrow.
Think you're on the list? Find out for just $1 and a secret of your own by clicking "trade secrets" at the top of the page!

~WWG

It's fun, writing my new blog. Some people have started to bite, and with their secrets it's way easier to make these blogs. I don't even need to snoop around anymore! I saved a few not-so-exciting tidbits for later, in case there was a day where not much went on, I could liven up the blog. I also made up a system for naming the people. You take the first three letters of their first names, and first one of their last name, make them into numbers using the old A=1, B=2 thing, and then smash it all together. So, for example, Justine Barton, is JusB, which translates to 1021192

(212119 is BlaS, or Blake Smith). Not too, too secure, but I can always change it if people start figuring it out.

It takes some time, but soon the cash really starts rolling in. I get $12 on Friday, up from $10 on Thursday. Of course, I have to use my $11 share of this haul to pay back the mama bear but at the rate it's going, I'll have some for myself soon. And only three posts up so far! I feel like a total genius. Maybe I'll make so much money that I can retire early and I won't even have to go to college or anything!

* * *

Monday, at school, I overhear the popular clique talking about a mysterious new gossip blog. Yes! They found it! I cheer, in my head, of course. They say they're trying to figure out who's who without paying but Britney says she's tempted just to send in the cash because she suspects the blog talks about her. Actually, she says she thinks 45127 is her (it's really this weird, unpopular girl named Delilah Geisman, who doesn't speak English real well and has a dorky orthodontic job; Britney is number 218919).

Ashley comments that she thinks back-stabbing 119813 should be punished, and the other two agree. What they don't know is that Ashley IS 119813. She secretly stole Kelsey's boyfriend, Carson Whittle, a baseball star, then told him to tell her he met some other girl at a different school. Then, he "dumped" the fake girlfriend and went out with Ashley.

I'm sitting at the table right behind them, with my back to them as they're saying this, and I have this terrible urge to laugh, so I get up and run to the bathroom. They look at me funny whenever they spot me after that.

* * *

Have I ever mentioned how much I hate Gordon Franc? That kid...when he and I were in sixth grade, we liked the same girl, this cute blonde named Clarissa, and she liked me best until that stupid boy came along and asked her what she liked best in a boy. She said that she liked nice boys, and so I made her a really soppy love poem, and she was about to kiss me when in he bursts, knocks me aside, and hands her a ring and a bouquet of flowers.

She had closed her eyes, and, not noticing that I was on the floor seeing stars, kissed who she thought was me and ended up being Gordon. I guess he must've been a really good kisser, or else she liked his expensive ring, because after that she went out with him, not me, and then she moved to Texas, and I never saw her again. It would've been my first kiss, and that guy ruined it. That's why I hate him.

So now I have all this power. I have a widely read blog, and people believe what I say. I did get a few couples together, like Maria D'Amato and Jason Henley. They're cute together, as those girls like to say. So I've done my good deed for society. I think my karma can handle it if I make a little mischief...just a teeny bit, and it'd be on an evil troll, so it serves him right...right?

I do a bit of research first. I need to find out Gordon's relationship status. I get Dan to send his girlfriend Alicia and her friends, Lily and Kayla, to find out if any girls like Gordon. Then I do a bit of digging on Gordon myself. I hear from one of Gordon's jock friends, Tommy, via Nick, that Gordon has a girlfriend, gorgeous, popular Tessa McAdams, who I know for a fact is a blog member, a very active one at that. She's the possessive type. Perfect.

I go online that evening and review my findings--three girls like him, Trisha Clark, Ginny Thompson, and Zoe Evans--then I begin writing.

Post #7

Hey folks! It's been a whole week now! Hooray! Well, today we have a special issue:

131184 and 101198 are officially hooked up because of yours truly! :)

It also looks like 119813 has their dream, though their friend 115125 is possibly not as happy...

Someone was caught kissing in the hall!!! Word is that

715186 (Currently dating 2051913!!!) was caught smooching 241555 before class a few days ago! :O

Shockers and more shockers! Find out the faces behind the numbers for just $1 per number!

~WWG

Ok. It's done. All my fans will now send in the moolah, and I'll let them in on this scandalous secret. So it isn't completely true. Well, it's actually not true at all. Gordon was talking to Zoe in the hall before social studies, but they never kissed or anything. As far as I know.

* * *

Soon the word is out around school. I let some people know who's who, and now everyone's talking about how bad of a boyfriend Gordon is. His popularity has taken a serious hit, and, of course, as soon as Tessa found out, she dumped him with a particularly nasty text message, or so I heard.

Gordon is a player, Tessa miserable, and Zoe has been receiving some dirty remarks lately. The only person who's happy, other than me, is Trisha Clark, because Gordon asked her out as soon as Tessa dumped him. He deserves his reputation, that's all I can say.

Then Dan tells me Kate, as in my friend Kate, is crushing on Nick. And for the first time, the gossip actually involves someone I care about. I have to make a choice. Do I keep my buddy's secret private, or do I post it? On the one hand, it would probably rake in the cash for me and Dan. I have been having to pay Alicia and her friends to keep quiet about who they're asking for, and it's adding up. I need to keep earning money. Also, she and Nick may realize they both like each other, and start going out! But on the other hand, Kate helps me with a lot of stuff, from homework to website design. This would be giving something of hers away.

Eventually, the lure of money and the possibility of seeing

my two friends together becomes too strong. I tell myself that it'll help her and Nick, and that it's a good thing. Then I post.

Post #11

Hello, followers!

Today, there are a few announcements in the gossip department.

141205 likes 181529! How cute!

312026 has a new admirer: looks like 2412210 is officially smitten!

And last but not least, 111206 seems to have an unexpected crush on 14931. Stay tuned for more developments...

Find out who these people are! Just one dollar (and a secret) per name! :)

~WWG

* * *

I walk into school on Monday, feeling pretty darn good about myself. I probably just helped my two buds get together. Hopefully Kate doesn't find out it's me, I think as I walk in the doors.

That's when I realize she already has.

She meets me at the door to school, looking angrier than I've ever seen her, even that time her Algebra 2 teacher got a problem wrong when he was grading their homework, and because he thought she had done it wrong (when it was actually him that was wrong and she was right), gave her a 99 out of 100 on the quiz. This is very, very bad.

"Hello, WWG!" She cries, grabbing me by both shoulders. "Do you know how many texts I got this weekend telling me I liked Nicholas Alder, and congratulations on having my first boyfriend?! I thought it was some stupid popular girl," here she stops to throw a glare at Kelsey and Britney as they walk past, gaping. They broke up with Ashley about the boyfriend thing when they found out it was her who was "that backstabbing 119813."

"But then I went to the post office, and pried until they told me it was Joseph De Luca who had reserved the P.O. box. I thought that he was playing some mean trick on us, but then I heard from Lily Yzinski that you were employing her to ask people who they liked. I was going to tell you to stop, when I get all these messages, and man, was that ever embarrassing! You have humiliated me!!! You ruined my reputation as well as nearly everyone else in the school! Happy now?! Or are you gonna sell this little story, too?"

She's fuming. Her face is red and her eyes livid. I'm starting to fear for my life.

"I-I'm s-s-so sorry..." I stutter, unsure what I should say. "I meant to help you...I mean, I thought--"

"You thought you were going to have a little fun at my expense, and earn some dough in the process, and I would forgive you and it'd all be just peachy. Well you're wrong, buster."

She turns on her heel and stalks away.

I feel positively awful. How can it possibly get any worse? I think, as I trudge towards science class. How wrong can you be?

During science, the P.A. system comes on and crackles a bit before announcing "Vincent De Luca, please report to the principal's office. Vincent De Luca, to the principal's office."

Feeling like I could really use a giant sinkhole right about now, I dash out the door, then slow to a walk down the hall, around this corner then a different one, till I come to Mr. Sylvester's office. I take a big breath, and step inside.

If Kate chewed me out, Mr. Sylvester pulverized me. He harped on "responsibility" and "respect" and "upholding others' honor," and a million other things. Kate must've spilled her guts to the guy. Finally, he told me to remove the blog that very instant, and, if I wanted to continue going to school here next year, I would also make suitable reparations to the people I'd "harmed" with my "damaging blog." I held my tongue on two remarks-- first, I wasn't going to be going here anyway next year; I'd be in ninth grade, and two, I didn't really want to go to school anyway, so he'd actually not be punishing me if he expelled me. I figured that voicing this opinion would probably just make the situation worse.

* * *

In the end, we had to pay back everyone who'd paid me for the blog. Me and Dan both. I never ratted on him, but someone else threw him under the bus for me. Some people actually didn't want their money back, mostly the people who hadn't been "victims" or people who got together with their crushes because of WWG. They were like, "Whatever, keep it." Gordon was really ticked at me, but there were teachers around so he couldn't maim me like he said he wanted to. Tessa was remarkably unaffected by my confession and said she'd hate me forever, except that she'd been getting sick of Gordon anyway, so my blog had given her an excuse to break up with him.

Then there was Zoe. I knew I owed her a really big apology, and it was hard, but she accepted it (though she was super mad and wouldn't forgive me).

Maria D'Amato, who, as I mentioned in post 7, hooked up with her longtime crush Jason Henley, on account of WWG, happily refused the refund, saying "You helped me out. Now I'm helping you out."

* * *

Then, at last, Kate. I ask as we're sitting on the bus. Up front, with the respectable kids, and where the bus driver is the only one listening. "Hey Kate," I venture, hoping I sound casual but repentant, "I really meant it, apologizing, you know, this morning. I did mean to help you. I'm friends with you and Nick and I thought it'd be so cute, if you guys, you know, were going out."

"Vince. There's something you need to learn. Sometimes, even the best intentions do not make a good deed. You sold my supposed secret, and involved the whole freakin' school in what should've been my business only. You destroyed our trust. You're gonna have to work to get it back." She has a point. Hard to argue with that logic.

"I know. But when I get going, I'm intractable!"

"Um... I think you mean, well maybe you do mean intractable. Its definition is 'difficult to manage or govern, unruly, or stubborn.' All those you definitely are. Where did you get that word?" She asks, eyebrows creased, looking genuinely confused. She must not remember.

"I got it from you, remember? On the phone the other day?" She nods, looking like she's starting to recall. "Then I just looked it up, cause I wanted to know what you were calling me."

Kate smiles a little. "Yeah, now I remember. I do believe I was a bit irritated with you then. You were smart not to ask about it."

"I kind of figured as much." Now, for the question that has been burning me up since I heard the words from Dan. "Do you like Nick?"

She laughs, looking happier than I've seen her all day. "You know what, I think it's actually the other way around. Nick has been ogling me lately. He has the IQ of a fruit fly. Maybe not even. There's no way I'd ever even consider going out with him." She chuckles a little.

"Yeah, he is a little slow sometimes. He's nice, though," I wink at her, "And he has huge biceps. Just your kind of guy."

"Don't you be trying to set me up with anyone, mister." She pokes me in the shoulder. It's funny how much taller she is than me. Middle school, I swear. It's so embarrassing for the boys with "short genes," cause all the girls are taller than us for a year or more. The tall boys never seem to have that problem. "I thought you'd learned your lesson."

"I guess." I grin maniacally. "But I'm here if you need me for the spring formal!" She burst out laughing.

"You little...inveigler!" She shoves me as we get off the bus, and walk toward home. I know better than to ask what she means...

The Twilight Time

Julia Di
10th Grade

I.

She sat down with a sad smile, staring out the window. A quiet blue reflection greeted her.

It was during this time, the twilight time, when she fd most of her thinking and remembering.

She smoothed out her wrinkled apron and gave her wizened wrist a little flick. Then she laid back to watch out the window:

The young men walked backwards, tugging their wives along, trying to avoid the historical house in which she perched. The birds flew from the sky down into the trees, . The lights flickered off, and the sun slowly rose back into the sky.

She closed her eyes, hoping the magic would hold:

The leaves fluttered past. The furniture in the room began reshuffling—ivy shrank down and crumbled pieces of mortar sprang up to meet the wall again. The dust disappeared; her curtains fluffed themselves and regained their velvet luster. The door stopped squeaking, the ornate carpets reappeared, and the room changed several shades of color before stopping at a quite respectable light green.

She held this image in her mind, daring not to open her eyes and see. Every night was the same—she held this image in a quiet solitude, waiting and waiting.

II.

"Honey? I'm home!"

He walked in with such tangible vivacity she almost thought she could reach out and touch him.

"Honey? Where are you?" he called again.

She was tempted to answer him, but couldn't bring herself to do it, not yet. Years of waiting and waiting had at least taught her a little bit of patience.

"Honey?"

She held this voice in her mind, daring not to open her eyes and see. The soft tenor of his voice...so magical....And even after all these years, still so crisp and fresh in the locked-away chest of her memories.

"Honey, are you--?"

She knew what would come next. The pained look on his face; the guilty stains of red-iron branded on her hands. The trial would come, the jury won over of course, for she was a true southern aristocrat.

But she hadn't wanted it to end like that.

She wanted him to come closer, to agree, to understand. Of course he didn't, and he later died from grief and sorrow....but, no matter, 'tis only collateral damage in the scheme of things, as she liked to say.

"WHY DID YOU--!?"

This was the part she hated; it was so distorted over time that some of his voice had been modified in the process. The memory grew hazy and black, omitting her darkest moments. She could still replay the scene in her mind, in the way that she wanted the scene to work out, daring not to open her eyes and see. She could control Father Time, and tempt the great Fate.

III.

The twilight time was almost over.

She had held the magic as long as she could, but the memories were slowly fading:

The light green of the room slowly faded to gray. The ornate carpets disappeared; the door regained its little creak; the curtains, damaged by years of sun, returned to ash; the dust reappeared.

She could smell the changes. She could hear the plaster begin to crack again and the ivy shoot back up over the walls. The furniture moved all around her—everything moved except the little wooden stool on which she sat.

The leaves fluttered past.

The sun began to set; the lights flickered on; the birds left their roost; the wives tugged their young husbands home.

Twilight time was almost over.

She was frozen there, staring at the last glimpse of the past. Her blue reflection quietly greeted her.

She reached up to touch her reflection's young, beautiful face. A quivering old hand nearly reached a young, smoothed hand. For a moment, it was almost as if two halves of her had nearly touched, only separated by a thin pane of glass.

The sun had set; the reflection disappeared.

It was over, done, vanished, gone, over. Then, and only then, did she finally weep.

Catori

Dakota Discepolo
9th Grade

Catori was the name my mother and father had given me. They said that when I was born the wind blew hard and the moon was full. They said that my screams filled the valley and scared the dear. I can't imagine why such a name would be given to me. I wasn't special, yet I was blessed to be named Catori. In Hopi language it means spirit, but I wasn't Hopi. It was said that Mother once ran into a Hopi medicine man while I was just an egg, and he muttered but one word, and that was Catori.

When I was younger I was never one to sit still very long unless something held my attention. I would sit and stare at the horses, walk in the creek, and lure animals as near as I possibly could. No matter what I did, there was one place I couldn't help but go to every day.

At the base of the mighty river was a willow. The tree was tall and strong. I would wrap my arms around it every day and see how much my arms would grow. I fantasized that one day my arms would be long enough to go around the whole thing, but that was impossible. I was four when mother and I first came to the tree. I can remember her voice that day. What she said has stayed with me my whole life.

"Trees are the most special creatures of all. They have roots that go deep into the world of the dark, they have their bodies that stay in this world, and they have their high branches that greet the sun and divine with their entire splendor."

Mother's voice was smooth and happy that day. That was before the time of great worry came upon us. It was when the women still went out and picked berries without fear. It hasn't been like that for a very long time, but surely I am getting ahead of my-self.

I returned to the Willow every day thereafter. It isn't surprising that it started to talk to me, I had inherited the endless curiosities my tribe was known for, and the tree couldn't help but answer to them. I remember my first question it answered, it was a year after mother and I had come upon the tree, and I was already maturing quickly.

"Mother said trees talk… I wonder why I cannot hear them…" Strangely I had said this out loud. I found it easier to sort my thoughts when I gave them to the wind to carry.

"You would hear them if you listened, Catori." The voice shocked me at first. I sat up from my laying position and looked all around. There was nobody.

"Who said that?" I wanted to hear the voice again.

"My name is not such for your ears to understand but I am the Willow. You may call me that." The Willow's voice was thunderous and strong, nothing like human voices; it sounded like a thousand voices made into one, always changing, always different.

Willow didn't talk to me often, but I seemed to be more aware of her presence after our first short conversation. When she did talk it was short and sometimes she left me wondering and questioning, but in the end what she said always made sense even if it took a while.

I was older when she began to talk to me at length. We would discuss the separation of tribes and causes. We had heard a few accounts of white men, but none seemed real to me. She always warned me that she could feel it in her roots and see it in her leaves that the stories were true, but I didn't want to believe her. She seemed to understand. Hearing of such men was like hearing of monsters. Men who carried sticks that shot explosions, and who wore clothes made of plants, not animals. They were everything we knew to be impossible.

We usually kept our conversations to more lively thoughts. She seemed to sway her leaves when she laughed, usually finding my questions amusing. She had once scolded me for climbing her when I was younger without asking, but she wasn't mad, she was entertained.

"A tree's limbs are sacred, that is why you must ask to climb them. We feel, but not to the extent that you do. Taking care is more out of respect than anything else. Trust me sapling, the worst enemy to have is a tree. They are the givers of life and food, and when you find yourself lost, they can either help you or deny you. " Her lessons always stuck to me. Every day thereafter I asked before climbing, and she always gave me permission and complimented me on my manners. It seemed though that her l essons weren't only those of tree etiquette but also worked at home.

It was a fall evening when I lay on her thick branch and thought of questions for her. She didn't always answer them. Some days, it seemed like she wasn't there at all. For the first time, she had spoken without me asking.

"Tomorrow is the celebration of your birth," she said joyfully.

"Yes, the fourteenth one."

"Are you not happy?"

"I am, but rumors of white men scare me."

"Ahh… I see your conflict…" I sighed and hung over her branch with my head dangling.

"Willow?"

"Yes, Sapling?"

"Are they coming?"

"Sapling. Tomorrow, after the morning celebration, come

see me. Tell no one of your whereabouts."

"Why?" My question went unanswered. I couldn't help but hear a twinge of worry in the Willow's voice, but her voice was always changing. I stayed there that day until late in the evening listening, to everything around me. Then I once again wrapped my arms around the Willow to find they were too short to come even near each other. I walked back to the tribe.

That night the wolves did not howl as they once did, and I could see the fear in many faces. I dragged my feet to my tent where my mother was waiting for me.

"Tomorrow you come of age."

"Yes, Mother."

"I am so proud, but may I ask where you go every day from day till night?"

"Mother…"

"I swear I shall not tell anyone. Tell me."

"I go to the willow."

"Does she speak to you?"

"Who?"

"The willow."

"Sometimes. Why do you ask?"

"Just curiosity forcing my tongue. Goodnight."

"Goodnight." It was actually not a good night. I found myself staring thoughtlessly into the fire until its embers turned to black nothingness. By then even the sun was starting to peak above the horizon.

I heard the thundering of hooves first. I thought the herd was moving, but they weren't. The herd was small compared to the herds of other tribes, and I could often hear and point out the different beats of different horses. These horses were different. I jumped up from my bed and readied myself in my clothes. When I ran outside the hoof beats had ceased, but I still worried. I couldn't have been the only one who heard them.

I looked around and soon found myself in a warm embrace from my parents. Food was set out. The morning celebration took my thoughts away from the disturbing event that had woken me from my restless relaxation. I was soon being greeted and congratulated by family. The morning celebration took a few hours; it should have lasted much longer, though.

It was only late morning when I heard the first shot. Our warriors rushed past, but I was dumbstruck still. Mother screeched as my cousin's limp body fell to the ground with a hole in his chest. Arrows flew through the air as I saw the incoming horses.

"Run, Catori!" I heard my mother scream. It was then that I came alive as a large white beast came rushing at me with a long tube pointed at my head. I ran as quickly as I could. Weaving through the trees, I could hear the horse's hooves thundering behind me, and I was running out of breath. Sharp branches tore at my leggings as I concentrated all my strength in continuing forward. It seemed like forever, but it was only a few minutes before I heard a name being called, and the horse came to a stop before swiveling and returning in the direction of the tribe.

"Little rat will end up dead any ways," I heard the rider mumble. I would much rather be a rat then to be a murderer. I wanted to yell it at him. What use is it? He can't understand me. No white man understands. I found that my intuition and instinct brought me very close to Willow. I ran to her and asked for permission to climb.

"Yes! Go and stay quiet. White men are not known to let their prey go. They can go a hundred years and not forgive or forget." I quickly climbed high into her branches, and began to sob. The full blow of what had happened finally hit me. I wondered what was going on, if my family were alive, and when if ever I would be able to go back. I sunk into such despair that I found not even the will to move my arms.

"Catori. Listen to me. I could not forewarn you of the attack because I am not to interfere. It is the very law of our kind, but I wanted you to be safe. The raid is still going on, but as long as you are here you are safe." I didn't argue or ask any more questions. I was scared even more bad news would come of it. "Don't worry, Sapling. All will be well."

It took hours for the screams and gunshots from the village to cease. I knew that the warriors of my tribe would never stop fighting, even when there was no chance, they would continue. I almost hated them for their martyrdom, knowing that as the last one died it would be the end of my tribe, the end of my home. As the last one did finally cease, I would be alone. I ended up falling asleep, my arms wrapped around the willow's branch. I just wanted to be numb to the world, just for the moment.

When I woke up I found myself to be even more upset than before. The willow had an empty feeling, a feeling that was common with her, as if all language or thought had left her and she was just an object. I hated it. How can she be so quiet at a time like this? I hopped down from her branches to find the moon high in the sky. I saw small billows of smoke erupting.

"You may go now. If you must see that your home is gone to believe it, then see it, but be warned, it will only bring you great sorrow." The Willow's voice returned out of nowhere, but I acknowledged it and continued forward to the where my home once was.

When I arrived I saw destruction. I saw Sadness. I saw monstrosity. I had heard of wars amongst brothers, but nothing in the stories came close to this extent. Familiar faces were piled, lifeless, one on top of the other. The horses. Gone. My family. Dead. Everything I had ever known was gone, everything but the willow. I reached down and retrieved a small wooden bowl. It was a common item among our people, something I never thought I would cherish. I rummaged through and found a bag, mine, from where the burnt ruins of my tent stayed.

I was about to leave, tears stinging my ash gray face, when I saw my mother's necklace on a tree that I had planted. A beaded symbol, at the base of the tree was my father's dagger. I looked around with the sudden hope that maybe out of all our people they, too, survived. A hundred yards over, there they were, dead, together. When I saw their faces I quickly ran back to the tree, taking the last momentos of my past, ripping branches out of my way, the pain fueling me.

When I arrived at the Willow, she was waiting, full of life. It was late in the night. "Will you not eat, Sapling? Fear and sadness will not be enough to live on. You are not a rat." I mumbled a response to the familiar phrase and reached into my medicine bag

,pulling the herbs and berries, munching on them.

Images of what I saw flashed through my mind, and I found that it was more relaxing to observe the nature of the night rather than close my eyes. Finally, out of all the questions that I feared to ask, I had one that I needed to know.

"Did you see it, Willow?"

"See what, Sapling?"

"The death of my parents."

"As I have said before, I see all." I sniffled, momentarily glad that I was not a tree and did not have to see such sadness. Willow spoke again.

"When you are as old as I, such sadness is common, but none have come so close to me. It is true that today is sad, and I shall mourn for a hundred years to come, but with great sadness comes great happiness. I have seen births of children who grow to be wonderful. I have heard the sweet song of lovers and their dance. The world is in balance. Peace. War. Happiness. Sadness. All is as it shall be." Her words were momentarily comforting, until again questions came to bother me.

"Why did they leave those things at the tree?" I needed to know.

"When the man returned so quickly without your head, they knew that you were alive. Your mother quickly grabbed your father, despite his warrior status, and pulled out his dagger. Only quickly explaining your survival, she put the stuff on the tree and ran as far away as she could before she was shot. Your father went to help her, but it was of no use." I winced as tears rolled down my cheeks. I cried myself to sleep.

When I woke the next morning I stayed still for hours. When I grew too hungry I went out picked roots and berries ate them, drank from the river, then returned and slept. I slept for many hours, letting my nightmares take their toll and grieve for my home. Willow didn't speak; she left me to deal with my loss the best I could. I refused to ask anything anymore. I spent weeks like this, dirty and hungry, but I did not care.

After a month I was found by passing brothers. They dressed differently from our warriors. Their paint was more severe.

Their weapons were sharper. The man who found me was startled, for I slept opposite of the river many follow, and the Willow hid my body. He had come around the tree to relax for a moment when he stumbled upon me, wound up tight and sleeping. Scared, I pulled the dagger as I woke up. I had prepared myself for the return of white men. Suddenly as my muscles screamed from the rude awakening, I saw that he was not white, but of copper skin; like me.

"What is your name, little one?"

"C-C-Catori."

"What has happened? Word of fighting came to us long ago, but very far East from here. We wanted to stop and stay with our brothers before battle." I couldn't help but burst into tears and turn my face into Willow's bark. The man could see I was upset. He promised me he would be right back, but I wished he would just leave. I could hear him giving orders to stop the march and stay here for the night. He soon returned to my side offering me food and new clothes. I was leery of accepting, but I did. He sat with me, talking of his home, and how happy they were to the west, where no white man has come. How it had taken them many weeks to come this far. He talked of other tribes farther west and how one of them had sent a medicine man to travel with them. I listened but did not speak.

"Catori, can you tell me what happened?"

"White men." I found that tears had finally left me and I stood stern faced, no emotions left to be felt. I hugged my knees as flashes of dead faces returned to my mind. I just wanted to go back to sleep. The man sat with me all through the day, talking to me calmly. He was very kind, and eventually he persuaded me to eat and clean up. It felt good being clean again. I washed up using the river, though it was cold. The man braided my hair and told me of his own sisters.

"How old are you?" he asked as he tied a string around the end of the braid.

"Old enough." He raised an eyebrow at me but did not ask again. I felt like my day of birth was forever cursed; just talking of my age would bring another disaster.

"Ahh, I see. Well, I wanted to know, are you willing to come with us? We would gladly offer you a home. Can you cook?"

"I have learned, but I cannot leave my friend."

"There are more of you?"

"No."

"Then who is your friend?" I looked up into the willow's canopy as if waiting for her to talk, but she just swayed in the breezeless evening.

"May I be alone for a few minutes?" The man was hesitant to leave, but he did. I asked for permission to climb.

"Yes, Catori."

"Willow?"

"Yes, Sapling?"

"I don't want to leave you."

"But you must. A life of solitude is a tree's life, not a woman's."

"But I will miss you."

"And I will miss you, Sapling, but it is time for you to continue. You are not alone.Jjust because my roots are planted deep, I can go to many places. I will always be with you, great Tree Talker."

"Tree Talker?" She was amused. I sat there with her for a while, until the light came to an end, and my eyes grew tired. "Willow?" I wanted to ask one more question.

"Yes, Tree Talker?"

"You will still talk to me, right? When I have questions…"

"Catori, you talk to me now as simply as you would your humans. When you are far, you need to try harder. Remember my voice and teachings, and ask me your questions. It may take longer for me to answer, but I will. I will always have an eye over you." I wrapped my arms around her branch one last time before jumping to the ground.

To my surprise an old man was waiting for me on the ground. He was laughing. I sat beside him waiting for the elder to explain what it was that seemed so ridiculous.

"Ahh, I shall, eldest, you must not worry; the tree talker will be safe amongst us. Thank you." He said all this while looking up into Willow's darkening canopy.

"Excuse me, but who were you talking to?" I asked. He smiled at me.

"Ah, she hasn't told you, Catori. Come with me. We have a lot of talking to do." He got up using his walking stick. Besides his old age he still looked strong and healthy. He wore a medicine bag around his neck and was quite tall. He hobbled out of the canopy toward the others. I was about to follow when I turned around and wrapped my arms around Willow.

At first it felt normal, the rough bark against my skin. Slowly, I started to feel it shift. The bark changed into softness, almost like human skin but not quite. It felt more like a blanket of endless comfort wrapped around me. I heard Willow's voice humming and my feet left the ground. And for the first time in a long time, I felt happy.

"I love you."

"I love you too, Catori, the tree talker of the Chabua tribe." Then I was safely put back on the ground and greeted once again with her cold dark bark. I was hesitant to pull away, but when I did, I wasn't sorry. I had been hugged by a tree spirit, and that memory could last me five life times of silence.

When I turned around I found myself being watched by the old man. I smiled at him as he held out his hand to me.

"You are loved, Catori. I warned your mother of your gift and how you would be loved for it."

"You are Hopi?"

"Yes, I am, I met your mother many years ago and told her of her egg." I looked up at the old man. He had known all these years that he would come to find me again.

"So where do I go now?"

"You shall see, Tree Talker. The unexpected lies ahead, but the trees will forever talk, and you will forever listen."

Discovering My Fear

Julia Dobel
7th Grade

"I'm cleaning the pool," I sung into the receiver.

"And that's a fun task?" Emma responded. I pulled together my patience and placed the phone on the ledge of the pool, putting it on speaker. I handled the net carefully, scooping out bugs and leaves from the water. I spot a squirming fly and dip the net in to rescue it from its death.

"Yes!" I screeched with a laugh. "It's fun, and besides, the more cleaner it is, the sooner it'll be open."

"Okay," Emma laughed. "Truth or dare?"

"Um, truth," I decided.

"Truth it is. Is it true you're scared of spiders?"

"Uh, NO!" I shouted. "I'm not scared of anything."

"Oh the brave one you are, huh? Do it to me now."

"Truth or dare?" I asked in the creepiest voice I could do.

Emma giggled. "Dare," She says in an equally creepy voice.

"Melanie!" My mom's voice rung. I sighed.

"Hold on Em," I called to the phone and then yelled to my mom, "What?"

Her and Shelby emerged from the house. My mom had her apron on, and Shelby was squirming, moaning.

"Can you hold her? She's so cranky and I can't do anything with her in my arms." She panted. I sighed again.

"But I'm talking to Emma right now," I grumbled.

"Melanie, if you want to eat tonight, let me cook and hold your sister." I stomped up the steps and grabbed her from my mom. Automatically, Shelby screeched in my ear and thrust her arms and legs. I clenched my fist to control my anger.

"Stop the attitude." My mom ordered. I closed my eyes and took a deep breath. Calm, I thought. Be calm.

"Got to go," I hissed into the phone and clicked it off.

"Eat the milk," I said through grinded teeth. I was holding her in my arms, and she was pushing away the bottle. Instinctively,

I felt her forehead and I softened. The baby girl is still sick, her fever never went away, and it's warmer than I remember…much warmer.

"Mom!" I called. She rushed in.

"What? What's wrong?" She says.

"Her forehead is really warm. I think you should take her temperature." Fear and worry danced across her face as she jogged to the sofa and sat down. I passed Shelby into her arms. Glancing at my backpack near the hanger, I remembered I had homework, still undone, and I inched away from the living room and the sofa. I still heard Shelby crying upstairs. About ten minutes later, I made out my dad's voice. I put down my science book, and crawled out into the hallway and down a few steps to hear what he was saying to my mom.

"…doctor…..so sick….yes?"

"…you sure..... Melanie?"

I overheard those tiny snippets of convo that I pieced together to form a conclusion. They were planning on going to the doctor soon because Shelby was so sick. I raced back to my room as soon as I heard footsteps. I threw my book open, sprawled some papers and poised my pen over a blank sheet of paper.

"Mel?' My dad asked.

"Yeah? And you can come in, you know." He opened the door and walked in.

"Listen, Shelby's fever is 104 degrees. It's been like this for a long time, and we have decided to go to the doctor really soon today. Can we trust you to stay home for an hour alone?"

"That high!?" I exclaimed. That was so unexpected. 104?! I realized I was gaping and retuned to reality.

"Sure," I told him. "I'm finishing up my homework."

"Great. Be careful. Don't open the door to anyone, don't answer the phone to unknown numbers, and most importantly, stay inconspicuous. We won't be gone long."

"Alright, Dad, I got it, usual plan. And I hope everything goes well with Shelby. I love her."

"I know you do. Okay, I think your mother should be ready to go in a minute or so, so I'll be back later. Call me if you need."

"Alright Dad, bye," I said as he exited.

I slid away from my desk and lay on my bed. I stared at the ceiling. Shelby is my baby sister. I love her so much. Goodness, I still remember the day she was born. We slept over at grandma's house, and I remember. I remember that feeling when I got the text from my dad, and there on that screen, was a picture of her. She was so precious. Hard to believe it's almost been a year. Now I'm thirteen years old. Last year I was twelve. I guess you can figure out that we have a twelve year age difference. But gosh, when I first met her was so incredible. It was the sweetest dream, and it didn't feel like reality at all. We drove to the hospital, and we saw my mom, and she was in the nursery, on the other side of glass. They were washing her up, or whatever, and it was unbelievable. I never experienced anything like that before. I cannot express the fact that something new and incredible moved into my life and it didn't feel real.

Shelby is not walking yet, at 11 months. She should though, because I did at that age. She still places her feet a bit awkwardly, but every day she improves and it's obvious. I love her so much, even though sometimes she annoys me to death! But her giggle, and the way she looks up to me. It's so amazing being a big sister. I don't know how being the youngest is the best. Emma is the youngest of three. Me? No. I love being the oldest. Being that example for the younger sibling, and taking care of them. I love walking out of school every day and walking into the parking lot, and seeing that gorgeous little face in the front seat of our Honda with my mom. It makes my day. When I'm fixed on reading or writing, or whatever, I catch her looking at me, and she always glances away, but she's so smart because she observes me. Maybe she's physically behind, but she can clap, say some short and not understandable words, almost walk, giggle when I giggle, throw her hands in the air when we ask how big she is, pat me when I say my name, and pats herself when I say her name, and so much more. I've invested so much love in a baby girl.

RING. RING. RING.

"Hello?"

"Melanie, you there? Melanie?"

"Dad, I'm here. What's wrong?"

"I need you to get ready and come outside when we honk the horn."

"W-why?" I stammered. I endured a momentary silence.

"Baby, uh, Shelby, listen, the doctor doesn't know why Shelby has that high fever…so they said we should go to the hospital. And we've decided to do so. The fever still hasn't gone away." My heart stopped, and I suddenly felt light headed. Was this a nightmare? I felt so woozy…

"Mel?!"

"I'm here," I managed.

"Get ready, okay?"

"Alright," I whispered.

Oh. My. Goodness. I pulled my jean jacket off the hanger and tied it around my waist. I felt frozen and disabled. It took a bit for that to sink in. My hand wobbled as I turned off the TV. I realized how terrified I was becoming. When I heard the honk, I managed out the front door somehow. Terrified, I got into the car and looked at my sister. Shelby had red blotches on her face from the crying which was so muffled and exhausted. I felt so helpless. I put my hand to her face and started singing. Tears were fighting to come out, but I suppressed them because I didn't want to cry. Now wasn't the right time.

Shelby fell asleep, but my mind didn't. I didn't want her to die, and that thought loomed around my head like a phantom. I regret ever being ungrateful for her, and all the things I've ever done to hurt her, if I did. I love her with all my heart. I don't want her to die. I would die too because I learned to depend on her for happiness and she was more than a sister to me. But a little girl that loved me back and inspired me. I was waiting for her arrival so long and curiously. I would sacrifice myself for her. And what if she had cancer? I wouldn't ever leave her side, but what would this baby have done to deserve this? What if her crying and fever revealed that she had cancer? I was never as scared as I was then, I was scared for her. I wanted to cry, but it would have made the moment sadder.

It was such a long ride, and I held my sister's hand as we

parked and exited the vehicle. I remember leaving the hospital on June 5th, her first birthday. Leaving the car and seeing her not crying in a sickly manner made my heart float. I suddenly felt better and relieved from my misery.

Shelby was snoozing soundly, which I could tell relieved my parents as well. The emergency room was quiet; I didn't expect that. My mom set down the carrier with Shelby on the chairs and she and dad went to the lady at the desk. I pulled a blanket from mom's purse and wrapped it around Shelby's legs. I sat back and listened as my parents talked to the lady at the desk. A few minutes later, the lady summoned a doctor. He was a tall man with round glasses. He told us to bring Shelby and follow him. From the chairs in the emergency room, I saw them take her into the room. That's when I noticed a man sitting five chairs down from me, as stiff as a board. He stared ahead, not evening flinching at the fact that I was staring at him. Wait, what am I doing? That's rude. I turned away. My phone vibrated in my pocket. I slid it out. I should have expected something from Emma. I opened the message.

Hey Mel, wuz up? Y did u hang up on me? I texted back, *an emergency. I will IM u later.* Soon after, she texted me saying, *kk., I might call u if I get too anxious.*

I took a deep breath and sped to the room Shelby was in. Gosh, the doctor had to wake her up. Agitated cries filled the room. My mom was putting her into a white gown. The doctor had a stethoscope on, ready to hear my sister's heartbeat.

I realized something while I was standing there. Despite everything, how much my life has changed, Shelby is that one puzzle piece that I can't live without. No matter what happens, I will always love her. Being in the car and thinking about all those horrendous possibilities terrified me. And my head swiveled to not too long ago, when I was on the phone with Emma. I lied to her. I lied about being not scared of anything. I am scared for my baby sister, and of anything happening to her. Through everything I will endure that I will consider frightening, I will remember what being scared really means.

True fear.

My fear.

A Thousand Words

Megan Ellenberger
9th Grade

"Do you think your brakes are good enough for the ride to Lime Kiln?" Eric asked, his brown eyes observing my bicycle doubtfully. "You know you said you were going to get them fixed soon after school ended." I had known Eric since I was born and had always lived next door to him. However, this was the first summer I'd be spending alone with him. I was used to my best friend nagging me instead of Eric.

"I'm sure if they were fine during school, they'll last one more day, all right? We don't have time to fix them this morning." He shrugged, but still looked a little concerned.

Eric's concern didn't last long. Soon we were zooming over the country roads to the park, with either trees or country scenes on both sides of us. We passed the Lavender Farm and inhaled the sweet and tangy smell of lavender.

"This is the life!" I shouted to him, and he grinned in agreement. The scenery on San Juan Island was enough so you could never get a full dose of it.

We struggled to ride up a large hill, since for the past ten months we hadn't ridden long distance or hills, but we did finally reach the top, even though I was breathing heavily – if Eric was, he was disguising it awfully well.

"Now to go down!" He grinned and started down, not waiting for me to follow.

"Thanks a lot, Eric!" I called after him. I knew I couldn't catch up; I did not enjoy going downhill on a bike speeding almost as fast as a car. I tended to use my brakes every now and then on the way down, due to a bike accident going down a hill when I was younger that resulted in a broken wrist and many bruises.

Taking a deep breath, I started down after Eric, keeping my feet still and just coasting. Occasionally I squeezed my hand brakes, but – I kept going faster and faster no matter how tightly I squeezed them. I was getting to the end of the hill where there was a turn, and I had to slow down.

"Oh no. Please, God, help me!" I frantically clutched my brakes but I wasn't slowing down. If I was still going this fast when I hit the curve, I could not turn correctly and fly off the road or skid on the loose gravel and twigs. "Eric, do something, my brakes aren't working!" I yelled down to him. His facial expression turned from neutral to immediate horror. Then it grew set and determined, and I dearly hoped that meant he had a plan. I was not too into the idea of trying to jump off or just hope everything turned out ok, as both were dangerous.

As I grew closer at a very alarming rate, Eric got closer to where my bike was headed. "Just steer straight on and don't hold too tight!" he yelled. As I was passing him, I saw his arms reach out and I felt him grab under my arms and haul up. My bike clattered to the ground. Eric holding onto my shoulders was the only way I managed to shakily stand.

"They'll last one more day, huh, Jo?" he was attempting humor, but his voice was as unsteady as I felt.

"Remind me never to make light of your opinion or your strong arms ever again," I answered.

Eric smiled and led me to the side of the road and I sat down as he picked my bike up and brought it over. "You sure you're ok? Here, drink some water," he said, handing me my water bottle from the holder on my bike.

"Yeah, thanks to you," I said, taking slow sips of water and feeling myself gradually calming down. "Just see what Nate and Nat are missing out on this summer already!" I joked, referring to our twin best friends who were visiting the east coast.

"You mean you almost getting killed or seriously wounded?" he answered wryly. "Next time you want action, please let me know. You practically gave me a heart attack!"

"Well, your heart may have stopped, but your brain worked just fine." I smiled.

"Yes, well, thank the Lord for that."

We sat on the side of the road as I got out my cell phone and dialed home. My parents had thought that it would be good for me to have a way to contact them in an emergency (like the brakes on my bike failing), since I was always going all over the island. When my mom answered, I told her that my brakes failed, without divulging details that would freak her out.

"Jocelyn, you should have gotten those brakes fixed," she scolded, "but I suppose I can pick you up when you're finished at the park."

"Thanks, Mom." I stood up and put my phone back in my pocket and said to Eric, "Looks like we have some walking to do."

"We? I still have a bike, you know. Do you remember how to ride on handlebars?"

"You're kidding, right?" His grin told me he was totally serious. I sighed. "All right, but be careful."

He sat on his bike to steady it while I climbed onto the handlebars and held on tight.

When we arrived at the park a few miles later, I gratefully scrambled off of Eric's handlebars and onto firm ground, feeling a bit sore from earlier events. It was a little early for lunch yet, and the sun was still hiding behind clouds. The evergreen and Madrona trees welcomed us; the latter's red skin peeling off of them like old paint. We followed the short trail until we came to the lighthouse, which was squarer and more squat than most. The trim on its white body was the same color as the ocean below it.

"How about climbing around on the rocks until lunch time?" Eric suggested, watching a couple of tourists go up to the lighthouse and take numerous pictures.

For a couple of hours we climbed around on the rocks, looking in the tidal pools for little creatures and stabbing out hands on the jagged edged rocks. We had climbed over them so many times, though, we didn't have to worry about falling – we were experienced.

When we decided we were hungry, we found the flattest rock that was furthest from the tourists and hidden by trees. We sat staring out to the west, across the ocean where the fog was slowly starting to lift and the sky beginning to clear. I knew that on the other side of all that water was Canada.

"All right, let's see what my mom packed us for lunch," Eric said, smacking his lips in anticipation.

"Whatever it is, it's good. Your mom is a fabulous cook,"

I answered, using my mini-bottle of hand sanitizer to be sure no germs lingered. "Here, use some of this before you touch everything up."

"Yes, Mother," he said.

"Eric."

"Sorry." I started pulling out items, and just as I predicted, there was a delicious variety of picnic food, ending with chocolate chip peanut butter oatmeal cookies. We started eating and I gazed out to sea, enjoying the cool breeze. I caught Eric watching me gaze.

"What?"

"Jo, why do you seem so…distracted today? It isn't like you to be so careless about your brakes, especially considering how much you rely on them going downhill. C'mon, what's up?"

"It's five years today that Jason's been gone," I said quietly.

Eric reached for my hand and squeezed it. "I'm sorry," he said. "I should have remembered."

Jason was my older brother by eight years. I looked just like him, and people joked we were twins born eight years apart. And we communicated as well as twins do – we were best friends, even though he could be a little overprotective. Jason and I were always playing together, or hanging out – even when he was a popular senior in high school he didn't abandon me or shoo me away. Everyone else esteemed him too highly to tease him about it, and I was never labeled a pesky little sister. In our neighborhood it was always me, Eric, Nate, Natalie, Eric's older brother Stuart, and Jason.

But five years ago, his second day as a high school graduate, Jason was driving home from a day in Roche Harbor when his car swerved out of control and into a girl on a bicycle in the other lane. When the ambulance came, she was unable to move her legs and they rushed her to the hospital. Jason was questioned briefly and allowed to go home while they finished up investigating what happened, even though Jason told them. They also kept his car.

When I woke up the next morning, he had left me a note on my dresser.

Dear Jo,

When you are reading this I'll already be gone. I'm leaving the island and I'm not sure when I'll be back. I didn't intentionally hit that girl; my tire blew out and I couldn't control the car. I don't know if they believe me and I'm scared, plus I feel terrible and I couldn't face her or her family right now, especially if she never walks again. I love you and Mom and Dad and I'm sorry I have to leave.

Love,

Jason

That very day the police found all the evidence needed to prove that Jason was telling the whole truth and his tire did blow – there were nails on the road and holes in his tire. He was not in any trouble. The family wasn't suing, because the girl was up and walking in no time. But we couldn't tell Jason, because he didn't leave any way to contact him or tell us where he was going. He never came back.

"You miss him a lot, don't you?"

I nodded. "I don't understand, Eric. We spent over a year trying to find him – he should've checked the papers to know he wasn't in trouble, he should've come back…" I felt tears coming and I hated them. I had cried enough about Jason – it wasn't bringing him back. I blinked hard. "Doesn't he love us anymore? Doesn't he love me anymore?"

"I know he does, Jo, he always did. You two were so close for being eight years apart. I'm sure he'll come home soon; maybe he's going through college and plans to come home and surprise you all with a big degree or something. He was always smart; he could do that."

"But what about the papers he'd need for all his applications and things?" I argued, glaring at my cookie.

Eric shrugged. "Didn't he take any of that stuff with him? Jason was always pretty thorough."

"Maybe he did. I never thought about asking my parents that, and they never mentioned anything about it." I finished packing away the lunch leftovers, Eric stopping me long enough to grab one more cookie, and we dropped the lunchbox off at our bikes. Then we headed down to Deadman's Bay, one of my many favorite locations on the island. Even there made me think of Jason.

We crossed the pebble beach, lined with blanched driftwood, and climbed to the other side of a cluster of rocks and watched the little crabs crawling around in the tidal pools.

"You have your camera with you?"

I nodded. "It's almost out of batteries, though. Why?"

"I just thought we'd take a picture of us and send a copy to our friends out east to show them what they're missing."

I laughed. "You're feeling mean today, aren't you? Here, you take it." I handed him my camera. "Better hurry before the battery totally dies. I forgot to get new ones before we left."

"All right, here goes. Lean in closer so I'll have a better chance of getting us both in the picture – smile!" The shutter opened and closed. "Maybe I'd better take a couple more and then we'll check them later, after you put fresh batteries in." That accomplished, we sat in the sun and watched the waves pounding incessantly.

On Monday afternoon at two o'clock I was ending my work day of taking orders for Friday's Crab House and Eric joined the throngs of busy tourists.

"Aren't you soon done, Jo?" Eric's lean face was tanned and shining from sweat.

"Soon. Been doing yards today?"

Eric grinned, running his hand through his sun-bleached hair and making it stand up in angry spikes. "How'd you guess? Look, how about lunch? It's on me. We can take it to the park to eat, if you want."

"Sure. I just have to let my boss know I'm leaving." Fifteen minutes later we were eating a late lunch of hamburgers at the small park overlooking the harbor. The fog had lifted a few hours ago and the sun made the aqua liquid sparkle. The numerous piers jutting out from the island looked like copious arms and legs with the small docks protruding off of them like fingers and toes. Tied along side of them, rocking on the water, were the usual assortment of boats. This was the life I was used to, the beautiful scenes of San Juan Island, Washington. The few times I went to the mainland, it bored me.

Eric interrupted my thoughts by swiping his fingers across my cheek. "Your napkin missed a splotch of Ketchup," he said when I looked at him in almost angry surprise.

"Oh. Thanks," I said. Eric, the last of his second hamburger stuffed hastily into his mouth, lay back against the warm grass.

"Busy day?" I asked, swallowing the last of my lunch.

"Yeah, lots of mowing and trimming. You?"

"Lots of tourists!"

Eric glanced over at me. "You still have your camera with you?"

"Yeah, I planned on going on a picture-taking outing after work." I relaxed on the grass beside him.

"And I guess I interrupted your plans. Where were you headed?"

"Oh, I thought I'd take some pictures of town today for my San Juan Island wall gallery in my room."

"Man, you really do want to be a photographer! I didn't know you have a wall full of pictures."

"Two walls, actually," I laughed. "You want to come with me, or do you have to go back to work?"

"Nah, I finished all my work this morning. Let's go." We dumped our trash into the waste can along the park trail and headed for the main street of town. "I guess you finally put new batteries in that thing?"

"Yeah, but I didn't think to look at the pictures we took on Saturday. I'll put them all on the computer at once when I get home – then you can stay and see which one turned out the best." We passed many tourists and many locals, not to mention the dozens of dogs whose owners always walked them around town.

A large group was walking toward us on the sidewalk, and Eric and I walked single file on the outside of the walk so there would be room for them. Before I even noticed what was happening, I saw a green blur as someone whisked by me, tearing my camera off of my shoulder and nearly knocking me over.

"Eric! Someone stole my camera!"

He had grabbed my arms to steady me and he kept them there as he asked, "What?"

"Someone stole it! As in, took it right off my shoulder!" I was very upset. That camera was a quality kind that I saved up a lot of money to buy. And now it was gone because some inconsiderate bozo.

"C'mon, we're going to the police to report this." Eric tugged on my arm and pulled me through the slightly bewildered crowd. After reporting all that I knew, we left the police station and headed for home.

"I still don't know why we had to report that. They practically rolled their eyes at me when all I could tell them I remember seeing was a flash of green," I complained.

"Because, they just might be able to help, and you need your camera back because you are going to be a professional some day and you worked hard to save up for it." Eric spoke soothingly, and I realized what a grouch I was being and wondered how he could be so patient with me.

"Sorry. You're right; I'm just being a grouch."

"And you have plenty of reason to be one. See you tomorrow, Jo." Eric patted my shoulder before he turned up his driveway, and I headed for mine.

I woke up still feeling downcast, with a lump in my stomach. My camera was gone. I might never see it again. I subconsciously stared at my walls of pictures, my life before my eyes. Pictures of the family boating, Jason and I climbing the rocks, all of us neighbor kids hanging out, a lazily blinking Popeye with her little harbor seal pup by her side, and the sun setting over the Madrona trees, making everything a fiery red-orange. Living anywhere else would be missing out on life. I fingered the frame of Jason's senior picture. Why wouldn't he come back?

Knowing Eric and I would be hanging out for the day, I thundered downstairs and threw open the front door and stopped. My camera was sitting in front of me with a brand new case beside it. I turned it on automatically and flipped through the picture review. All of my pictures were there except for the ones of me and Eric out on the rocks.

I pounded on the Jacobsons' front door. Eric opened it, looking barely awake. "I'm not ready yet, Jo, I just got up."

"No kidding. Eric, look what was on my porch this morning."

"Your camera! Jo, that's great. Can I go eat breakfast now?"

"You're such a guy," I admonished him. "My camera's fine, whoever it was even bought a new case to replace the one that he tore. All of my pictures are still here...except for the ones you took of us out on the rocks. They're gone."

Suddenly Eric looked awake. "Gone? Why would someone do that?"

"I've been asking myself that, too. It's not like we witnessed a crime or anything."

"You guys planning a big hold up or something? What's the racket all about, Jo?" Stuart, Eric's older brother by two years, came up to the doorway, looking as disheveled as Eric. "Morning, Stuart. We're trying to figure out why someone would steal my camera and delete a couple of pictures, then buy me a new case and leave everything on my front porch. Any ideas?"

"Nope, I just want to go back to sleep. Have a nice day," he said, hastily retreating up the stairs.

"Way to be helpful," Eric said, shaking his head. "Did you eat yet?" When I shook my head no, he invited me in for breakfast. "Since it looks like I'm officially awake, I might as well have some company for feeding time." Once in his kitchen, I said hello to his mom and ate some toast and yogurt while Eric stuffed his face.

Over breakfast, we decided to go kayaking; we were pretty skilled in ocean kayaking and had permission to go as long as we stayed together. Eric's mom offered to drive us to our destination.

Down at the docks of historic Roche Harbor, among the swarms of tourists and citizens, we found a mostly unused dock and I lowered my kayak down on one side; Eric lowered his on the other. As I was straightening up, a tourist bumped into me, making me lose my balance, and I would have fallen in except for a hand that grabbed my arm and pulled me back up. The lady who had bumped into me apologized profusely.

"Oh, dear, I'm so sorry! You almost got all wet on this frigid morning!" Oh yes, a tourist for sure. They're always cold.

"It's fine, ma'am, really. I mean, you pulled me back up."

Her eyes widened. "Oh, no, dear, that wasn't me; a nice young gentleman was standing nearby and helped you before I could even move."

Confused, I didn't even hear her good-bye as I made my way over to Eric.

"Was it you who stopped me from falling in?"

Surprise was written on his face when he turned around. "You almost fell in? I was busy fixing the seat of my kayak. What happened?"

I explained what had occurred and concluded, "I wonder who that guy was and why he disappeared so fast."

"Who knows. Questions seem to follow you around like puppies. Let's just go." I obediently climbed into my kayak and Eric gave me a shove. Soon we were gliding smoothly across the colorful Puget Sound. For the next three hours we paddled across kelp beds, past harbor seals, and over jellyfish. We saw big purple starfish clinging to the jagged rocks and eagles landing on the tops of pine trees. I could feel the salt drying on my arms as the water splashes evaporated.

When we landed again in Roche Harbor, we decided to stop for ice cream before calling Eric's mom to come pick us up. We sat at an outside café and ordered drinks and ice cream cones.

After carefully eating the last bite of cone, Eric handed me money and told me to go pay while he called his mom.

"But…I can pay for myself…" I said, confused. "It's not a…date or anything."

Eric looked disappointed as he said, "No, it's not a date, but…I can still pay for you."

I shrugged. "Well…ok. Just this once – thanks." I took the money and headed inside to the cashier.

The young woman smiled. "No need, honey! A cute young gentleman about my own age paid for you." She raised her eyebrows. "Isn't he a little old for you?"

I ignored the lady as I turned to go back to Eric, confused as ever. It hadn't been Eric…who was it? The only "young gentlemen" that I knew were my brother's friends, but I hadn't talked to any of them since Jason left.

Jason.

No.

Could it?

"ERIC!"

He almost dropped his cell phone. "What?" Someone had stolen my camera to delete a picture, but had returned it safe and sound, with a new case. Someone – a young gentleman – had stopped me from falling into the Puget Sound. A young gentleman had paid for my ice cream…

"Eric, I think Jason's come back," I whispered.

"Are you sure?" Eric expressed his doubt and his hope at the same time, resulting in a very odd facial expression.

"No, I'm not. But what other "young gentleman" would have paid for our ice cream?"

"Some guy who has a crush on you," he said with a faint grimace.

"Our ice cream?" I pointed out. Eric sighed.

"But where is he if he's here and why isn't he showing himself?"

"I don't know." I stared at Eric's bewildered face as I realized something. "Stuart knows. That's why he acted so weird when I told him about my camera. Usually he'd want to help us figure it out. But he left. He ran. And he knows where I work, he knows from you where we're always headed…Stuart knows."

After showering and changing back home I headed over to Eric's house to find him sitting on the porch steps waiting for me. I swallowed deeply, and my hands were sweaty and fluttery. Was I soon going to see my brother after five long years?

We rode our bikes to where Stuart worked, at The Toy Box.

"Hey, Jo – Eric."

"Stew, we want to talk to you – say, down at the park – after you're finished here. Which you should be in the next five minutes." Eric's steady gaze seemed to affect his brother, who shifted uncomfortably and clasped and unclasped his hands before giving a curt nod.

Down at the park, standing on the rocks watching the tide go out, Eric got right to the point.

"Stuart, where's Jason?"

He stiffened. "Jason? What do you mean? I know as well as you do that Jason left, what…five years ago by now?"

I felt frustrated. Why wouldn't Stuart help us? Jason was my brother, and I wanted to find him! "But…"

Stuart glanced at his watch. "Sorry, guys, but I gotta run my car to the shop for an inspection." Without waiting for a reply, he ran out of the park and was swallowed up by tourists.

Eric's eyes were narrowed. "He got his car inspected in February."

"How are we going to find Jason?" I said, feeling like a ten year old again.

Eric put his arm around me, and it felt only natural to lean into him. "We will," he whispered. "We will."

Wondering around town the next day, I absently mindedly found myself strolling down the long dock where I would find Popeye. Everyone in town knew Popeye, the female harbor-seal-in-residence, most likely named Popeye because she was blind in her left eye.

Harbor seals are very cat-like in the way they just float around, watching you, with their eyes blinking slowly and sometimes staying shut like a sleepy kitten. Popeye's multiple whiskers were thick and white. The sun glinted off of the light-colored spots on her head.

I knelt down on the wooden slats and tossed a shrimp to her. "Hey, girl," I said, "I hope your life is less complicated than mine. I bet seals don't have missing brothers." Popeye just blinked at me, having gulped down her shrimp.

Just then a little boy and his younger sister came up beside me. "Be careful, Sissy, don't fall in," the boy said, holding tightly onto his sister's hand as she leaned close to toss the seal a shrimp. Then they ran back to their mother, still holding hands.

"That's how Jason and I were," I said to Popeye. "He'd always look out for me…he was a good brother. I just wish he would have stayed. He wouldn't have been in trouble or anything, but…maybe he was tired of us. Maybe he is going to college. Maybe he just came back here to see his friends. I really wish he'd show himself, though. I miss him so much! Maybe, some day, he'll come back." A tear slid down my cheek as I whispered the last words.

"I'm so sorry, Sis. I'm sorry I caused the family such pain," said a husky voice, thick with emotion, behind me.

I was facing my brother in an instant. My eyes drank him up, making sure he was really there, afraid to speak as if he would vanish like the morning mist.

He reached out a hand and wiped the tear off of my cheek. "I thought you said you missed me. Jo, Honey, it's really me."

"Oh, Jason!" I finally cried, launching myself into his strong arms. His embrace felt the same as it always had. Jason or I, or perhaps both, held on tight until finally we pulled away.

"I'm sorry I left, Jo. I was anything but the brave older brother I always pretended to be. I should have stayed to face the music, no matter the tune."

"I'm sorry, too, Jay. But it's ok. You're here now…to stay?"

"Yes, I've finished college…I'm here to stay." I leaned against him as we made our way up the dock into the park.

"That's good. We've got a lot to catch up on. Oh, but…do you have a job here?"

"Yeah. I'm your new principal." He tried to hide his smile.

"My what?" I gaped at him in surprise. I hugged him. "You have a lot of explaining to do, brother."

Jason laughed out loud then. "Don't I know it. Say, Jo, you've really grown up since I last…last saw you. You're even prettier."

"Thanks, Jay. You've gotten even more handsome. But why did you only talk to Stuart and hide from the rest of us, following me around? You stole my camera…to delete a picture…" I was rambling, but Jason knew what I meant.

"Well, they say a picture is worth a thousand words, and they're right. I had to be sure what…what really happened and that I'd be welcome, and that I could get a job before I showed up. I followed you around because I missed you, and I wanted to see if you were still…the little sis I remembered. But you're not; you've grown up to be a pretty young woman that I can be even prouder of, and…apparently I'm not the only one who thinks you're pretty special," he said with a grin, calling my attention to Eric, who was running down the sidewalk calling to me.

"As for the picture…I couldn't have you see me around before I wanted to be seen. I was watching out for you, and making sure that your boyfriend treated you right, like he used to as a little kid."

I frowned. "He's not my boyfriend."

"He wants to be." I looked up at my brother in surprise, and then at Eric, who was coming closer. Was that really what Eric wanted? Was that what I wanted?

Eric caught up to us, breathing slightly heavier. "Hey, Jo, Stew said…" He took a double look at who was beside me. "Jason?!"

"Yep. Good to see you again, Eric."

I grabbed Eric's arm. "He's here to stay."

Eric gave me a warm smile, put his arm around my shoulders, and said, "That's great, Jo." He laughed, and said, "Nate and Nat sure picked a bad time to go on vacation!"

Everyone we passed stared at us three laughing young adults as we made our way home.

A Day at the Park

Hannah Fuerstenau
7th Grade

It was a wonderful day. The sun was shining and it was the middle of summer. Lily couldn't have been happier. She was just learning how to roller blade, and she couldn't wait to show her friends. Lily was at the park when she noticed a strange glimmer in the distance that seemed to be growing. It was getting closer and closer to her. Then all of a sudden there were flashes of light everywhere, but Lily seemed to be the only one to notice it. She was starting to get scared and then a magical portal came and sucked her into blackness. She couldn't see anything and she couldn't keep track of time.

Lily was so scared and she thought that she'd never get out. It could've been five minutes that she was in there, or it could've been five days. But then she found herself sitting in a white room. Lily started to panic and she got even more scared.

Looking around Lily saw nothing in the room; it was completely bare and boring. But then a hologram popped up in the middle and started playing a message. This is what it said:

Hello there Lily,

You probably don't know where you are right now but that doesn't really matter. All you have to know is that you will be stuck here forever and ever...unless you can complete this challenge.

Outside of this room is a magical land filled with magical storybook characters. If you can find all of the things on this list then you will find yourself back at your home.

You have 24 hours to find everything. If you don't then you will live here for the rest of your life. This is the list of things that you will need to find:

1 unicorn, 2 leprechauns, 3 fairies, 4 trolls, 5 ogres

You will find everything that you will need to accomplish these tasks in this bag.

Just then a bag flew out of the floor and landed in front on

Lily. She looked inside and there was a net, tranquilizer darts, and shrinking powder. Lily couldn't believe that, if she didn't find everything, she would be trapped here forever. She would never see her family or family again.

So Lily decided to look for a way out of the room and a secret door opened. Outside there were lollipop trees, gummy animals and pink skies. It was beautiful! Lily was amazed, but she didn't have time to gaze at it. She had to find the things on the list. But where did she start? Out of the corner of her eye Lily saw something move. She spun around quickly and saw the tip of a unicorn horn. But how would she catch the unicorn? Lily grabbed some licorice vines from one of the trees; she could use it as a lasso. She chased after the unicorn and threw her lasso at it. It caught and Lily had one less thing on her list. She pulled the unicorn behind her on the licorice vine.

Now she had to find two leprechauns. Lily had an idea of where she could find them. There was a rainbow in the sky; all she had to do was follow it to its pot of gold at the end. Then she would find her leprechauns. So she set out in search of the end of the rainbow. After what seemed like ages, Lily had finally found the pot of gold, but it was empty. Lily saw a trail of coins leading into the bushes. She followed it, and she found two leprechauns sitting there looking frightened. They were small enough to fit in Lily's pocket, so she scooped them up and threw them in. The whole time they were screaming in their very high-pitched voices.

With a unicorn trailing behind her and two leprechauns in her pocket, Lily went in search for three fairies. All of a sudden she started to sneeze. There was something floating in the air around her. It was fairy dust! Lily looked up and saw three little fairies above her. They were beautiful. She looked in her bag to see if there was anything that could help her catch them. There was a net that she could throw over them. So Lily grabbed the net and flung it over the fairies to trap them. Then all she had to do was throw the fairies into the bag. Now she just had to get four trolls and five ogres.

Lily was walking over a bridge when she heard some weird noises coming from underneath it. When she looked under, she saw a family of trolls sitting there! She had to act quickly or they might notice her.

Lily grabbed the tranquilizer darts from her bag and shot them at the trolls. Then they were unconscious. She threw some shrinking dust on them and they shrunk to the size of mouse. Lily snatched them up and stuck them in her bag. All that was left to do was find five ogres.

Lily kept walking straight when she noticed the lollipop trees, gummy animals, and pink skies turning into dark, creepy forests. Lily was starting to get scared. She was deep into the forest when she saw something move in the trees, but it wasn't an ogre. It was a little puppy. Lily walked toward it, but it started to run. So she chased it. The little puppy lead her to a campsite where the ogres lived. But they were so big, how would Lily bring them back? Lily threw the shrinking powder at the ogres and they all shrank. So all she had to do was grab them and stuff them in the bag with the trolls.

With everything that was on the list, Lily headed back to the place where she had started. Finally she would be able to go home. When she got back to the white room, a portal came and took everything that she had just found. Then another hologram popped up and said:

Congratulations Lily! You found everything on the list. Now you can go home.

Lily was so overjoyed that she screamed. Then a giant trap door fell out from underneath Lily, and she fell for what seemed like an eternity. Then she found herself back at the park, roller blading. Time seemed to have stopped when she was gone. No one noticed that she had just disappeared. Well, now Lily will have a great story to tell her friends.

Rising Heat

Christina Gibbs
7th Grade

Smoke stung my eyes and seemed to crawl in my throat. I choked as I desperately called Johan's name. But I couldn't stand the pressure. I collapsed and felt my eyes close. I knew that I would probably die if I stayed where I was, because I was in the middle of the street during the first of many air raids on Berlin, the capital of the glorious Third Reich.

My heart thumped so hard as I pulled my eyelids open, but immediately the smoke forced them to close. I felt like I was suffocating. But I had to go on. "Come on, Rachel! You have to save Johan!" Every muscle in my body screamed as I pulled myself up. And for the first time I noticed the burns on my face.

The sirens screamed and the bombs whistled. Explosion after explosion made it impossible to hear myself think. Johan would never hear me above this noise.

"What if I found him, but it was too late? What if he was crushed under a falling building?" I picked myself up and ran.

My mind spun as I raced along the streets. I felt like I was in a horrible maze, and I knew one wrong move would be the death of me. I tried not to think about the burning buildings or the exploding bombs, but focus on only one thing…saving Johan.

I didn't know where I was running as I raced along the burning streets, but I think my mind was unconsciously running through all the places where Johan might be. Of course. He would go to the person he trusted most. Papa.

My steps slowed as I caught sight of a little boy in front of Papa's work building. Johan was here. My head was spinning, and I felt like I was going to faint and throw up at the same time.

Johan turned and looked at me. "Rachel!" he screamed in terror.

But it was too late. A falling piece of wood hit me, and everything went black.

My eyelids felt very heavy, but I forced them to open. It must have been a few hours later, but I have no way of knowing exactly how long afterward it was. All I knew was that something wasn't right.

Then it hit me. Silence. Total silence. No sirens or bombs or explosions.

I tried to get up, but my shoulders screamed in agony. With a yelp, I lay back down on my stomach.

A sudden surge of energy electrified me as the realization swept over me that it wasn't over yet. I may have escaped being blown to bits, but I might die out here because no one would find me, meanwhile I was unable to move.

So I did the only thing I could think of doing. I screamed.

But it was useless. No one heard. I was alone.

And for the first time I thought over the events that had taken place.

Johan and I had both been in school. Then the air raid sirens sounded and the teacher told us to move down to the shelters in an orderly fashion. I met Johan down the hallway outside his classroom. He looked at me with a scared look in his eye. I was panicking too. Was Mama okay? Would Papa's building get bombed? What happened to all of what the Fuhrer had told us? About us being prosperous? Now we are getting bombed! What was going to happen? These doubtful thoughts crossed my mind, one by one. But I looked at him with a steady glance, trying to be brave. "It'll be okay, Johan." But Johan just shook his head.

We headed down the corridor and rushed to get outside. The shelter was so close! When we got outside, it was complete chaos. Most of the kids were running and screaming. Fear held me in its tight, suffocating grip. The shelter was so close…

I looked back over my shoulder to reassure Johan, but he was gone.

I started to run away from the group of kids. I screamed, "Johan! Johan, come back!" My steps quickened as I started toward the street. One of my classmates stopped me. "Rachel! What are you doing? You'll die out there!" She was probably right, but how could I be safe in a shelter, knowing Johan was out there all alone?

I raced out onto the street, screaming his name. Sobs racked my body. All I wanted was for things to be normal. All I wanted was to be in our flat with Mama and Papa. All I wanted was to be safe.

But now, here I am, all alone. What I needed was a miracle. And there was only one person who could supply that miracle.

"Oh, God, send someone to help me!"

I pressed my ear to the ground and tried to hear vibrations. But I could neither feel nor hear anything. I closed my eyes, feeling defeated.

At first, there was nothing. The street was completely silent, deathly silent. And then, I felt vibrations. Was it possible? No, it couldn't be. I must have just imagined it, like how people in the desert see water that isn't really there....

But no. A couple minutes later a truck rolled down the debris filled road. I knew they could probably see me, but just in case, I screamed for all I was worth.

The truck jerked to a stop. It was a military truck, with a swastika on its side. Out jumped what I hoped was a doctor, and he ran to my side.

First he took the weight off my shoulders, and then he moved his fingers all over my shoulder area. "Uh-huh. Looks like a dislocated shoulder. But we'll just get you to the hospital and it will be alright. What's your name, young lady?"

"Rachel Hirsch." I was desperately looking for any sign of Johan.

"You don't happen to be the daughter of Hildegard Hirsch?"

"Yes, yes I am." I curiously looked back at him.

"Very good! She is at the hospital this very moment. Come along, I'll help you to the truck."

We were halfway to the truck when I jerked around. "Johan! I have to find Johan!"

"What?"

And then, to my terror and dismay, I saw a small hand poking out of a pile of debris. "Johan!" I screamed. I started running toward him, but I fell hard on my side. I could almost hear my ribs crack.

The other men leaped from the truck and ran to the debris. They started digging for all they were worth until they found Johan's crushed body.

"Nooooooo!" I screamed. The men half carried, half dragged me back to the truck, with me kicking and screaming the whole way. The rest of the ride was a blur, I only remember screaming and sobbing.

I remember seeing my mother, collapsing into her arms. My mama started sobbing harder than even I was when she heard the news. I don't remember who told her. It all seems like broken pieces to some great puzzle, a puzzle I didn't understand, a puzzle that seemed to be turning me inside out, wringing me until every last tear was shed.

A few days later, my mother and I were in front of a truck, on our way to the train station, though not the train station in Berlin, of course. That had been completely destroyed, what remained was only a skeleton. We were going to have to travel quite a ways in a car before reaching train tracks that were intact.

Unfortunately, Papa had to stay in Berlin because of business, which worried both Mama and me. We knew that the Allies would bomb again, and when they did, Papa may not be so lucky.

As I stood in front of the truck, I felt completely hollow. I had no more tears, only a dull ache.

Out of the corner of my eye, I saw movement. I turned to see a girl, and, although she wasn't wearing a yellow star, her facial features gave her away. She was a Jew, and she was dancing. She tried to conceal her face with a big hat, but I knew. "Dirty Jew," I whispered. I felt the hatred flickering in my eyes. She saw me, and with one look at my hate-filled eyes she knew where I stood. With tears trickling down her face she turned, as if to run. Serves her right! It was her parents that started this war! Her parents were the reason my brother was dead! And look at her! Now she is dancing!

Then she turned back around and looked steadily into my eyes. "I overheard your mother saying your brother is dead. So is mine. But it was you Germans that killed him."

I scoffed at her. "I thought you consider yourself to be a

‘German.’”

“I don’t want to be German. I don’t want to be you. You know what, I am Jewish! And I will wear it like a badge of honor! Because when all is said and done, I can turn to my God, when you can only turn to your Hitler.” She spewed out the last word with both anger and pain.

And then I did what I would regret for the rest of my life…I turned and walked away.

The ride in the car and then on the train was agonizing. It was so long, and it gave me much time to think about what happened. I should have held on to Johan! What was I thinking! I should have watched him more carefully! I should have run faster! I should have seen the wood fall before it fell on me! It’s all my fault!

Of course my mind knew this wasn’t the case, that there was nothing I could do to stop it, but my heart didn’t. I felt the tears stream down my face for the first time that day, and, though my heart ached for Johan, it was a relief to cry. At the same time, it was also a heart-wrenching moment, because I felt like I was letting go of Johan. I would have done just about anything to have him by my side right then.

After that really long ride, we finally pulled up to the train station just outside of my aunt’s town. She was already there, and after hugs and kisses and tears were exchanged, we started for her house.

It was an old house with a door that creaked open every time the wind blew. I stared at it, comparing it to the spacious flat that we owned in Berlin. And right then I wanted to go home.

I wanted to go home to a Berlin that didn’t look like a bombshell. I wanted to go home to our flat, where Johan would be. I wanted life to go back to normal. Because right then life seemed anything but normal.

Seeing as there was no way this situation could be helped, I took my bags and ran into the house.

The kitchen was old, and it had none of the modern appliances that our kitchen had. I frowned at the sight of this, and I felt like I had gone back in time to about 60 years ago.

Pretty much the whole town seemed to go back to 60 years ago. True, there were men with swastikas on their sleeves and people saluting in the street and saying, "Hail Hitler!" but the air wasn't as electrified as it was back in Berlin. In Berlin, we screamed and clapped our hands when we heard the Fuhrer's voice, and we held our breath for news of the war. But, in this town, the people seemed barely touched by the war or the coming of the Third Reich.

My aunt then came in, and she wore a broad smile. "Why, Rachel, I see you have seen my kitchen! Now, come along, I must show you your room."

I followed her up the stairs into my room. And then, I wanted to cry.

The whole room was red.

Red was Johan's favorite color.

After I cried my eyes out, I went downstairs for dinner. Despite the antique kitchen, delicious smells wafted up to my room. I dried my eyes and dragged my feet to the dining room table.

In the kitchen with my aunt and Mama was a very pretty young girl, with curly brown hair and hazel eyes. They didn't know I was there.

"Now, Anna, you must understand what Rachel's been through. She saw her brother dead, and I'm sure she thinks it was her fault. Be understanding, okay? She might be a little jumpy, but it will all wear off over time."

Wear off? Like how one takes off a sweater? You mean one day I'm going to live a normal life again? Without Johan?

I ran back up to my room and cried. I was no longer hungry.

I spent the next few weeks mostly in my room, crying until my throat hurt from the sobs and my eyes itched from the salty tears.

My aunt would bring food up to my room, though usually I would eat only about a quarter of what she brought. Every day the routine was the same, "Dear, won't you please come eat supper with us?"

But I never felt like it. I would just continue crying.

At night my dreams were haunted with that day in Berlin, and I realized that a lot had changed because of that day. I mean, I knew a lot had changed because Johan was no longer with us, but I had changed too. I had been care-free before. Now, I always kept an eye to the sky to make sure no planes were coming to bomb us. I knew that they never would because we were in a small, secluded town, but my anxieties got the best of me.

I was absolutely heart-broken.

One morning, my stomach growled furiously. I had cried all night long, like usual, and my eyes were very red and scratchy. I was very tired, but I couldn't go back to sleep, and I had gotten tired of just sitting and crying. I decided to go downstairs.

At the dining room table sat my mother, my aunt, and that Anna girl. They were all eating breakfast.

I looked down at my mussed up self, suddenly embarrassed of how I looked. My cheeks turned red as I said, "Um, I should probably go change…"

But before I could finish, Anna jumped up. "No, no, come, sit down." She eagerly patted the seat next to her. And at that moment, I couldn't help loving her.

I smiled back and sat down beside her. She took my plate and put eggs and toast on it, than she handed it back to me. One bite told me that I hadn't eaten a good meal in a very long time.

Anna cupped her chin in her hands. "So, my name is Anna Gottlieb."

"Rachel Hirsch." I stretched out my hand, and she shook it heartily.

Her smile was so bright, and her eyes were so merry, that I felt like nothing could ever have gone wrong in her life. I was hoping it would rub off on me, that nothing bad would become of either of us ever again.

How wrong could I possibly be?

After breakfast, Anna tugged at my hand. "Come on. I want to show you something."

She began dragging me through the house toward the door. I laughed. "At least let me get dressed first!"

The house became silent. The silence was so thick, I felt like it was suffocating me. "What? Did I do anything wrong?"

Mama jumped up to me and pulled me into a bear hug. "No, no, sweetie! You haven't done anything wrong! You…you laughed!" Tears ran down her cheeks, and I knew that they weren't tears of sorrow. She stepped back and cupped my chin in her hands. "We're going to be alright, aren't we?"

"Yes, Mama." Tears ran down my own cheeks as I looked into her deep blue eyes.

"Oh, I'm so glad you laughed!" Anna paused before she tugged on my arm again. "But I want to show you something!"

She dragged me upstairs to my room and pulled out a dress and a pair of shoes. She handed them to me. "Here. Put these on."

I laughed as I struggled to put on the dress as fast as she wanted me to. "Hurry! We're burning daylight!" she half-teased.

I laughed again. My laughter sounded so sweet as it hung in the air, because I knew that even though I may not be perfectly happy now, I would be soon. I would get through this.

But I didn't have much time for deep thoughts before Anna was pushing me out the door. "Come on! Let's go!"

So with one shoe only half-buckled I ran across town with Anna. We skipped and laughed and ran, and for a little while, I forgot why I was in this town. I forgot that we came to escape a war-torn city.

We came to a field that ended with a long line of trees, but Anna was pushing me to a small cluster of trees that stood a few meters in front of the tree line. She ran ahead of me, and she looked beyond beautiful with her brown hair blowing in back of her, and wisps of her bangs falling in her eyes. She looked strong.

Anna ducked beneath the trees' branches, and I followed suit. I found myself in a small grove of trees, with soft green grass covering the ground. The grass felt so soft, so we both kicked off our shoes, no matter how un-ladylike we both knew it was.

It was very private, and I liked it in there. Wildflowers grew between the trees, and the air smelled so sweet.

Anna turned to face me. "I've always liked it in here." She smiled. "It always seemed so private, and I've always felt like I could be myself in here." She pointed to her feet. "And I can be as un-lady like as I want."

I laughed, and then I just smiled. I lay down on my stomach. "I feel like…I feel like time has stood still here."

For a brief moment, Anna just smiled, but then her smile vanished. "But time can never stand still." What I beheld in her eyes scared me to death. I saw fear in her eyes. I knew that I had only known her for a day, but she had seemed so care-free, so happy. But she only had that look in her eye for a second, before she was smiling and chatting on again. I tried to forget about it, but I could not forget what I had seen.

We chatted on about different things, until the sun was high in the sky, and my stomach growled. I blushed, and Anna laughed. "Hungry? Me too." Anna tugged at my hand. "Come on; let's go get something to eat."

The days passed pleasantly, with the weather being always nice. Most of the time, I went with Anna to the grove. But sometimes she showed me different brooks and streams, and we would wade in the icy water, laughing and talking about anything and everything.

Over the weeks, I would still cry at night for Johan. I still hadn't shaken all of the guilt, and I still wished with all my heart that this was a nightmare that I would wake up from. I wished that one of these days Anna would knock on the door and when I answered, she would look around and ask, "Where's Johan?"

But she never did and I knew that she never would, but she did know enough about him to recognize him. As the days passed I would tell her more and more about Johan, slowly opening up and letting what I had locked in my heart free. One day I told her everything. I told her about the day that Berlin had gotten bombed, about how Johan had looked so scared, about how he had just run off. When I was finished, she took me in her arms and whispered, "Oh, Rachel, I'm so sorry." And I knew that even though I may have lost a brother, I had gained a sister.

The day had begun like any other day. I had gotten dressed and slipped downstairs for breakfast. Anna was sitting at the table, and I sat down next to her.

We began eating our breakfast like any other day. And then, I heard a car rolling down the street.

Now, may I remind you that this town seemed to have gone back about 60 years. No one had a car before the war, and no one had a car now.

Anna and I rushed to the window to see a car with a swastika stopping in front of the house. Out stepped a tall man who looked a good deal like Anna.

"Noooooooooooooo!" Anna screamed. Terror was written all over her face, and I too was scared to death, though I didn't know why.

My aunt ran to us. "Out the back door, now!" she ordered Anna.

Anna didn't need to be told twice. She ran like a deer outside. "What…" I began.

My aunt held up her hand. "Not now."

A man banged on the door and yelled, "Open up!"

Mama opened the door and the man stormed in. I had never been afraid of the Gestapo; on the other hand, they had never banged on our door and yelled at us, demanding to come in. Anyway, right then, I was deathly afraid of that Gestapo man.

"Are you harboring a Jew?" The man's face was bright red from yelling, and his veins were bulging from his neck. I was beyond scared. I was terrified.

"Why would we harbor a Jew?" my aunt evaded the question. Why would she do that? Unless…no, it couldn't be… she wouldn't… would she? Harbor a Jew?

The man pushed my aunt aside like a rag doll. "Search the house!" he commanded the other men.

It was then that I noticed that the man who was yelling was not the man that I had first seen step out of the car. I looked out the door to see the man walking purposefully down the street. Why? Who were they looking for? I refused to think of how my aunt had commanded Anna to run.

The men tore the house apart. Tears ran down my face. Anna was right. Time can't stand still. Sooner or later the new Germany had to catch up on this town. And for some reason, I wished with all my heart that it wouldn't.

And then, someone barged in the back door. "Is this her?" A man tugged Anna in with him, yanking her around. Her face was white, and I didn't know why. Maybe that was what terrified me the most.

Then the man I had seen on the street walked in the door. He nodded. "She is a Jew."

"How could you betray your own daughter?!" My aunt spat in his face. The man ignored her, pretending not to hear.

"Should we arrest her also?" Another man pointed to my aunt.

The man who had been called Anna's father shook his head. "No." His smiled twisted into an evil grin. "Seeing Anna being arrested will shut her up."

My mouth may have been sealed from fear, but my mind wasn't. It tried to analyze the situation as best as it could, and then the facts began to fall into place.

Anna's father was a Nazi, like mine. But Anna's mother was a Jew. Anna was a Jew.

"No! You can't be! You're… a dirty Jew!" I blurted out the words before I could think about them.

Anna looked at me with tear-filled eyes. "I trusted you!" she screamed. "I thought of you as my sister! When my mother told me that all Germans hated us and wanted to destroy us, I defended you! I told her that you can't judge them all by one!" Then she choked on her tears. "But she was right! You are all out to get us! Well, are you happy?!" Than the man jerked her out the door and forced her into the car.

And I sat down and cried. Because I didn't know what else to do.

* * *

To be honest, I was glad when the war was over and the Allies won. I didn't want the world to be ruled by Hitler. Because he would have killed tons of innocent lives. He would have killed Anna.

After that day when Anna's father had turned her in, I had wondered about who Jews really were. At first, I thought that she had been manipulative when she didn't tell me that she was a Jew. Then again, I had never really asked.

My aunt had retreated into silence after that day, but when I asked her whether or not the Jews were really bad or not, she immediately snapped out of it. She showed me in the Bible verses of how the Jews were God's chosen people.

The verse that really caught my eye was Genesis 12:3. "I will bless them that bless thee, and curse them that curseth thee: and in thee shall all families of the earth be blessed."

My aunt explained that the they in that verse were the Jews, so according to that verse, God had cursed me, because I had cursed one of His people.

As soon as the war was over I immediately ran out the door into the cool air. Literally, I didn't even stop to pack. Mama laughed as she called to me to come and get some clothes before going on a cross-country trip.

First I went to the Jewish relocation center and searched for Anna. I found out that she had probably been taken to Auschwitz. When the woman told me she looked at me with pity. "I'm sorry, but…there are very few that made it out of Auschwitz alive. Very few."

But I had to search anyway. I caught a train ride to a town near the concentration camp Auschwitz, and I asked everyone I met, "Do you know Anna Gottlieb?"

It was bright and early when I got up and put on my shoes. I thought about the day when Anna had rushed me to put them on, and I put my face in my hands, and I cried.

A knock sounded on the door. "Come in," I somehow managed to call.

A slender young woman came in. Seeing my tears, she wrapped her arms around me. "Are you okay?"

"Yeah, I think so." I wiped my tears with my hand. "By the way, thanks for letting me stay with you. You're very generous, especially since you barely know me."

"Well, I knew your mother, so that's good enough for me!"

she said cheerfully. Then she lowered her voice. "And, when I heard you were looking for a Jewish loved one, well, I just couldn't turn you down," she sighed. "I just hope you have better luck than I did.

She had already told me about her Jewish friend who had perished in another major concentration camp, Berger-Belsen. I hoped I had better luck than she did, too.

But, maybe it wasn't luck that I needed.

"Oh, God, please help me find Anna!" I silently prayed.

I was all ready to go before the woman spoke again. She put her hand on my shoulder. "You are dreadfully young to go search for your friend alone," she said.

I nodded. "But I have to. Mama had things that she needed to take care of, and my aunt is searching for Anna's mother.

"Just, be prepared for what you might see." Then, softly, to herself, she whispered, "Though I don't think that anyone could truly be prepared to see what we Germans did to human beings."

I pretended that I hadn't heard that last statement as I rushed out the door and onto the street.

This time, there weren't any burning buildings or whistling bombs or loud explosions. There weren't any screaming sirens, and there definitely weren't any of my own screams. At least, not yet.

But there was death. Though the survivors of Auschwitz that surrounded me were indeed alive, it was obvious that their spirits had died long ago.

Maybe the little Jewish girl who I had seen on the street that day in Berlin was like them. Maybe she had survived, but her spirit hadn't.

It was a random thought, but it forced me to relive that day in Berlin. I felt like I was once again on those streets, screaming Johan's name. But I couldn't stand the pressure. I collapsed and felt my eyes close. My heart thumped so hard…

Every scene flashed before my eyes. I ran the streets, screaming his name. I was in front of Papa's building. The falling piece of wood hit me. Everything went black. I was conscious again. A doctor came. And then…Johan's crushed body. I was pulled away, kicking and screaming and sobbing.

It took a moment for me to realize that I really was screaming and sobbing. A woman put her hand on my shoulder. "Can I help you?"

I turned around to see a girl a little older than me. She was obviously a survivor from some concentration camp, but there was something different about her. Something that set her apart from the other survivors. And then, it came to me. It was her face. It seemed so bright, and she seemed so cheerful, so optimistic. As if she knew that things would eventually get better.

And then I blurted out my question. "Do you know Anna Gottlieb?" I prayed that she would give the response I wanted.

Her face lit up, and she looked like a child does on Christmas morning. No, she looked more joyful than that. "Anna! I know her! She slept on the bunk across from me at Auschwitz! She was the one who kept this alive." She pointed to her heart.

"Do you know where she is now?" I asked excitedly.

The girl nodded. "Follow me." She waved her hand.

I was so excited I could barely contain myself. Joy bubbled up inside of me, and I wanted to explode. Tears of joy stained my cheeks, and when we broke free of the town and the woman pointed to some trees, I ran for them.

I ran as fast as I could until I came to… a stone. And on the stone was written… Anna Gottlieb.

It took a moment for my mind to realize that this was a gravestone.

"Noooooooooooooo!" I screamed. I fell down on my knees and sobbed and sobbed and sobbed. And this time there was no one there to pull me away.

*   *   *

It was several years later when I was at a graveyard in Germany. My husband was waiting a few feet away, letting me be alone with my thoughts.

I had set up a proper grave for both Johan and Anna. I had told my husband that I needed to do that, and though I don't think he understood, he let me do it.

I sat down on the wet grass, and I lifted my finger and traced the engraved words. "Johan Hirsch." "Anna Gottleib."

I moved my finger down to where it was supposed to say, "Son of Wilhelm and Hildegard Hirsch," and "Daughter of Lars and Sarah Gottlieb." But that didn't seem fitting for Anna's grave. So instead I put:

The truest friend, unto the end,
Closer than a sister,
Joyfully she gave to her friends
The best gift.
Hope.

It was all true, and I knew that. The girl who had showed me the "gravestone" that she had set up had told me all about her and what Anna had said and done in Auschwitz. She never complained, and was always trying to help. As I thought back to the days at my aunt's house, that didn't surprise me.

I stared at the grave for a long time before I burst out crying. And though I was crying for Johan and Anna, I was also crying for someone else. For someone who may have never known that there was a soul in the world who cared about her.

I was crying for the little Jewish girl on the street.

I never knew her name.

But she was engraved in my memory as, "the girl I called a dirty Jew. The girl who I thought was evil because she danced because she knew that the bombs meant that she was that much closer to freedom."

She never knew that I cared.

I cried and sobbed and I cried some more. I couldn't stop. The grass became not only wet from the dew, but also from my tears. My tears of sorrow and regret.

I heard light footsteps behind me, too light to be my husband. I didn't bother looking, I just went on crying.

The footsteps stopped behind me, and I heard someone kneel down. A womanly voice asked, "What's wrong?"

And I told her the whole story. I told her about the little

Jewish girl on the street who I had hated.

“And she’s probably dead now, and I will never get to tell her that I cared, I will never get to tell her that I’m sorry!” I sobbed.

“Oh, I wouldn’t say that.” I turned around to see the grown-up face of the little Jewish girl who had been on the street. She opened her arms. “I forgive you,” she whispered.

23465493R00145

Made in the USA
Lexington, KY
11 June 2013